DANDYISM

CULTURAL FRAMES, FRAMING CULTURE
Robert Newman, Editor
Justin Neuman, Associate Editor

DANDYISM

Forming Fiction from Modernism to the Present

LEN GUTKIN

UNIVERSITY OF VIRGINIA PRESS
Charlottesville and London

University of Virginia Press
© 2020 by the Rector and Visitors of the University of Virginia
All rights reserved
Printed in the United States of America on acid-free paper

First published 2020

ISBN 978-0-8139-4389-3 (hardcover)
ISBN 978-0-8139-4390-9 (paper)
ISBN 978-0-8139-4391-6 (ebook)

9 8 7 6 5 4 3 2 1

Library of Congress Cataloging-in-Publication Data is available for this title.

CONTENTS

ACKNOWLEDGMENTS

I have been thinking about the topics discussed in *Dandyism* for a long time and have incurred many debts along the way. At Bard College, Deirdre d'Albertis's course on Anglophone modernism planted the seed from which this book grew, and Nancy Leonard's literary theory courses were formative. At Yale, coursework with Tanya Agathocleous, Jill Campbell, Wai Chee Dimock, Lanny Hammer, Pericles Lewis, Michael Warner, and Ruth Yeazell shaped the direction of my subsequent work. Anthony Reed alerted me to Lyotard's book on dandyism. Paul Grimstad shared his sensitive responses to detective fiction and to William Burroughs. A visit to New Haven from Cathryn Setz taught me much of what I know about Djuna Barnes. I am especially grateful to Amy Hungerford and Katie Trumpener. Their breadth of knowledge, their commitment to argumentative clarity, and their personal encouragement were invaluable.

I can't imagine having enjoyed graduate school more than with Maggie Deli, Anna Dubenko, Merve Emre, Sam Fallon, Edgar Garcia, Matt Hunter, Tom Koenigs, Tessie Prakas, Glyn Salton-Cox, Justin Sider, and Josh Stanley. I owe particular intellectual debts to Justin Sider, Merve Emre, and The Anchor.

At the Harvard Society of Fellows, I benefited particularly from conversation—often very late into the night—with Alex Bevilacqua, Michaela Bronstein, Stephanie Dick, Marta Figlerowicz, Abhishek Kaicker, Marika Knowles, Jed Lewinsohn, Hannah Walser, Moira Weigel, and Daniel Williams.

I have presented versions of this work at conferences sponsored by the Modernist Studies Association, the American Comparative Literature Association, and the English departments at Indiana–Bloomington and UMass–Amherst, as well as at meetings of the Yale Americanist Colloquium and the Yale British Studies Colloquium. I would like to thank all involved. A compressed version of my second chapter appears as "The Dandified Dick: Hardboiled Noir and the Wildean Epigram" in *ELH* 81.4 (Winter 2014): 1299–1326, copyright © 2014 The Johns Hopkins University Press; it is reprinted with permission by Johns Hopkins University Press. A portion of my fourth chapter appears as "Djuna Barnes's *Nightwood* and Decadent Style" in *Literature Compass* 11.6 (June 2014). And a shorter version of my third chapter appears as "Modernist Genre Decadence from H. G. Wells to William S. Burroughs" in *Affirmations: of the modern* 5.1 (Autumn 2017). At the JFK Library, Stephen Plotkin made visits to the Hemingway archive run smoothly. The University of Virginia Press's anonymous readers were diligent, intelligent, and scrupulous; they improved the book immensely.

My family was never less than supportive. And Cori O'Keefe was always more than supportive, and still is.

I am deeply indebted to the late Sam See for his attentive reading of portions of this book in its very early phases, and for his friendship. I miss him.

DANDYISM

INTRODUCTION

THE DANDY IN LONG MODERNISM

In different ways, the search was to recover a sense of the numinous in the human depths, including sexuality and aggression, a power which could be tapped through aesthetic presentation.
—CHARLES TAYLOR, *A Secular Age*

Surface, surface, surface was all that anyone found meaning in . . .
—PATRICK BATEMAN, in *American Psycho*

In his afterworld fantasy novel *Malign Fiesta* (1955), Wyndham Lewis works in a not-so-sly dig at Ernest Hemingway's 1927 story collection *Men without Women*. Lewis is describing the clientele of an all-male hotel in Purgatory: "[T]his huge collection of men-with-out-women . . . were grey flannel-suited, with flowing Byron collars, horticultural lapels, a heavy swaying of the hips, and great sweeping gestures of the arm in order to pat the back of the hair, or to maintain a silk sleeve handkerchief in place." (Lewis was scornfully fond of the "men-without" formula, as attested also by his 1934 critical collection *Men without Art,* in which Hemingway is a primary target.) This is a womanless superterrestrial milieu with, as one character puts it, "Alfred Lord Douglas thrown in!"[1] Lewis's canny association of Hemingway with Douglas and, by extension, Douglas's lover Oscar Wilde, suggests a surprising affiliation between Hemingway and the figure of the dandy. By locating Hemingway in Oscar Wilde's fin de siècle, Lewis points to an important continuity between the masculinist homosociality of the boxers, bullfighters, and soldiers who make up Hemingway's men without women and the apparently very different social type of the Victorian dandy, whom Lewis depicts, pejoratively, as homosexual.

Dandyism takes Lewis's cue seriously, as more than just a mischievous challenge to Papa's presumptive straightness. In *Sartor Resartus* (1837), Thomas Carlyle offers an appealingly pithy characterization of the dandy: "A Dandy is a Clothes-wearing Man."[2] But across the remainder of the nineteenth century and well into the twentieth, the dandy would come to be much more than just a clotheshorse.[3] The first canonical dandy was Beau Brummell (1778–1840), whose famed wit and sartorial innovations established dandyism as a social force. Jules A. Barbey d'Aurevilly's 1844 *On Dandyism and Beau Brummell*—the first work of dandy theory—analyzed a repertoire of dandiacal traits that echo across the Victorian and modern period, and across this book. First, the dandy is a figure of supreme autonomy: "[T]he Dandies, of their own authority, make rules that shall dominate the most aristocratic and the most conservative sets, and with the help of wit, which is an acid, and of grace, which is a dissolvent, they manage to ensure the acceptance of their changeable rules, though these are in fact nothing but the outcome of their own audacious personalities." Or put even more strongly: "Independence makes the Dandy. There would otherwise be a code of dandyism, but there is not."[4] Second, the dandy is elementally cold, dispassionate: "Byron was only [a dandy] on certain days, for passion is too true to be dandyesque."[5] This coldness can even tend toward a kind of asexuality, "for to love, even in the least lofty acceptation of the word—to desire—is always to depend, to be the slave of one's desire."[6] Third, and relatedly, the dandy is a figure of reserve—he holds something back. Barbey d'Aurevilly connects this reserve to Englishness and to Protestantism (although, as fate will have it, later on the dandy will come to be associated with Catholicism): "Dandies never completely get rid of their original puritanism. Their elegance, however great it may be . . . never quite abandons reserve."[7] Fourth, the dandy's wit is a kind of violence, "a shield with a javelin in the centre, that turned defence into aggression."[8] Fifth, the dandy is a gourmet: "His love of dining well, delicate as a taste, and exacting as a passion, had always been one of the most highly developed sides of his sybaritism."[9] Sixth, the dandy (who for Barbey d'Aurevilly is male) is essentially androgynous—"a Dandy is a woman on certain sides"; dandies "are the hermaphrodites of History, not of Fable."[10]

In the pages that follow, I will return to these six traits—autonomy, coldness, reserve, verbal aggression, culinary connoisseurship, and androgyneity—again and again.

Oscar Wilde, who has supplanted Brummell as the proper name most synonymous with "the dandy" right up to our own time, united dandyism as a style of personality with the theories of aestheticism developed by Walter Pater and the extravagant decadence—the representation of psychic and aesthetic refinements pushed to the point of pathological perversity—offered in Joris-Karl Huysmans's 1884 novel À Rebours. Wilde met Pater while a student at Oxford; he had committed passages of Studies in the History of the Renaissance (1873) to memory.[11] He would go on to combine Paterian aestheticism—broadly mistrusted as a hedonistic religion of art—and the decadence he associated with Huysmans into a single project, a blend that, as Richard Ellmann says, "had been foreshadowed, but forsaken, by Pater. Wilde had more courage."[12] To Wilde, Huysmans's À Rebours seemed "the exfoliation of Pater's theory."[13] The dandy's association with aestheticism and decadence—formal movements, social dispositions, zeitgeist—is especially important here. For aesthetes, as Leon Chai says, aesthetic "intensity" conducts "a light of consciousness that illuminates all objects in its clear brilliance until things themselves become but reflecting surfaces."[14] Conversely, what "characterize[d] the Decadence," as Regenia Gagnier puts it, were "nerves, rather than the more Romantic-Victorian senses."[15] Decadence entails, at its limit, the biologization of both aesthetic appreciation and introspection; aestheticism, the epiphanic transformation of surface. These twinned forms of subjectivity occasion related but distinct aesthetic projects. Often treated as synonymous, the two modes might better be understood to name competing proximate tendencies emerging from Victorian culture, climaxing at the fin de siècle, and continuing on, subdued, scrambled, but very much alive, in modernism and beyond.[16]

While in actual use the terms often describe overlapping phenomena, in their general drifts "aestheticism" tends to describe surfaces and "decadence" depths. For the dandy, an aestheticist cult of surfaces—his attention to clothes and makeup, to dispositional composure, to fine objets d'art, to affective control, to the well-turned phrase—complements his decadent pursuit of fascinating, messy, and perverse interiority. The aestheticist dandy is continent, clean, well-turned. The decadent dandy,[17] conversely, revels in grotesque disproportion; in emanations of decay; in libido as unchecked, monstrous, vampiric, abject, sticky. As Ellmann puts it, Wilde could see "the possibility of uniting the two movements" because he "had always been both *comme il faut* and *à rebours* too, Apollonian gentleman and Dionysian subverter."[18]

To set up the binary this strongly is to oversimplify, and caveats are easy to imagine.[19] But much of the writing I will look at might be understood as the result of the dialectical interpenetration, different in every case, of these two tendencies. We might think of *The Picture of Dorian Gray* (1891) as an allegory about the ingredients that make up the fin de siècle atmosphere. The aestheticist/decadent binary is expressed melodramatically and moralistically, as the novel's big reveal exposes the "truth" of corruption underlying overrefined aristocratic surfaces. *Dorian* schematizes the binary starkly, and with a (perhaps sarcastic) susceptibility to Victorian moralism: the rotting portrait is the "inside" (moral and aesthetic) of the outwardly lovely Dorian, a dandy shaped by another dandy, the corrupting Lord Wotton, and a decadent forbidden book, Huysmans's *À Rebours*.[20] "To [Dorian] man was a being with myriad lives and myriad sensations, a complex multiform creature . . . whose very flesh was tainted with the monstrous maladies of the dead."[21] Corruption is thus the "truth" of surface beauty, or its complement, or its price.

Dorian articulates a cultural logic that would continue to echo across the fin de siècle through modernism and beyond: the themes of aestheticism and decadence will remain inextricable from representations of queerness. From the Wilde trials onward, the dandy was definitively marked by suspicion of his indeterminate or unspeakable sexuality, which might also be said to constitute his appeal. (In this, the dandy is a queer variation on those earlier figures of charismatic masculine transgression, the rake and the libertine.)[22] Dandiacal trappings thus become almost de rigueur for a tradition of queer modernism practiced by such diverse figures as Charles Henri-Ford and Parker Tyler (in their under-read *The Young and the Evil* [1933]), Cyril Connolly, Christopher Isherwood, or the Harlem Renaissance novelist Wallace Thurman (in *Infants of the Spring* [1932]).[23] The novels of Ronald Firbank probably go further than any other in forging a modernist version of dandiacal form. If one of modernism's projects is a newly energized investigation of the operations of sexuality, it receives its impetus in part from dandyism.

One conventional way of periodizing modernism begins with Baudelaire, from which point of view it is not at all surprising to assert that the dandy is a central modernist figure. Peter Nicholls has linked the dandy's "aloofness from practical necessities," as discerned by Baudelaire in his essay "The Painter of

Modern Life" (1863), to the modernist development of aesthetic autonomy.[24] And in the twentieth century, one thinks of such minor and as it were symptomatic cases as the "Romantic Egotist" Amory Blaine in Fitzgerald's *This Side of Paradise* (1920), whose dandyism is cobbled together from templates at hand. Here, for instance, is Amory's affinity with Catholicism, a familiar topos of dandyism: "He was not even a Catholic, yet that was the only ghost of a code that he had, the gaudy, ritualistic, paradoxical Catholicism whose prophet was Chesterton, whose claqueurs were such reformed rakes of literature as Huysmans and Bourget . . . a Catholicism which Amory found convenient and ready-made, without priest or sacraments or sacrifice."[25] Just so "convenient and ready-made" is Amory's whole character; he is a dandy by default.

Dandyism, however, examines the dandiacal not primarily as it appears overtly, as in early Fitzgerald, or in the work of such unabashed dandy novelists as Firbank, but instead in the work of authors, like Hemingway, not necessarily associated with dandyism either in their public personae or in their work. I suggest that for many twentieth-century authors, the energy of dandyism could be harnessed only by strategically rinsing it of suspect associations with the queer, the effeminate, and the recherché. For macho authors like Hemingway and Raymond Chandler, the masculinist recoding of dandiacal aestheticism was not a simple, unidirectional process: the goal was not utterly to expunge the queer from the dandiacal, but to develop strategies for managing its embrace that would be acceptable to a large mainstream readership. In the very complicated case of William Burroughs, dandyism and decadence provided templates both for authorial self-fashioning and for methods of formal innovation, even as Burroughs's reliance on a hard-boiled idiom he'd adopted from Chandler would involve him in ambiguous repudiations of the dandiacal. For Djuna Barnes, decadent interiority has been subjected to the pressures of high modernist parody. For writers as different as Patricia Highsmith, Anthony Burgess, and Bret Easton Ellis, the dandy as a stock type would provide a point of entry for highly idiosyncratic explorations of the aesthetics of violence in the novel.

Like Hemingwayesque machismo, dandyism is a species of gendered charisma. It exists, necessarily, within a field of competitors: its value is relational, and it accomplishes its goals by defining itself against alternative modes of gender performance. Although the dandy is originarily male, the female dandy enables some of dandyism's most radical formal possibilities, as my discussion of Djuna Barnes and Coco Chanel will show. Dandyism achieves charisma by the codification of costume and taste, the cultivation of habits of speech reflective of continence and power, and, in many cases, the suggestions of a queer (variously androgynous and homoerotic) substrate to masculine performance. In the period of the fin de siècle through modernism—that is to say, from the period of the trials of Oscar Wilde on—this last would assume special prominence. From the turn of the twentieth century, the dandy is always assigned an originary queerness, which is, alternatively and as the case may be, intensified, exaggerated, and celebrated; repressed and reconstituted; tentatively embraced; obliquely referenced; or denied outright. The authors covered in *Dandyism* run the gamut from suppression to embrace, sometimes within their own oeuvres.

Celebrity, Form, and Masculine Style

Hemingway set a standard for authorial fame that remains unbeaten in American literary history. As Loren Glass puts it in his work on literary celebrity in the United States—in a chapter called "Being Ernest" (the wink to a Wildean Hemingway anticipates my project)—"Hemingway found himself straddling a line between modernism and mass culture that literary critics would understand as an almost-heroic struggle between the ascetic demands of the 'style' and the worldly temptations of the 'personality.'"[26] Glass goes on to show that literary style and worldly celebrity were for Hemingway not at odds but reciprocally constitutive. The dandy is always a kind of celebrity, and dandyism has since Oscar Wilde been a particularly available posture for male celebrity authors: think of Truman Capote, Gore Vidal, Evelyn Waugh, F. Scott Fitzgerald, and Tom Wolfe. Dandiacal celebrity was celebrated and suspected in equal measure. As Max Nordau said of Wilde in his stigmatizing, pseudoscientific magnum opus *Degeneration* (1893), "What really determines his actions is the hysterical craving to be noticed, to occupy the attention of the world with himself, to get talked about."[27]

But celebrity, dandyish or otherwise, in modernism and after has to do with more than just the public self-fashioning of a handful of authors. It is profoundly a question of literary, not just personal or sartorial, style. As Aaron Jaffe has shown in his *Modernism and the Culture of Celebrity* (2005), "The same way modernists and their publicists fetishize authorship, celebrities and their publicists fetishize the production of self."[28] For Jaffe, this fetishization involves the modernist establishment of a brand (what he calls the "imprimatur") by which "the modernist literary object bears the stylistic stamp of its producer prominently."[29] The imprimatur promotes modernist art as the rarified emanations of charismatic, stylistically recognizable personalities, or even offers modernist art as itself *a kind of personality*.[30] Or as Wyndham Lewis, that most ambivalent navigator of the pressures of modernist publicity, supposedly said to Ford Madox Ford, "I display myself all over the page. In every word. I . . . I . . . I."[31]

The modernist culture of celebrity is substantially predicated on the culture of the dandy, whose insistence that style was a very serious business indeed was a necessary condition for the elite imprimaturs of modernist authorship. Just as the modernist author disappears into his brand, so the biographical personage (Oscar Wilde, b. 1854) disappears into a version of himself as pure style, "Oscar Wilde, dandy." The performance of dandiacal personality prefigures modernist "impersonality." Jessica Feldman traces this lineage back to Théophile Gautier—a major influence on macho modernists like Ezra Pound and, as my first chapter discusses, Hemingway—and the aestheticist androgyny topos: "What will become the aesthetic doctrine of impersonality, refined throughout the remainder of the nineteenth century, begins to flourish on the divide between Gautier's male and female dandies."[32] And like modernist impersonality proper, the poses of the dandy aesthete aren't so much impersonal as they are personality hypostasized, or translated into the hieroglyphic lineaments of pure style. In this respect, the distance between Wilde and Hemingway isn't nearly so great as normally presumed. In the medium of celebrity, both convert personality into style.

The dandiacal stylings of Ezra Pound ("He would wear trousers made of green billiard cloth, a pink coat, a blue shirt, a tie hand-painted by a Japanese friend, an immense sombrero, a flaming beard cut to a point, and a single, large blue earring")[33] and even of T. S. Eliot (he of the Baudelairean green makeup)[34] are well known, and in general modernist dandyism represents a fairly direct Victorian transmission, as Leo Braudy observes in his canonical study of fame: "The appeal of the outsider [is] perhaps our most widespread psychological inheritance from nineteenth-century Europe. . . . The dandy especially took that alienation and turned it into a badge of style and honor."[35] Wyndham Lewis affected a broad-brimmed black hat throughout his career, an aspect of what Paul O'Keeffe calls his "vigorously self-promoted personality."[36] Raymond Chandler's lifelong nattiness helped make him a recognizable figure, especially in England, where he enjoyed an extraordinary burst of late-in-life fame; his "bright ties and white gloves," one biographer tells us, "made him immediately recognizable" in London.[37] Djuna Barnes's eccentric stylishness was famous among her contemporaries; her penchant for a black cape seems especially to have made an impression. Robert McAlmon was struck by what he called her "cape-throwing gestures"; Burton Rascoe claims that he "never saw her wear anything except a tailored black broadcloth suit with a white ruffled shirtwaist, a tight-fitting black hat, and high-heeled black shoes; and I rarely saw her without a long shepherd's crook which she carried like a Watteau figure in a fete galante."[38] And even Hemingway, wounded and hospitalized during the Great War, felt it necessary to have a bespoke Italian uniform, decked out with cape and cane.[39]

At the most general level, dandiacal texts, like dandies, can be recognized as stylish—that is to say, their style will be strongly marked *as* style.[40] Stylishness courts desire and fantasy identification, as attested by the broad popularity of Hemingway and Chandler, my two exemplars of modernist dandiacal style in a macho mood. As Rhonda Garelick puts it, "Dandyism . . . conflates textual and human seduction."[41] As I see it, dandiacal textual seduction is identificatory rather than possessive. This identificatory spur is common to dandies and celebrities alike, as Garelick recognizes when she claims that "[t]he media cult personality . . . whose image appears and reappears on television and movie screens" has its roots in nineteenth-century dandyism.[42] The key to dandiacal seduction is that the interest we extend to the dandy holds out the promise of a rise in our own status. As Rosalind Williams puts it, "The sense of social superiority assumed by the dandy extended to his admirers."[43] Hemingway's whole corpus might, from one angle, be thought of as a virtuoso exercise in facilitating the collapse of author into character, and of reader into both; one function of Hemingway's clipped prose is to activate in the reader the desirable sense of being as composed as his heroes and, implicitly, as their author.[44] I mean "composed" in the sense of "having one's feelings and expression under control" (*New Oxford American Dictionary*, 2nd ed.) but also of "written." One of the pleasures of Hemingway's dandiacal prose is the pleasing suggestion that one's own life might, even in defeat, be arranged with as much cool aesthetic vigor as a line of his narration or dialogue: "Isn't it pretty to think so?"

Hemingway's celebrity depended on the imaginary conflation of biographical author and authorial persona which the dandiacal novel had courted at least since Edward Bulwer-Lytton's *Pelham* (1828). What if, Norman Mailer asked, Hemingway's work had been "written by a man who was five-four, wore glasses, spoke in a shrill voice, and was a physical coward"?[45] We couldn't read it the same way. Although this kind of interpretive dilemma has informed the Western authorship concept from at least the seventeenth century (as Foucault reminds us in his 1969 essay "What Is an Author?"), the literature of dandyism raises it to a peculiar pitch. Dandiacal authors were dangerously liable to buy into their own myth, a process that, in the modernist period and after, was inseparable from that myth's media propagation.[46] Braudy attributes the high rate at which twentieth-century artists committed suicide to increasing media saturation and the modes of celebrity it enabled: "In such a fragmentation of self and public image, suicide is the final act of cohesion, the final good faith. . . . The more public, the more famous the person, the more sacramental and ritualistic the act."[47] Whatever the cause, Hemingway, Chandler, and Barnes all attempted suicide, sometimes more than once. Hemingway, of course, eventually succeeded.

Less tragically, the dandiacal pressures of authorial image management could be very amusing, particularly when, like Wyndham Lewis, the author is putatively antidandiacal. A wonderful passage in O'Keeffe's biography describes Lewis's contemporary Winifred Gill witnessing Lewis "building up what would now be called a public 'image'":

> Without realising it, he afforded Miss Gill a rare glimpse of this image cultivation. She was resting on a bedstead in the back showroom, concealed by a shadow to the left of the window and opposite the door. It was late afternoon and getting dark. "Suddenly the door burst open and in rushed Wyndham Lewis carrying a large paper bag which he threw onto a small table." The bag contained an outsize cloth cap made in a large black and white check material: the height of fashion. "Lewis . . . tried it on in front of the looking glass on the mantel piece. He cocked it slightly to one side to his satisfaction, then, taking a few steps backward, raised his hand as though to shake hands with someone and approached the mirror with an ingratiating smile. He backed again and tried the effect of a sudden recognition with a look of surprised pleasure. Then, cocking the cap at a more dashing angle his face froze and he turned and glanced over his shoulder with a look of scorn and disgust." Throughout this embarrassing would-be solitary performance, the reluctant spy feigned sleep, terrified at what he might do to her if he discovered he had been observed. Finally, Lewis snatched the cap from

his head, thrust it back into its paper bag and left. She heard his boots clattering down the stairs. The coast clear she went back to the studio and recounted the incident to her fellow worker. . . . "Ye were never nearer being murdered in yer life," he told her, "no man could have let yer live."

I have quoted at length because this anecdote wonderfully evokes the fraught nexus of celebrity, performance, and gender in modernism's early period. As the fellow worker's comment suggests, Lewis's potential humiliation inhered in the threat that exposure would have posed to the integrity of his masculinity: "no man" can afford to let the performativity of masculinity be discovered.

"Literary style," as Peter Schwenger puts it, "has an important relationship to sexual style; it can be used both to render an existing sex role and to change it."[48] Schwenger's observation complements leading masculinity theorist David Buchbinder's insistence that gender should be considered "a *rhetorical* system" which is "designed to persuade the viewer [or reader]."[49] By bringing both literary style and sexual style to a peculiarly high pitch, the dandy offers opportunities for intensive sex role consolidation—but also for sex role *transformation.* The metamorphic pressure put on sex and gender by the force of the dandy's style is a running theme throughout this book, most clearly in the chapters on Barnes and on Hemingway. Dandiacal form is constitutively androgynous, though it can often appear, as Schwenger says, "supermale." In an apparent paradox, such supermale style—"overcivilized diction," a "penchant for absurdity and ludicrous exaggeration," "moments of languor"—is "one which most people would call effeminate."[50] The contradictions captured by "supermale effeminacy" go to the very heart of the dandy, and of the dandiacal forms the dandy inspires.

What do I mean by dandiacal "form"? And what might it mean to think about modernist form—famously "impersonal"—as conditioned by the very accented "personality" of the dandy? Jaffe's conception of the imprimatur points toward one answer: the dandiacal novel effects the formalization of authorship linked to a biographical personage who disappears in a magical puff of literary style. But what about the dandy as character? How do character types come to have formal ramifications? From one point of view, it's hardly surprising that novel form follows character: think of the expansive, episodic structure of the picaresque as necessitated by the divagations of the *picaro,* or the repetitive pornographic scenarios of *Fanny Hill* as its "woman of pleasure" encounters yet another "furious battering ram" or "Maypole, of so enormous a standard."[51] And fictional narratives in the first person, from Clarissa's fractured "rape letters" to Humbert Humbert's sinister subtleties, can express character through form with special intensity. (In his amoral curation of forbidden pleasure, Humbert Humbert is a dandy in the evil mode.)[52] As the example of *Lolita* suggests, though, novels of dandyism render form and character peculiarly inextricable because the dandy himself is precisely a figure of form: his speech, his body, his clothing are dandiacal insofar as they are subjected to the shaping influence of creative discipline.

The dandy's "form" might be thought of as a specific, intensified instance of the "formalism" of masculinity in general, which, in Anthony Easthope's evocative phrase, our culture conceives as a "castle of the self,"[53] whereby men rigorously police the boundaries between their interior states and the outside world. As Buchbinder puts it, "Weaknesses or gaps in the bodily surface must be repaired and vigilantly patrolled in order to prevent the outside and the inside from merging and overpowering man's sense of himself as an autonomous entity."[54] Far from repudiating these masculinist prerogatives, the dandy, in one of his most common guises, amplifies them: he is a creature of sheer, protective surfaces, pure mask, impenetrable and unassailable. Like Schwenger's "super-male," this version of the dandy exaggerates masculinist cultural imperatives—and in exaggerating them, threatens to undo them by rendering them *spectacular*. He becomes a self-conscious "male impersonator," to borrow Mark Simpson's suggestive label. More precisely, he exposes masculinity itself as a performance and, as such, an object for public visual consumption—a role otherwise reserved for (or imposed on) women. Although the dandy is not his specific subject, Simpson's account of traditional masculine phobias around the spectacularization of the male body (in advertising, for instance) illuminates what is scandalous about the dandy's insistence that masculine form is, after all, an *image*: male spectacle "invite[s] a gaze that is *undifferentiated*: it might be female *or* male, hetero *or* homo."[55] The dandy's exaggeration of the bounded form of masculinity might scandalously render him less a "castle of the self" than a beautiful objet d'art. The conversion of oneself into a beautiful object is after all one of the dandy's projects. Here we have a clue to the drama of personal autonomy which animates the dandy in so many of his manifestations and which links him to that specifically aesthetic autonomy associated with the modernist artwork—a connection I will take up most explicitly in my third chapter, on William Burroughs.

The "castle of the self" metaphor for male subjectivity deployed by theorists of masculinity like Buchbinder and Easthope implies an interiority that must be vigilantly protected. Every castle, after all, hides a dungeon inside.[56] In the history of the dandy, such interiority emerges under the sign of decadence. Decadent literature develops the dandy's forbidden or secretive interiority. The very excessiveness of that interiority is a function of the exaggerated control of dandiacal surface: hard, even brittle, on his outside, the dandy's immaculate surface hides strange joys and stranger sins within. All of the authors discussed in *Dandyism* might be understood as developing, in different proportions and to different degrees, the interaction of dandiacal surfaces and decadent interiors. The surface/interior binarism animating the dandy's whole existence receives a schematizing theoretical treatment in the work of Lewis, an author who was more preoccupied with the problem of "manliness" than perhaps any other modernist, even Hemingway. An examination of Lewis and such avant-garde fellow travelers as T. E. Hulme and Ezra Pound will set the stage for the modern and postmodern dandies who follow.

BLAST and the Binarisms of Modernism: The Prehistory of *Dandyism*

Modernist dandies (fictional characters and authorial personae both) encode a formal history extending from the period of Pater onward.[57] The conditions against which ambivalent dandies like Chandler's Philip Marlowe or Hemingway's Jake Barnes can emerge are chiefly a product of tensions around aestheticist formal modes, tensions that would sustain a debate whose flash points include the reception of Paterian aestheticism, the trials of Oscar Wilde, and, crucially, the macho formalisms of such high modernists as Wyndham Lewis and Ezra Pound. Macho formalism of this quintessentially modernist type aims to purge Victorian aestheticism of any lingering Romantic subjectivism, a gambit achieved through a distinctly gendered rhetoric the aim of which is less to eliminate the dandy and the aesthete entirely than to reclaim them for a modernism understood as hard, dry, and male.[58]

Take, for instance, the Vorticist *BLAST* (1914). The inaugural *BLAST* (a second issue, the "War Number," came out in 1915) is the most important early document in that tradition of Anglophone modernist machismo often considered, both contemporaneously and by literary historians, as opposed to the gentler tendencies of Bloomsbury. It published drawings, poems, plays, and fiction by a range of figures, including Ford Madox Ford (then Hueffer) and Rebecca West, but its presiding aesthetic was the hard, angular "Vorticism" exemplified in its pages by the drawings of Lewis, Jacob Epstein, and Henri Gaudier-Brzeska, and by the poems, plays, and manifestos of Pound and Lewis. At first glance, *BLAST* would seem the opening salvo of modernism's masculinist abjection of the more dandiacal energies of the fin de siècle: among those quantities being "blasted" are England's "effeminate lout within," with the "BRITANIC AESTHETE" one of the first to go.[59] Indeed, a single dismissal is insufficient; a few pages on, in an amplified typeface: "CURSE WITH EXPLETIVE OF WHIRLWIND THE BRITANNIC AESTHETE," and curse too the "PEDANT," "PRACTICAL JOKER," "DANDY," and "CURATE," not to mention "SNOBBERY (disease of femininity)." The manifesto's valorization of "bareness and hardness" is the most succinct statement of the strain of modernist aesthetics *BLAST* inaugurates, an aesthetics here presented with much macho bombast. This posture of aggression especially marks Ezra Pound's poem "Salutation the Third," the first item in *BLAST* after the prefatory material. Pound concludes: "HERE is the taste of my BOOT, / CARESS it, lick off the BLACKING."[60] An aggressive "salutation," this poem's placement immediately after the Manifesto gives it something of the charge of a climax or a peroration, a proto-Fascist boot stomp from the right wing of bad modernism.

But all those dismissed aesthetes and dandies, all that vicious deployment of footgear, shouldn't mask *BLAST*'s rootedness in the aestheticism of the previous century. Nor did Pound, at least, attempt any cover-up. In his closing entry on the "Vortex," he adumbrates Vorticism's "Ancestry" through three quotations, from Pater, Pound himself, and James Whistler:

ANCESTRY

"All arts approach the condition of music." –*Pater*

"An Image is that which presents an intellectual and emotional complex in an instant of time." –*Pound*

"You are interested in a certain painting because it is an arrangement of lines and colours." –*Whistler.*[61]

What does it mean for Vorticism's "ancestry" to comprise formalist dicta from these three figures, Pound and his flanking Victorian predecessors? In Pater's and Whistler's quotations, we are given a now-familiar narrative about the modernist drive to abstraction, each formulation directing aesthetic attention away from reference or representation. Pound's own quotation, beyond its unabashed self-promotional function, introduces the doctrine of Imagism in what might seem a shorthand version of the Coleridgean "symbol." From one point of view, this might look like little more than an economic articulation of modernism's debt to Romantic aesthetic theory.[62]

But by positioning his statement on the Image between formulations by Pater and Whistler, proponents of an art for art's sake strongly associated with the figures of the "dandy" and "British aesthete" elsewhere vociferously cursed in *BLAST*, Pound acknowledges Vorticism's roots in aestheticism proper, even as he distances it from a Romantic poetics.[63] One effect of the name "Whistler" is to summon, pejoratively, the legacy of Ruskin, who famously attacked Whistler as a "willful imposture" guilty of "flinging a pot of paint in the public's face."[64] T. E. Hulme, whose ideas were formative for Pound's conception of Imagism, later in his essay "Romanticism and Classicism" dismissed Ruskin as a romantic with "a bad metaphysic of art": "I see quite clearly that [Ruskin] thinks the best verse must be serious. That is a natural attitude for a man in the romantic period. . . . He wants to deduce his opinion like his master, Coleridge, from some fixed principle which can be found by metaphysic."[65] Ruskin's aestheticism, according to Hulme, suffers from the Romantic prejudice that "[p]oetry that isn't damp isn't poetry at all"; his "bad metaphysic" can be repudiated only by showing, as Hulme and his Vorticist allies Pound and Lewis would set out to do, "that beauty may be in small, dry things," and that "dry hardness" is the condition of good art.[66] Pound's triple epigraph, then, means to highlight Vorticism's "ancestry" in one strain of aestheticism (Pater's) at the expense of another (Ruskin's). This is also to underline Vorticism's dandyism, since, as Ellen Moers put it in her early and important history of dandyism, Ruskin's criticism of Whistler "brought to an inglorious end the grand Victorian tradition of anti-dandiacal invective."[67]

Although Pater is often thought of as an aesthetic psychologist, a theorist of the "impression" and of the phenomenology of art, his aestheticism involved an emphasis on surfaces and externality absolutely necessary for the development of macho modernism's emphasis on "hardness."[68] The experience of the Paterian "moment," that historical mediator between Romantic and modernist varieties of epiphany, is in the conclusion to *Studies in the History of the Renaissance* (1873) given its best-known formula in language anticipating the very "hardness" so valorized by Hulme, Lewis, and Pound: "To burn always with this hard gem-like flame, to maintain this ecstasy, is success in life."[69] Pater is describing a subjective disposition, a state of perceptual intensity, that involves at the level of figuration a set of implications about the qualities of aesthetic objects: they are marked by a maximum concentration of energy (they "burn"), they present a complex play of surfaces (they are "gem-like"), and they are "hard." If, on the one hand, Pater's empiricist impressionism could risk reducing the subject to, as Judith Ryan puts it, "a bundle of sensory impressions precariously grouped together,"[70] on the other hand, the "hardness" of the trained percipient was a necessary condition for the aesthetics of Hulme, Lewis, and Pound.[71] If Gaudier-Brzeska's famous 1913 bust of Ezra Pound was, according to Lewis, "Ezra Pound in the form of a marble phallus"[72]—a characterization Hugh Kenner relates to Pound's theories on "the brain as a localization of seminal energy"[73]—then this aestheticizing "hardness" has at the level of figuration and metaphor antecedents in the Paterian perceiver's "hard, gem-like flame."

Pound's "ancestry," ultimately, insists that Vorticism is an outgrowth of those currents of the aestheticist movement whose force is anti-Romantic, a tendency repeatedly figured by the "Men of 1914" in terms of dryness, hardness, externality, even deadness. As the titular character insists in Lewis's novel *Tarr* (1918), "[D]eadness is the first condition of art. A hippopotamus' armoured hide, a turtle's shell, feathers or machinery on the one hand; that opposed to naked pulsing and moving of the soft inside of life."[74] The 1928 version continues, "Deadness is the first condition for art: the second is absence of soul, in the human and sentimental sense. With the statue its lines and masses are its soul, no restless inflammable ego is imagined for its interior: it has *no inside: good art must have no inside*."[75]

The *Recherche* of Proust (a great reader of Ruskin) is roughly contemporary with these developments, and might be taken as the extension of aestheticism distinctly *not* purged of Romantic subjectivism, a mode related to what I have above called "decadence." Its example can throw light on the Lewisian and Poundian avant-garde by contrast. While the Proustian *memoire involuntaire* is analogous to the Poundian Image insofar as both are epiphanic, Proust, like Wordsworth with his "spots of time," elaborates a complex psychology and temporal philosophy.[76] The Wordsworthian/Proustian epiphany unfolds a subjective temporality and draws on a tradition of Christian-humanist psychobiography structured by moments of revelation around which the meaning of life gets told. "Decadence" names the extreme limit of this kind of psychologizing, its "revelations" often demonically or pathologically inverted. As Baudelaire's protodecadent Cramer says in *La Fanfarlo* (1847), "We have psychologized like madmen, which increases their madness by trying to understand it."[77] In contradistinction to such "psychologizing," the Vorticist Image and its affiliations—Lewis's opposition to the "time-cult," Hulme's celebration of "classicism" in the visual arts—are atemporal, formal, and broadly antipsychological and antihumanist.

The foregoing interpretation rests on an admittedly streamlined and tidied-up account of the modernist "image," the history of which is complex and contradictory, but which, as Michael Levenson has shown in his pathbreaking *A Genealogy of Modernism* (1984), inherits a surface/depth dialectic from Jamesian and Conradian impressionism which it never ceases to negotiate.[78] The "dual movement" of Jamesian form—"the initial commitment to life's surface and the subsequent enhancement provided by subjectivity"[79]—will have decisive formal ramifications across all of modernism, will, indeed, constitute its two "major lines . . . the increasingly radical egoism and the similarly extreme formalism":

> On the one side the representative figures have been Pater, Bergson, Stirner, Upward and Ford, who, despite divergences in detail, shared a fundamental outlook: each offered a skeptical critique of traditional beliefs and institutions, and a renewal through retreat to the self—the existing order criticized from the standpoint of ego. On the other side stood Worringer, Husserl, Lasserre, Maurras, G. E. Moore, Gaudier-Brzeska and Lewis, all denying the ultimacy of the human subject and insisting on the autonomy of art, logic, politics and ethics, whose laws were independent of human will and whose values were objective—the existing order criticized from the standpoint of objective truth and objective value.[80]

These "major lines"—generative of such suggestive but imprecise binarisms as formalism/egoism, objective/subjective, mechanical/vital, classicism/romanticism,[81] and, in a recent study by Jessica Burstein, cold and hot[82]—are all subsumed, for the purposes of *Dandyism*, to the binarism aestheticist/decadent. (Behind all of these is the Nietzschean pair Apollonian/Dionysian, which Ellmann associates with aestheticism and decadence, respectively, in the case of Wilde.) I do not suggest this pair as an improvement in precision over the others—it has as many problems as they do. But I like aestheticist/decadent for three reasons. First, both terms are implicitly evaluative, and so reflect the intense social contestation around modernist form. Second (and relatedly), both are as much personality traits or types as they are formal categories, and so reflect the role of modernist celebrity, or at least modernist personality, in defining the contours of debate. Third, "aestheticist" and "decadent" are not starkly opposed in the way that, say, "objective" and "subjective" are; one has much less trouble imagining a decadent aesthete than a subjective objectivist, which sounds flatly contradictory.[83] This is, I suggest, a strength and not a weakness because it more accurately reflects the slippery way in which, in actual use, the aesthetic terms used by the modernists (image, subject and object, impressionism and expressionism, romanticism, classicism, and so on) have a range of values and uses that transcend their merely logical applications. After all, an objective image is not the opposite of a subjective impression the way north is the opposite of south. Thus Pound can at one point suggest that the role of the artist is to be, as it were, objective in his subjectivity: "The serious artist is scientific in that he presents the image of his desire, of his hate, of his indifference as precisely that, as precisely the image of his own desire, hate or indifference."[84]

Levenson is quite aware of the failure of such terms as, say, egoism and formalism to maintain their positions in a strict binary. His own reading of Pound's triple epigraph in BLAST situates Pound's self-quotation—"An Image is that which presents an intellectual and emotional complex in an instant of time"—as a mediator between competing poles: "[Pound's] remark reminds us of the personal and psychological basis on which the formalism of his experiments depends."[85] But by opposing Pater to Whistler—as proponents of "internal" and "abstract art," respectively—Levenson does not allow the mobility between poles that he elsewhere insists on. After all, the aspiration of the non-musical (traditionally representational) arts to music involves a drive toward abstraction absolutely consonant with (not opposed to) Whistler's "arrangements of lines and colours." (And abstraction has its roots in that "art for art's sake" associated, in the Anglophone world, most famously with both Pater and Whistler.) Lewis, at least, seemed to recognize the consonance of abstraction with Pater's line about music when, in 1954, he denounced his own abstract prewar painting: "I saw that it was irrational to attempt to transmute the art of painting into music—to substitute for the most naturally concrete of the arts the most inevitably abstract."[86] If Pater is the supreme theoretician of the impression, of egoism, of aesthetic psychology, he is nevertheless also one of the major forerunners of the abstraction associated with Pound, Hulme, and Lewis.

Pater is both egoist *and* formalist, both humanist psychologist *and* antihumanist abstractionist—which is to say he is decadent (egoism at its furthest extreme) and aestheticist (devoted to an aestheticism of surfaces anticipating modernist abstraction) at once. As the quintessential theorist of an aestheticism seen by others, if not by himself, as decadent ("in Pater's case theorizing the subjective also meant taking the first misstep down the slippery decadence of public homosexuality," as Jesse Matz puts it),[87] Pater has pride of place among the Victorian forerunners to the twentieth-century authors examined here. He embodies both sides of the aestheticist/decadent dialectic.

Two Paths for the Modernist Dandy: *Hugh Selwyn Mauberley* and *Snooty Baronet*

For the early modernists, the scholastic details are perhaps less important than the polemical fury underlying the debates, a polemical fury that, for macho modernists like Hulme, Pound, and Lewis, could sustain surprising reversals in position. A fighting style was at least as important as the subject fought over. Like Hemingway, the macho modernists in the *BLAST* set were all of them in it for the fight. In this, too, they were not as far from the dandy as might be assumed.

Verbal combat is one of the dandy's modes, so it should come as no surprise that the modernist personality in its most polemical phase was often dandiacal. The dandy has always been a locus of masculine oppositionality, an oppositionality which Martin Green, in his cultural history of the English upper classes in the first half of the twentieth century, understands as a form of Oedipal revolt: "[T]here is an alliance between the dandy-aesthete and the rogue-rebel [two Oxford types] in a common cause, the cause of defying their fathers' mode of seriousness."[88] What better standard-bearer for the serious antiseriousness enacted by *BLAST* than the dandy in his antisentimental and aggressive guise, a Lord Wotton who has read Marinetti? The "Britannic aesthete" and the "dandy" are repudiated in *BLAST* because they are too close for comfort—and Ezra Pound, at least, seemed to know it. Pound's early poetry systematically negotiates the heritage of dandiacal aestheticism and art for art's sake, developing a strategy for preserving aestheticist formalism for a toughened, indeed a martial, avant-garde.

Green recounts that when Harold Acton—noted British dandy and author of *Memoirs of an Aesthete* (1948)—lived in Europe, "he shunned the writers he called 'bogus Bronco Bills,' with their vaunted virility, like Hemingway and Pound—'they lived in dread of betraying their emotions, except by hic-cups.'"[89] But in 1944 Paul Rosenfeld could criticize Pound's "dandyism," a trait one would assume to be at odds with Acton's characterization of the poet as a "Bronco Bill." Nothing, though, is more dandiacal than the dread of betray-ing emotions; Acton's resistance to Pound and Hemingway is over means, not ends. The quarrel is not with the mask as such, but with the style of mask chosen. Bronco Bill and the dandy may represent competing styles of masculinity, but they are alike in their shared dependence on performative masquerade. Rosenfeld's account points toward the way Pound's status as a "literary dandy," a "self-worshipper" like "Whistler, and Oscar Wilde" involves both *too much* personality (his poems "persistently and complacently have brought us face to face with the personality of Ezra Pound") and *too little* ("To achieve self-expression . . . Pound has always to wear a costume, to enact some role proposed to him by other minds").[90] How can one maintain, even em-phasize, one's "personality" while hiding behind costumes and masks? The working out of this paradox is one business of modernism's intensely per-sonal theories of impersonality.[91]

Pound's own masks, in life and in verse, were as likely to be of the aes-theticist as of the Bronco Bill variety. And while Hemingway's negotiation of Victorian precedent happens mostly (like so much else in Hemingway) be-neath the surface, Pound openly stages his anxieties, and debts, of influence. There is the "Ancestry" section of *BLAST*, there is the poem to Walt Whitman ("let there be commerce between us"), there is Canto 2 ("Hang it all, Rob-ert Browning"),[92] and there is *Hugh Selwyn Mauberley* (1920), in which Pound presents and discards a series of literary masks in order to effect a partial—but only partial—containment of dandiacal aestheticism. *Mauberley* might be said to represent the normative avenue by which a chastened and ironized aes-theticism makes it into modernism. In that poem, Gautier's prosody—which Pound valued for its hardness, its externality—is adopted as a bridge between nineteenth-century art for art's sake and the twentieth century's imperative to "make it new."[93] Along the way, such literary dandies as Max Beerbohm (ap-pearing Hebraicized as "Brennbaum, the impeccable") and Mauberley him-self are engaged with, inhabited, and found wanting. *Mauberley's* most famous lines, on the devastation and disillusionment wrought by the Great War, an-nounce a break with tradition thematized elsewhere in the poem by the rejec-tion of the persona of the aesthete.

There died a myriad,
And of the best, among them,
For an old bitch gone in the teeth,
For a botched civilization,

Charm, smiling at the good mouth,
Quick eyes gone under earth's lid,

For two gross of broken statues,
For a few thousand battered books.[94]

Mauberley enacts a post-*BLAST* modernist mythography in which literature's relationship to the world and to its own past is changed irrevocably by the war. It does so, importantly, in verse bearing no resemblance to the compressed Gallic quatrains that are the default mode for the rest of the poem. Taken altogether, the poem suggests a literature in revolt against but haunted by the past—haunted by the ghost symbolism of Gautier's meter, by the ghost dandyism of Beerbohm's "impeccable" lines.[95] As Anne Quéma puts it, "The modernism of Pound consists in the explosive combination of radicalism and *nostos*, revolution and tradition."[96] The tactical literary masquerade by which *Mauberley* anxiously negotiates an aestheticism at once embraced and scorned represents the most familiar model of modernist aestheticism.

A consideration of the inter-war work of Wyndham Lewis reveals a more surprising path by which modernism absorbs the energies of the fin de siècle. I have already suggested that Lewis's *BLAST* owes more to aestheticism than is commonly assumed, but can the rest of Lewis's career be considered under the rubric of dandiacal authorship? There are tempting details in the biography, for instance Lewis's positively Wildean devotion to forging a public persona ("my publicity pursued me," as he put it in his 1937 war memoir *Blasting and Bombardiering,* which means that he pursued his publicity) and his late-life flirtation with Catholicism. But at the level of both aesthetic theory and public position-taking, Lewis is generally considered a committed antiaesthete and antidandy. Douglas Mao sums up the consensus position when he writes that Lewis finds in the label "aesthete" "a capacity to dismiss and denigrate peculiarly his own," a stance proceeding from motivations both promotional and phobic: "'[A]estheticism' and 'aesthete' were especially useful in attack [because] they combined suggestions of obsolescence (the nineteenth century against the 'modern') with an air of the unsavory that still clung to the memory of Wilde."[97] Lewis's strenuous bellicosity certainly seems at odds with what Heather Love calls Pater's "queer modernism," which "cultivates a modernist aesthetic based not on violent transgression but rather on refusal and passivity."[98] After all, according to Lesley Higgins, the "Men of 1914" found it "necessary to protect modernist discourse . . . from the doubly-tainted undertones of effeminacy and homosexuality so often associated with Pater and Wilde."[99] As this yoking of Pater and Wilde implies, for the prewar avant-garde, aestheticism and the figure of the dandy were, the thinking goes, linked in a common abjection.

But the very violence of Lewis's renunciation should make us suspicious.[100] What makes Lewis's love of surfaces different from aestheticism's? As he put it in *Blasting and Bombardiering*, "I enjoy the surface of life, if not for its own sake, at least because it conceals the repulsive turbidness of the intestine. Give me the dimple in the cheek of the Gioconda . . . and you can have all the Gothic skeletons and superrealist guts you like!"[101] Between *Tarr's* earlier celebration of "deadness" and the later text, an interesting shift of emphasis has occurred: an antihumanist "deadness" and hardness, which we might have expected Lewis to associate with "skeletons" if not with "superrealist guts," has been brought to bear on the psychologically evocative—that is to say, humanist—countenance of the Mona Lisa.

This is, I would suggest, less a reversal than a conflation: Lewis means to make "deadness" relevant to all artistic representation, rather than limit it to his own avant-gardist preoccupation with "feathers or machinery." His invocation of the Gioconda as an emblem of the anti-Gothic and of surfaces, then, both confirms and counters Pater's famous ekphrastic description of her in *The Renaissance*: "[L]ike the vampire, she has been dead many times, and learned the secrets of the grave; and has been a diver in deep seas."[102] "Confirms" because of the echoing resonance of aesthetically productive "deadness" across the divide of the fin de siècle; "counters" because of Lewis's pointed rejection of the probing Gothic interiority Pater's ekphrasis evokes. In fact, though, Lewis's preference for exteriors bears a distinct debt to nineteenth-century aestheticism, particularly that of Pater—who after all, as James Eli Adams has it, "seeks to evoke hidden depths of intention and meaning in order ultimately to return us to the surfaces of an image."[103] Such aestheticized deadness fulfills one of the dandy's longstanding ambitions, as Giorgio Agamben recognizes: "[T]he dandy-artist must become a living corpse, constantly tending toward an *other*, a creature essentially nonhuman and antihuman."[104]

I want to take up this aesthetic history with regards to *Snooty Baronet* (1932), Wyndham Lewis's most eccentric production, a novel that, more than any other document of modernism, dramatizes the intellectual and aesthetic impasses reached by the avant-garde's strained, anxious negotiation of aestheticism. A rambling, manic first-person picaresque, *Snooty Baronet* treats the adventures of an author and wounded Great War veteran (the war has left him with a prosthetic leg and a metal plate in his head) named Michael Kell-Imrie, or "Snooty Baronet," as he travels around London, France, and, finally, Persia. There, his literary agent, Humph, has arranged for him to be kidnapped by desert bandits and ransomed by the British government, all part of an effort to promote Snooty's forthcoming book and to defraud Britain out of the ransom money, which will be split among Snooty, Humph, and the bandits. Toward the end of the novel, Snooty sabotages the kidnapping scheme by shooting and killing Humph, much to the consternation of the bandits and the surprise of the reader.

By profession, Snooty is a kind of ethnologist whose work focuses on "behavior"—he is a caricature of the behaviorist psychologist J. B. Watson. Not merely a student of behaviorist psychology, Snooty is also an instance of its emphasis on classical conditioning and on automaticity, and his climactic killing of Humph in particular is presented as automatic and unmotivated. Lewis had rejected behaviorism in his theoretical treatises *The Art of Being Ruled* (1926) and *Time and Western Man* (1927), and it is possible to see *Snooty Baronet* as an extension of that critique. As a "satire on Behaviourism," the novel is, as Paul Edwards puts it, "simple and devastating; [behaviorism] leaves no room for rationality, humanity or morality, and it is part of the ideology that destroys the conception of the integrated human subject."[105] But, crucially, *Snooty Baronet* presents Lewis's hated behaviorism in terms very similar to those by which he has described his own vaunted aesthetic of externality. David Trotter observes of *Snooty* "a certain equivalence between the doctrines of behaviorism and Lewis's eversive technique, which often treats human beings as though they were animals, or machines."[106] And there is yet a further equivalence with satire itself, which, as Fredric Jameson observes, Lewis "understood to be a non-ethical, purely external mode of representation, cubist-caricatural, its objective and materialistic techniques fundamentally set against all the shapeless warm organic flux of inner monologue and psychology-oriented subjectivism."[107] In an audacious frenzy of self-critique, *Snooty Baronet* systematically recasts Lewis's own aesthetic theories in the idiom of behaviorism, while also suggesting that satire as such—Lewis's preferred mode—might be assimilated or reduced to behaviorist observation.

The novel's pivotal scene is not the murder of Humph but an encounter between Snooty and an advertising puppet in a London shopwindow, an apparently mundane occurrence taken as an occasion for Snooty's most sustained theorizing on "behavior." Strolling along in search of a gin fizz and an American club sandwich, Snooty becomes distracted by a large crowd entranced by the puppet, who is advertising a straw hat. "The puppet was a good size. . . . He was a sturdy well-kept puppet. He was fashionably dressed, in a somewhat loud, I thought, summer-suiting." Snooty, too, finds himself transfixed as the puppet mechanically removes and replaces his hat, staring all the while at the spectators staring at him. "[T]hen straightening himself out, [the puppet] put on his hat again at a somewhat rakish angle in his particular, a little dandyish, manner . . . and I could swear that his eyes lightened as he looked down for a moment in our direction."[108]

The puppet prompts a revelation for Snooty: not only are his fellow spectators puppets, *"but equally so am I!"*[109] Snooty is reminded of a past visit to the zoo: "How surprisingly small is the difference between a mandrill and a man! Certainly—but still slenderer was the difference between this stiffly-bowing so-called automaton, and my literary agent, for example. . . . But this automaton *looked*, was dressed and behaved itself, far more like a man than did a mandrill. And that word *looked*, that was for me *everything*."[110] The puppet—or "The Hatter's Automaton," as the chapter in which he appears is called—is an extreme icon of Lewis's fascination with surfaces and his repudiation of depths. He represents the uncanny possibility that interiority, psychology, consciousness, and intention are merely the deduced effects of surface appearance. It is no surprise that the puppet emblematizing this problem should be "dandyish." Not only is the "dandy" attached to the Paterian aestheticism from which Lewis draws his emphasis on externality, but he is also, at least in one of his major strains, a personality type with a thesis: surface is everything. Agamben observes that Baudelaire, in the founding moment of aesthetic (which is also to say, aestheticist) autonomy, "immediately assimilates the human being to the statue, that is to say, to a divine and superior being."[111] Lewis, by assimilating the human being to the advertising puppet, both continues and deflates the aestheticist trajectory that Baudelaire inaugurates.

In *The Sense of Things* (2003), Bill Brown takes William Carlos Williams's slogan "No ideas but in things" as an occasion for theorizing what he calls the "object matter" of American fiction from the late nineteenth century through modernism.[112] Williams's dictum, Brown writes, "may be read as the mark of a limit within modernism's effort to accept opacity, to satisfy itself with mere limits." For Brown, "the idea that there are ideas in things amounts to granting them an interiority and, thus, something like the structure of subjectivity."[113] But Lewis's puppet represents a different kind of limit to this strain of modernist aesthetics: the apparent subjectification of things rebounds upon the subject himself, who discovers not that things have a mysterious inner life but, rather, that people do not. At some level, this was always a consummation devoutly to be wished in Lewis's aesthetic thinking. But its allegorization in the episode of the hatter's automaton is distinctly uncomfortable, as if dramatizing, at mid-career, the internal conflict that eventually led to Lewis's rejection of artistic abstraction, for instance in *The Demon of Progress in the Arts* (1954): "[B]eyond a certain well-defined line—in the arts as in everything else—beyond that limit there is *nothing*."[114]

Snooty's worldview results as much from his creator's interest in the problems of the visual arts as from his own Watsonian theories; he, too, evinces a phobic preoccupation with the intestines, which, in a bravura description of appetite immediately preceding his encounter with the puppet, he invokes only to rescript in the language of sculpture and painting:[115]

> My intestines had thrown up the picture in bold plaster-cast relief of a big chicken-hearted club-Sandwich. My spittle-ducts had squirted with a will and all together at the sight of it: so with the above life-size model, in crisp yellow-crusted impasto, of a super-Club-sandwich swelling inside me (blocked out in wind in mid-stomach—a cave, a receptacle—my thunderous belly had modeled a cavity, with a contour of such an object as a monstrous Club-sandwich, to attract my attention) and with my hat hanging in my hand, I took the route my destiny had traced out.[116]

Indeed, Snooty's quest for a sandwich frames the episode with the hatter's automaton: "[I was] a very thoughtful and important puppet—wandering in this sinister thoroughfare, in search of an american Club-sandwich—a place in my breadbasket, scooped out in wind, the size of a small melon like a plaster mould."[117] If, as Brown has written of *The Golden Bowl*'s Adam Verver, "To become a self-possessed connoisseur, [Verver must] reify his mind in order to take possession of it,"[118] then Snooty's own reification of thought (here, thought about appetite, as if to underscore consciousness's material underpinnings), accomplished by metaphors about the fine arts, transposes the operations of Jamesian psychology to a comic key. *Snooty Baronet* is a kind of parody of the way that, as Brown puts it of James, "[t]hought assumes a physicality of its own."[119] While for James and other novelists of the nuances of interiority, reification via metaphor achieves a deepened sense of subjective complexity—as when Maggie Verver's commitment to a renewed erotic engagement with her husband is likened to "seeing her jewels again a little shyly, all but unmistakably, glow"[120]—for Lewis, such interiority is the occasion for a spasmodic, stuttering narrative herky-jerk serving not to multiply subtleties but to provoke laughter.

Like Adam Verver's "connoisseurship," Snooty's self-objectification proceeds along distinctly aestheticist lines. He substitutes for his insides and their associated appetites the materials (paint, plaster) and forms of the visual arts. But while aestheticist metaphors, from Pater's "hard, gem-like flame" to Maggie's glowing jewels, reify consciousness in order to present it as richer and stranger, Snooty's aestheticist reification reduces him to the status of a "puppet." As Jameson puts it, in Lewis "an almost pathological depersonalization releases the personality from all favoritism."[121] With his antic, bizarre humor, Snooty takes the aesthete's credo—to live one's life like a work of art—and literalizes it so as also to deflate it: the very intestines become material for ekphrasis. Snooty's compulsive, aestheticized conversion of his intestinal activity into plaster casts and crisp impastos bears ambivalently upon Lewis's own professed theories: Snooty is both an enactment of Lewis's thought and a parody of it. Like all of Lewis's rebarbative puppet fiction, *Snooty Baronet* translates the aestheticist cult of surfaces into a worldview, one Jessica Burstein characterizes as "not antihumanism, but ahumanism."[122] That is to say, Lewis is not interested—as contemporaneous thinkers as different as Heidegger and Hulme were—in critiquing the hubris of a humanism that makes man the measure of the world, but rather in imagining a world without the human as such.[123] Snooty represents Lewis's half-joking rejection of both the novel of consciousness associated with James, Woolf, and Proust and the ideal of the "rounded character" propounded in 1927 by E. M. Forster. For Snooty, whose views are Lewis's hyperbolized (and therefore partially rejected), one can ascribe interiority to a puppet with as much validity as to a human being—which is to say one cannot properly do so at all.

In the most nuanced account to date of Lewis's thoughts on "impersonality," Heather Arvidson demonstrates beyond any doubt that Lewis's depiction of a puppet world ought not to be taken as an endorsement—at least not at the level of theory, where Lewisian puppetry is a monitory part of his "many-pronged defense of the autonomous subject."[124] But it seems to me undeniable that the representation of humans as mechanized puppets presents profound affective satisfactions for Lewis—that, at the level of *feeling,* a fully mechanized human-kind, the comprehensive reduction of persons to things, is a source of aesthetic gratification.[125] In *Snooty,* such nihilistic gratification extends to violence. When he shoots his agent twice in the desert, Snooty experiences the killing in a distinctly aesthetic, indeed aestheticist, register. He is particularly pleased with the second of his two shots: "I think I shall never lose that pleasant feeling of immediate satisfaction. . . . It will never lose that quality—. . . A thing of beauty is a joy forever! That second one was a *beauty!*"[126] The ironic invocation of Keats perversely yokes aestheticism (for which Keats was a major Romantic source) to murderousness.[127] Snooty, as Paul Edwards observes, is a "psychopath," a pathology resulting, here, from an aesthetic theory carried too far.[128] In *Snooty Baronet,* the reduction of subjects to surfaces entails rather shocking consequences, as every subject is converted to an object and thereby rendered disposable.[129]

Psychopathy, then, is a characterological disposition consonant with modernist aesthetics at their most masculinist, and Snooty accordingly provides a theory for the gender performance of macho modernism. His objectification of interiority is linked to a theory of gender performativity. Describing his poet friend Rob, Snooty says, "Now like myself Rob is an actor—he is the artist in action. . . . I am the man-of-action incarnate. So is he. But I *act* at being in action. And he too! What man-of-action has not?"[130] Because interiority is so uncertain, in order to be anything at all one must perpetually act—one must, as it were, pull one's own puppet strings. As a "man-of-action" and former warrior, Snooty prizes a bellicosity requiring continual performance, since "to *fight* is as essential as the drawing of breath, to the man-of-action—that is what m.-of-a. means I conclude."[131] Fighting, acting, and a determined rejection of the organic constitute, for Snooty as for Lewis, a complete system. With his prosthetic leg and metal plate, Snooty is closer than most (one senses that he is pleased about it) to the objectivity of the puppet, which means he is better able than most to exemplify the discursive construction of gender—the ways in which one pulls one's own puppet strings in conformity with gender's imperative stage directions. For Lewis, as he explains in *The Art of Being Ruled,* masculinity is not at all natural: "[The male] had to be propped up into that position with some ingenuity."[132]

Replace "dandyism" with "manliness," and Ellen Moers's classic formulation could be Lewis's: "[D]andyism is a pose: not a *'mere'* pose, but an immensely difficult, conscious and effective pose. It is a training for power."[133] But *Snooty Baronet's* manic style, and Snooty's swing into psychopathy, register the risks of overperforming a potentially toxic masculinity: one might turn into a chattering hollow man, or a murderous robot, or an unthinking chunk of bone matter. When Snooty tries to conceive of his own psychic insides, he describes himself as possessed of ossature rather than brains. It is as if, taking as cue Tarr's preference for the "armoured hide" over the "naked pulsing and moving of the soft inside of life," he has replaced all insides with armor: "I understand only too well the meaning of the american 'bonehead.' . . . [It] meant *a head like mine*—just opaque and solid skull, or it feels like that if you happen to own one, as I do."[134] Snooty Baronet's bonehead both satirizes and revels in Gaudier-Brzeska's rendering of Pound as a "marble phallus"—it is an emblem of aesthetic machismo's flailing failure, and one of aestheticism's surprising termini.

As I hope the example of *Snooty Baronet* has shown, much of modernism's (and postmodernism's) dandiacal masquerades are a good deal less familiar than Pound's *Mauberley*—hidden, like all masks, in plain sight. And even when the texts themselves are familiar, the dandyism is not. *Dandyism* begins with Hemingway's macho dandyism, which seems to have gone unremarked by all observers other than Lewis himself, who sensed early on that Oscar Wilde was Hemingway's unacknowledged daimon. I read Hemingway as heir not only to Wilde but to Pater, and more broadly to Victorian aestheticism's interest in refined sensory experience. The epic rounds of dining and drinking in all of Hemingway's novels are a conscious inheritance at the level of theme of Pater's aesthetic connoisseurship—Hemingway's tough heroes are Paterian aesthetes brought out of the art museum and into other, humbler surrounds. And Hemingway's clipped sentences and famous strategy of "omission" (the "iceberg method"), so markedly different from Pater's rhetorical lushness, in fact involves a complex engagement with the rhythms of aestheticism. From the Hemingway hero I turn, in my second chapter, to the wisecracking dick of detective fiction, considering Chandler's Philip Marlowe novels alongside the trial transcripts of Wilde. In both cases, a certain kind of talk—what I call "epigrammatic speech"—serves as the verbal signature of self-contained masculinity and oppositionality to bourgeois norms. And the actual dandies who

appear in Chandler's fiction, usually as abject victims or villains, are the oc-
cluded sign of Chandler's appropriation of dandiacal verbal style.

My third chapter treats William S. Burroughs's "cut-up" technique as extending the concerns of fin de siècle decadence. Burroughs's novels inherit a set
of Victorian anxieties clustered around the class stratification associated with
the later phases of the Industrial Revolution, anxieties that, as H. G. Wells's
novels *The Time Machine* (1895) and *The Island of Dr. Moreau* (1896) demonstrate quite keenly, took apocalyptic, pseudoscientific coloring in the wake of
Darwin. I suggest that Burroughs's formal experimentation, rooted in decadence and in early science fiction, can shed critical light on theories of modernist impersonality. In my fourth chapter, on Djuna Barnes and the female
dandy, I turn back to the period of modernism proper to explore connections
among cross-dressing, degeneration theory, and Barnes's stylized imagination
of the literary past in *Nightwood*. For both of these chapters, the interiority so
feared by Lewis will return with a vengeance: Burroughs was as phobically
fascinated by "the repulsive turbidness of the intestines" as Lewis was, while
Barnes's elaborate animal metaphors strive to make present that "naked moving pulsing of the soft inside of life" denigrated in Lewis's *Tarr*.

My final chapter returns to "the psychopathic dandy" as he appears in a
range of texts including Anthony Burgess's *A Clockwork Orange*, Bret Easton
Ellis's *American Psycho*, Patricia Highsmith's *Ripley* novels, Norman Mailer's essays and journalism, and in psychoanalytic and sociological literature ranging
from Robert Lindner to Theodor Adorno. In doing so, it extends my interest
in the relationship between form and character type—as rebel and psychopath, the dandy becomes the personality assumed by aesthetic flatness in late
capitalism. As David Joselit has observed of twentieth-century painting, "flatness may serve as a powerful metaphor for the price we pay in transforming
ourselves into images—a compulsory self-spectacularization which is the necessary condition of entering the public sphere in the world of late capitalism."[135]
Baudelaire noted in 1863 that the dandy is a figure of "opposition and revolt,"
and the dandy-as-psychopath carries this oppositionality to its most shocking limit.

Each chapter might be thought of as addressing different facets of the post-
Victorian dandy—though there are, I hope, countless continuities between
them. The book's first part, on dandiacal machismo, begins with Hemingway
to ask: how does the dandy *eat*? More broadly: how does the dandy inherit
a nineteenth-century aestheticist emphasis on taste? And of Chandler: how

does the dandy *talk?* How does Wildean epigrammatism inform popular machismo? The book's second part, on the perverse interiority of the decadent dandy, picks up on Burroughs's absorption of Victorian science fiction to ask: how does the dandy *dream?* How does decadence inflect Burroughs's visionary sci-fi fantasias? Decadent metaphor is also the core of the chapter on Barnes, which asks: how does the dandy *love?* More broadly, what kind of emotional suffering does decadent dandyism promote? The next chapter, on the dandiacal psychopath, asks: how does the dandy *kill?* Or, how do some tendencies long latent in the dandy eventuate in psychopathy? And briefly, in my conclusion, I turn to the twenty-first-century hipster to pose a question I cannot answer: will the dandy survive?

Like a number of recent studies of modernism, including Douglas Mao's broadly phenomenological *Solid Objects* (1998), Jessica Burstein's broadly historicist *Cold Modernism* (2012), and Andrew Goldstone's broadly sociological *Fictions of Autonomy* (2013), *Dandyism* engages a renewed interest in the formal stakes of modernist aesthetics, but by routing this interest through the figure of the dandy, it suggests that modernist form depends much more centrally than has been recognized on a certain set of character traits: modernist "impersonality" turns out to depend on the marked "personality" of the dandy. Looking backward from modernism, then, *Dandyism* brings the study of modernist form into conversation with Victorianist scholarship on dandyism and its affiliated aesthetic modes, especially aestheticism and decadence. And, in the other direction, it extends the Victorian-to-modern trajectory well into the latter half of the twentieth century, demonstrating that Victorian aesthetic concerns continued to exert profound influence long after the period of modernism proper. It furthermore contributes to the collapse of those disciplinary boundaries that have sometimes prevented us from seeing how much twentieth-century American literature and culture draws from British aesthetic and social precedent. *Dandyism's* central contention is that dandyism's formal implications remain relevant long after the period conventionally associated with it—that, indeed, dandyism constitutes a point of maximum intensity around which the gendered stakes of aesthetic form are worked out.

PART I

MACHO DANDIES

1

FINE AND DANDY

Ernest Hemingway's Androgynous Connoisseurship

The heavy bear who goes with me
A manifold honey to smear his face.
—DELMORE SCHWARTZ

Good, Fine, Nice, Pretty: Hemingway's Aestheticism

In Cyril Connolly's 1935 novel *The Rock Pool,* a rather sour portrait of queer expatriate bohemia in interwar France, a platinum-haired young man named Jimmy (in whom "[t]he tradition of Oscar was still preserved") offers a startling judgment of literary taste: "[T]he two greatest modern writers were Firbank and Hemingway."[1] The conjunction of Hemingway and the extravagantly dandiacal (and today largely forgotten) Ronald Firbank recalls Wyndham Lewis's allusive yoking of Papa to Alfred Lord Douglas; Hemingway would not have approved of either. "Firbank," as Hemingway puts it in *Death in the Afternoon* (1932), "wrote very well about what he wrote about but was, let us say, a specialist."[2] Let *us* say that Hemingway's faux politeness does not conceal his suspicion of Firbank's queer aesthetic.

Nevertheless, with the retrospective clarity granted in part by the 1986 publication of Hemingway's gender-bending novel *The Garden of Eden,* it has become necessary to credit Hemingway, from *The Sun Also Rises* onward, with far more analytical self-awareness regarding questions of gender and sexuality than some of his earlier detractors could recognize. As published, *The Garden of Eden* depicts a love triangle of sorts involving a young writer, David Bourne, his wife, Catherine, and their new friend Marita, whom they meet in Europe and with whom each is sleeping. David and Catherine's erotic relationship involves androgynous identity mergers (they cut their hair to resemble one another) and sexual role reversals (David is anally penetrated by Catherine). Hemingway, as a number of critics in the last three decades have shown, is not so much the preeminent fictional chronicler of stereotyped machismo as he is a deliberate, if ambivalent, investigator of highly ambiguous sexual territory.[3] This chapter will argue that Hemingway's psychosexual explorations hinge on his absorption and reconfiguration of a tradition of aestheticism inherited from Pater and Gautier and inseparable from the figure of the dandy. For Hemingway, as we will see, these aestheticist inheritances will revolve around two of the dandy's signal traits: his androgyny and his love of fine dining (not for nothing was his posthumously published memoir called *A Moveable Feast*). Hemingway, indeed, is a bridge connecting the androgynous aestheticism of the nineteenth-century dandy to something very like contemporary foodie culture.

In *The Garden of Eden*, the word "dandy" appears, during a tense three-way exchange between David, Catherine, and Marita, as a problem of lexical definition:

> David made two martinis taking his time and the girl [Marita] came in. She was wearing a white sharkskin dress and she looked fresh and cool. "May I have one too, David? It was very hot today. How was it here?"
>
> "You should have stayed home and looked after him," Catherine said.
>
> "I got along all right," David said. "The sea was very good."
>
> "You use such interesting adjectives," Catherine said. "They make everything so vivid."
>
> "Sorry," David said.
>
> "That's another dandy word," Catherine said. "Explain what dandy means to your new girl. It's an Americanism."
>
> "I think I know it," the girl said. "It's the third word in 'Yankee Doodle Dandy.' Don't please be cross Catherine."
>
> "I'm not cross," Catherine said. "But two days ago when you made passes at me it was simply dandy but today if I felt that way the slightest bit you had to act as though I was an I don't know what."
>
> "I'm sorry, Catherine," the girl said.

"Another sorry sorry," Catherine said. "As though you hadn't taught me what little I know."

"Should we have lunch?" David said. "It's been a hot day, Devil, and you're tired."[4]

"Dandy," here, is first of all an interpretive problem, something whose meaning needs to be explained. As Jessica Feldman notes of the term's crossing and recrossing of the English Channel, the "international proliferation of dandyism suggests the very displacement crucial to 'placing' dandyism: it exists in its purest form always at the periphery of one's vision, often in a foreign language or a text requiring decipherment."[5] Here, its use as part of an exotic American vernacular must be deciphered for the Spanish Marita, who identifies its Americanness with "Yankee Doodle Dandy."[6] By the twentieth century, "dandy" in American usage had become a kind of all-purpose term of approval, rather drained of any connotative specificity.[7] By making, here, "dandy" an occasion for interpretive activity, Hemingway works against the word's very broad applicability in American colloquial speech.

Catherine further associates "dandy" with lesbianism: "But two days ago when you made passes at me it was simply dandy." In the larger context of *The Garden of Eden*, nonheterosexuality is always aligned with the troubling of gender binaries. As Marita say to Catherine later on, "You aren't really a woman at all," to which Catherine responds, "I know it. I've tried to explain it to David often enough."[8] In the unpublished manuscript version of the novel, the experiments in sexual role reversal between David and Catherine are inspired by seeing Rodin's sculpture *Metamorphoses*, which depicts the mythic transformation of the female Iphis into a man so that she can appropriately wed her lover, the female Ianthe. The sculpture shows the two in an erotic embrace, Iphis midtransformation, with female breasts and a male head.[9] Such emphases on androgynous boundary states are, as Feldman notes, regular features of "the literature of dandyism," which "challenges the very concept of two separate genders."[10] This is especially true of the French literature of dandyism, particularly Théophile Gautier's *Mademoiselle de Maupin* (1835), which Hemingway had certainly read and which is mentioned in the manuscript version of *The Garden of Eden* as well as in *Islands in the Stream* (1970).[11]

The word "dandy" does some of its subtlest and most important work in this passage as a vernacular alternative to "good," "fine," or "nice," those mainstays of Hemingway's diction. Throughout his oeuvre, Hemingway deploys the adjective "good" literally hundreds of times as an all-purpose index of aesthetic appraisal, competent craftsmanship, and gustatory approval. In *A Moveable Feast*, for example, Hemingway in the course of a half-dozen pages writes of "the good Martinique rum," "a very good story," "good wood for sale," and "the good cafés."[12] Besides food (and booze), art and writing are, for Hemingway, especially susceptible to this adjective. As a favorite term of his aesthetics, "good" might be read as the most compressed expression of Hemingway's famously pared-down style.[13]

Indeed, it is necessary to draw a distinction between "good" on the one hand and "fine" or "nice" on the other as they are used in Hemingway. Michael North has discussed the word "nice" as deployed both by Gertrude Stein and by Hemingway. In North's reading of Stein's line "All nice wives are like that" in "Idem the Same: A Valentine for Sherwood Anderson," the word "nice" both cites and subverts its conventional associations with respectable femininity. " 'Nice wives,' " North writes, "are those who fit comfortably within the category of 'wife,' so that 'nice wives is almost, as the assonance and near-rhyme suggest, a tautological phrase."[14] Given, though, that Alice Toklas was the original dedicatee of "A Valentine" in its manuscript form, North suggests that "nice," here, expresses a masked homosexual erotic.[15] North connects the complicated polyvalence of "nice" in Stein to Hemingway's own deployment of the word: " 'Nice' is the precisely measured term of approval that Jake applies to Lady Brett and Hemingway applies to Stein herself."[16] The word's applicability to these ambivalently embraced female figures, the real-life master and the fictional phallic woman alike, suggests that "nice," for Hemingway, can continue to encode some of the queer potential North finds for it in Stein. In a recent study, John S. Bak has extended the analysis of the gender work done by Hemingway's adjectives to track the word "pretty" in *The Sun Also Rises*; Jake's famous concluding line—"Isn't it pretty to think so?"—might be read as a particularly ironic engagement by the Hemingway hero with dangerously feminized aesthetic descriptors and all that they entail.[17]

"Good" does not fit into the feminized adjectival series "fine-nice-pretty," though Hemingway often uses it in places where "fine" or "nice" (if not "pretty") might seem to do just as well. In an important sense, the semantic range of "good" is more restricted than that of "fine" or "nice"; "good" uttered as a judgment does not necessarily suggest a speaker's capacity for subtle distinction, for minute discrimination, carried by the other two words. In short, "good" as a term of approbation is blunter than "fine" or "nice"; it does not require that its pronouncer possess *refinement* or *niceness* of vision, traits proper to an aestheticist mode of observation derived from Pater. It is because of their redolence of a queer aestheticism that Hemingway uses "fine" and "nice" as fitting adjectives for Brett on the one hand and for the bullfight on the other (I will discuss Hemingway's perfectly deliberate representation of the queerness of the bullfight below). Not unrelatedly, Hemingway and his contemporaries might well have seen "nice" as a kind of women's word; as North discusses, the linguist Otto Jespersen had claimed in his 1922 book *Language: Its Nature, Development, and Origin* that "there are a few adjectives, such as *pretty* and *nice,* that might be mentioned as used more extensively by women than men."[18] Complementarily, as Heather K. Love has argued from etymology, "good" can be aligned with "straight" in a binary the other half of which is "bad/queer," since "*bad* originally derives from the Middle English *bad-de,* a variation on the Old English term *bœdel* ('homo itriusque generis, hermaphrodita') and its 'derivative *bœdling* "effeminate fellow, womanish man," applied contemptuously.'"[19]

This is not to suggest that Hemingway never calls a bullfighter "good"—he does, often—or that he always deploys "good" according to some strict system of differentiation from his uses of "fine" or "nice." My point is that Hemingway's introduction of "good" within a series that also includes "fine," "nice," and, terminally, "pretty" doubly reinflects both the masculine and feminine poles ("good" and "pretty" respectively) of an adjectival spectrum of aesthetic connoisseurship. That is to say, a Jake Barnes can attempt to appropriate "pretty" as a macho descriptor because it, along with "fine" and "nice," has been rendered macho by proximity to Hemingway's trademark "good."[20] (This more or less works with "fine" and "nice," but with the more determinately feminized "pretty" the effect is sardonic.) On the other hand, there is the risk that "good" itself may be feminized by the terms Hemingway means it to subsume and supplant. It is this risk that Catherine exposes when she refers to "good" as a "dandy word" and then yokes "dandy" itself to lesbianism.

Hemingway's nearly fetishistic commitment to certain terms of aesthetic evaluation marks him as an important participant in the long afterlife of late Victorian aestheticism. As Hugh Kenner observed long ago, "If Hemingway is to be equipped with a sponsoring philosopher we shall not find better than Walter Pater, the aesthetician of appreciative intensities."[21] "Fine" is one of Pater's favorite words and appears many times throughout *The Renaissance,* but it doesn't get something like a theoretical formulation until the "Essay on Style" in *Appreciations* (1889):

The line between fact and something quite different from external fact is, indeed, hard to draw. In Pascal, for instance, in the persuasive writers generally, how difficult to define the point where, from time to time, argument which, if it is to be worth anything at all, must consist of facts or groups of facts, becomes a pleading—a theorem no longer, but essentially an appeal to the reader to catch the writer's spirit, to think with him, if one can or will—an expression no longer of fact but of his sense of it, his peculiar intuition of a world, prospective, or discerned below the faulty conditions of the present, in either case changed somewhat from the actual world. In science, on the other hand, in history so far as it conforms to scientific rule, we have a literary domain where the imagination may be thought to be always an intruder. And as, in all science, the functions of literature reduce themselves eventually to the transcribing of fact, so all the excellences of literary form in regard to science are reducible to various kinds of painstaking; this good quality being involved in all "skilled work" whatever, in the drafting of an act of parliament, as in sewing. Yet here again, the writer's sense of fact, in history especially, and in all those complex subjects which do but lie on the borders of science, will take the place of fact, in various degrees. . . . For just in proportion as the writer's aim, consciously or unconsciously, comes to be the transcribing, not of the world, not of mere fact, but of his sense of it, he becomes an artist, his work *fine* art; and good art (as I hope ultimately to show) in proportion to the truth of his presentment of that sense; as in those humbler or plainer functions of literature also, truth—truth to bare fact, there—is the essence of such artistic quality as they may have. Truth! there can be no merit, no craft at all, without that. And further, all beauty is in the long run only *fineness* of truth, or what we call expression, the finer accommodation of speech to that vision within. (emphases in original)[22]

Pater, here, distinguishes between two distinct but related functions of truth. On the one hand, there is truth as mere fact, the literary horizon of which involves "various kinds of painstaking." On the other hand, there is that imaginative truth proper to the "writer's spirit . . . his peculiar intuition of a world . . . changed somewhat from the actual world." The writing of history, Pater suggests, occurs on the border of this impressionistic subjective truth and the transcription of the facts of the actual world. A whole epistemology is enfolded in this rich and difficult passage, but for my purposes I want to seize on the introduction of "*fineness*" as index of impressionistic or imaginative truth. "Fineness" for Pater indicates the degree of precision with which artistic expression corresponds to subjective impression—the "finer" the art, the more accurate, the more precise, is the representation not of the "actual world" but of the impression of that world on a particular subject, the artist.

Hemingway, likewise, considered "truth" the paramount criterion of art. In *Green Hills of Africa* (1935), the third sentence in the three-sentence "Foreword" is as good an instance as any of Hemingway's frequently reiterated commitment to "truth" in writing: "The writer has attempted to write an absolutely true book to see whether the shape of a country and the pattern of a month's action can, if truly presented, compete with a work of the imagination."[23] Here, "true" means both nonfictional and authentic in some deeper sense, straight reportage always constituting one horizon of Hemingway's conception of truth. Hemingway's statement on *Green Hills of Africa* seems to distinguish it, though, from journalism; like "history" for Pater, Hemingway's account of African big-game hunting occupies a marginal position between the objective transcription of facts and "a work of the imagination."

But Hemingway certainly does not confine the application of "true" to purportedly factual memoirs. In an emblematic statement from *A Moveable Feast* (1964), he describes his process of fiction writing thus: "So finally I would write one true sentence, and then go on from there."[24] In a famous statement about *The Old Man and the Sea* (1952), Hemingway again emphasizes a quality of "truth" or "reality" in fiction: "I tried to make a real old man, a real boy, a real sea and a real fish and real sharks. But if I made them *good* and true enough they would mean many things" (emphasis mine).[25]

In a discussion of Tolstoy's *Sevastapol* in *The Green Hills of Africa*, Hemingway, like Pater, aligns "fine" writing with "true" writing, and then grounds such writing in personal experience, specifically the paradigmatically Hemingwayesque experience of war.

> It was a very young book and had one fine description of fighting in it, where the French take the redoubt and I thought about Tolstoi and about what a great advantage an experience of war was to a writer. It was one of the major subjects and certainly one of the hardest to write truly of and those writers who had not seen it were always very jealous and tried to make it seem unimportant, or abnormal, or a disease as a

subject, while, really, it was just something quite irreplaceable that they had missed.[26]

Hemingway inherits both an aesthetic vocabulary and an emphasis on experience from Pater, but his model of "truth" differs somewhat from Pater's. The raw data of Hemingwayesque "experience" hews closer to the raw data of journalism, with combat considered the ultimate object of experience just as it is the ultimate subject for the newspaper reporter. But the mere experience of war, this passage suggests, is a necessary but not sufficient condition for the production of a "fine description of fighting"; indeed, of all subjects war is "one of the hardest to write truly of" and it is this difficulty, a difficulty which indicates its importance, that renders "those writers who had not seen it . . . very jealous." Here, we can see something like Pater's theory of subjective expression; if war is what Pater calls the "mere fact" in the "actual world," the task of the artist is the communication not of raw data but of "his sense of it," a task difficult in proportion to the importance of the fact in question.

But the kinship of Hemingway's style with journalistic reportage and colloquial speech places a heavy rhetorical accent on what Pater calls the "bare fact," apparently (but only apparently) unadorned or untransmuted by aestheticist intensities. (Hemingway's rhetoric of facticity inaugurates a tradition in American letters extending at least to Raymond Carver and the "dirty realism" of the 1980s.) Hemingway's "truth" relies on the privileging of the colloquial he shared with Stein and Sherwood Anderson. As North puts it, "The chief characteristic of the Anderson-Stein-Hemingway brand of modernism was to be its restoration of direct, colloquial language. For Hemingway more purely than for any other male modernist this was a masculinist project, and clarity of reference was to be a masculine virtue."[27] North is correct to note that colloquiality was part of a masculinist rhetoric for Hemingway, but its precedent in Stein considerably complicates its gendered valences—and its further inflection by Pater suggests a surprising aestheticist genealogy for what might at first look like blunt machismo.

"Very fine and very mine": Stein's singsong line locates the aesthetic as, properly, a kind of privately possessed and implicitly libidinal experience. This reflects the Paterian turn to the subjective-impressionistic, recalling us to the distinction between solid fact and subjective impression Pater draws in the conclusion to *The Renaissance*:

And if we continue to dwell on this world, not of objects in the solidity with which language invests them, but of impressions, unstable, flickering, inconsistent, which burn and are extinguished with our consciousness of them, it contracts still further; the whole scope of observation is dwarfed to the narrow chamber of the individual mind. Experience, already reduced to a swarm of impressions, is ringed round for each one of us by that thick wall of personality through which no real voice has ever pierced on its way to us, or from us to that which we can only conjecture to be without. Every one of those impressions is the impression of the individual in his isolation, each mind keeping as a solitary prisoner its own dream of a world.[28]

This most famous description of the psychology of the aesthetic impression invests the impressionable subject with a grandeur at once tragic and sublime, and suggests that the experience of what Pater will later call "fineness" might offer a kind of immanent salvation, since "[n]ot the fruit of experience, but experience itself is the end."[29]

Hemingway's Dandiacal Connoisseurship

But there was always a risk that the Paterian emphasis on subjective aesthetic experience might fail of its exalted register, and that "fineness" would become the criterion not of high aesthetic experience but of the feminized sphere of expanding consumer culture.[30] Stein's "very fine and very mine," with its emphasis on acquisition and possession, playfully acknowledges this facet of the aesthetic. So, in its different way, does Hemingway's endless return to scenes of fine eating and drinking. In *Green Hills of Africa*, not only can a Tolstoy war scene be "fine," but so can chilled duck: "[T]raveling, we had cold teal, the best of ducks to eat, fine, plump, and tender, cold with Pan-Yan pickles, and the red wine we had bought at Babati."[31] For Hemingway, aestheticist criteria are as applicable to edibles as they are to art.

Hemingway transforms the involved appreciations associated with Victorian aestheticism—Pater's most prominently—in the service of appropriating aesthetic connoisseurship for his own idiom. When Catherine sarcastically mocks David's use of "good"—"You use such interesting adjectives. . . . They make everything so vivid"—she means to expose David's, and Hemingway's, working assumption that the humble word "good" contains within it an accreted history allowing it to function as a master term of aesthetic evaluation, of "appreciative intensities." When she goes on to refer, sarcastically, to "sorry" as "another dandy word," her meaning is double: "dandy" here means "good" in the sense of "a good word," but it can also be read back onto David's original "good" such that "good" becomes a "dandy" word in a very different sense—as an index of aesthetic evaluation, it is a word used by dandies. By translating "good" into "dandy," Catherine renders explicit the dandiacal logic of Hemingwayesque connoisseurship. The rhetorical downshifting from the solemn complex sentences of Pater's art criticism to the clipped sentences and simple "good" of Hemingway are part of a larger effort to produce a new style for the dandiacal connoisseur, who was, by the end of the nineteenth century, a decidedly unmanly figure.

It is with connoisseurship, then, that any examination of Hemingway's inheritance and reconstitution of nineteenth-century dandiacal precedents should begin—connoisseurship not just toward writing and the visual arts but, perhaps above all, toward food. As Colonel Cantwell puts it in *Across the River and Into the Trees*, "A market is the closest thing to a good museum like the Prado or as the Accademia is now."[32] As Rosalind Williams puts it, "Of all the paradoxes of dandyism, none is more striking than the way the loftiest theories of spiritual superiority all depended on the vulgar act of shopping."[33] Or as *The Garden of Eden* describes Catherine's trips to Cannes and Nice, "The big winter season shops were closed but she found extravagances to eat and solid values to drink."[34]

Close attention to the pleasures of dining occupies the dandiacal novel from the Regency to the fin de siècle. In Edward Bulwar-Lytton's extremely popular fashionable novel *Pelham, or, The Adventures of a Gentleman* (1828), the titular character carries around a custom-made spoon of "peculiarly shallow dimensions" allowing him the better to linger over his repast. This is, after all, a world in which "a bad dinner is a most serious—I may add, the most serious calamity."[35] *Pelham* was one of the most famous of the "silver fork" novels, so-called after Hazlitt's derisive description of "the dandy school" of fiction in an 1827 essay.[36] Hemingway's connoisseurship is a late entry in that history of aestheticized gastronomy which Denise Gigante, in *Taste: A Literary History*, traces to the Romantics: "Having a taste to distinguish between pickles and seasonings may seem a far cry from distinguishing among the finer shades of poetry or painting, but by the final quarter of the eighteenth century, the two were becoming pragmatically conflated." By the nineteenth century, "gourmands and their sartorial counterparts—dandies" expanded their range of appreciation to accommodate a growing market, "for as taste was increasingly expressed through choices of consumerism, it expanded to encompass all the arts, including the culinary."[37] Baudelaire would give culinary consumption a gothic twist in his *La Fanfarlo* (1847), whose title character "loved meats which dripped blood and wines which bring intoxication."[38] By the latter half of the century, with the rise of the decadent dandy, culinary connoisseurship takes on pointedly sinister overtones, as the cultivation of rarified appetite becomes associated with pleasures both forbidden and dangerous. In J. K. Huysmans's *À Rebours*, Des Esseintes constructs a "mouth organ," an elaborate device designed to dispense synesthetic mouthfuls of various liquors. As Jonathan Freedman has observed, Des Esseintes is a kind of limit-case Paterian, "will[ing] himself into Pater's prison of the self: by seeking to explore and refine every possible sense experience and combination of sense experiences, he seems to live as closely as possible to Pater's ideal life of perpetual 'sharp and eager observation.'"[39] His extravagant contraption apotheosizes decadent-dandiacal consumption:

> The organ was now open. The stops labelled flute, horn, celestial voice, were pulled out, ready to be placed. Des Esseintes sipped here and there, enjoying the inner symphonies, succeeded in procuring sensations in his throat analogous to those which music gives to the ear.
>
> Moreover, each liquor corresponded, according to his thinking, to the sound of some instrument. Dry curacoa, for example, to the clarinet whose tone is sourish and velvety; *kümmel* to the oboe whose sonorous notes snuffle; mint and anisette to the flute, at once sugary and peppery, puling and sweet; while, to complete the orchestra, *kirschwasser* has the furious ring of the trumpet; gin and whiskey burn the palate with their strident crashings of trombones and cornets; brandy storms with the deafening hubbub of tubas; while the thunder-claps of the cymbals and the furiously beaten drum roll in the mouth by means of the *rakis de Chio*.[40]

Huysmans's synesthetic equivalence between taste and hearing, between liquor and music, was self-consciously perverse, for, as Gigante says, "Taste has always ranked low on the philosophical hierarchy of senses as a means of ingress to the mind. Whereas sight and hearing allow for a proper representative distance from the object of contemplation . . . taste, like its closest cousin smell, is bound up with the chemical physiology of the body."[41] Huysmans's perverse emphasis on the mouth over the ear, or, better, the mouth *as* an ear, locates his "mouth-organ" within the dynamics of commodity culture, for which oral "consumption" is the dominant metaphor. His "mouth-organ" represents the self-consciously perverse pinnacle of "the use of commodities to create a dream world"[42] that Rosalind Williams associates with France in the second half of the nineteenth century.

Rita Felski has discussed the way in which Huysmans, Wilde, and other male nineteenth-century aesthetes "alienated and disaffected from the dominant norms of middle-class masculinity" registered resistance through modes of consumption coded as feminine. In Felski's influential account, the aesthete, having rejected norms of bourgeois masculinity, ends up aligned with "an emerging commodity culture, which provides an important precondition for his own strategies of stylistic differentiation and self-consciousness."[43] The feminine coding of aestheticist consumption has, perhaps, less to do with the objects consumed than with the subjective mode of consumption as registered through the literary style in which consumption is depicted. Thus, while bravura eating and drinking sessions may seem typically male activities in the nineteenth-century, they become feminized through discursive emphases on things like delicacy and fineness of sensory experience. The style of *À Rebours,* writes Felski, "is reminiscent of nothing other than the lavish prose of a consumer catalog."[44] (Such observations are continuous with Nordau's dismissive remarks in *Degeneration:* Huysmans "has evidently been forced to copy the catalogues of commercial travelers dealing in perfumes and soaps, teas and liqueurs, to scrape together his erudition in current prices.")[45] Jettisoning "the romantic myth of the creative genius," the aesthete eschews the masculine prerogative of production for feminized patterns of consumption.[46]

The dangerous or sinister element in the elaborate consumption projects practiced by figures like Des Esseintes or Dorian Gray—their curation of objets d'art, fine fabrics, exotic flowers, rare liquors—has to do, then, with the internal transvestism such consumption involves, and marks the stage at which aestheticism passes over into decadence. Under the sign of the medicoscientific categories of "inversion" or "psychosexual hermaphroditism" codified by the end of the century, the feminized aesthete becomes associated with the unnamed content of Dorian Gray's "wild joys and wilder sin." Decadent sensory consumption carried to extremes is part of the dangerous experimental self-analysis that Henry Wotton, in *Dorian Gray,* describes as a kind of auto-vivisection: "Henry Wotton had always been enthralled by the methods of natural science, but the ordinary subject-matter of that science had seemed to him trivial and of no import. And so he had begun by vivisecting himself, and he had ended by vivisecting others. . . . There were poisons so subtle that to know their properties one had to sicken of them."[47] The vivisection of others, and especially the vivisection of oneself, will go on to offer an essential model for modernist psychologizing in the following century.[48]

Hemingway picks up on the literature and terminology of decadence most overtly in *Death in the Afternoon,* a text not coincidentally obsessed with homo-sexuality.[49] He characterizes modern bullfighting as "a decadent art in every way," which "like most decadent things . . . reaches its fullest flower at its rot-tenest point, which is at present."[50] Early on, he compares the pleasure of the spectacle of the bullring with wine drinking, a comparison that, he insists, "is not so far fetched as it might sound. Wine is one of the most civilized things in the world and one of the most natural things of the world that has been brought to the greatest perfection, and it offers a greater range for enjoyment than, possibly, any other purely sensory thing which may be purchased."[51] Like his decadent late Victorian predecessors, Hemingway valorizes his favored modes of aesthetic consumption in terms of their opposition to what he figures as received norms of bourgeois masculinity. *Death in the Afternoon's* portrait of hapless American bullfight spectators evokes smug, self-satisfied, and aes-thetically deficient upper-middle-class men—"well-fed, skull and bones-ed, porcellian-ed, beach-tanned, panama-hatted"—fleeing the spectacle "when the women with them wanted to stay." After all, "If they didn't leave and liked it there was something wrong with them. Maybe they were queer. There was never anything wrong with them. They always left."[52] As a decadent art, bull-fighting can inspire dangerous forms of self-rumination. By making his flan-neled, sport-shod Yale men comically insecure about how their relationship to the decadence of the bullfight might implicate their masculine self-image, Hem-ingway aligns aesthetic philistinism with defensive heterosexual chauvinism.

In *Islands in the Stream,* decadent culinary habits are given comical ex-pression in Hudson's friend Johnny's discussion of Caribbean chiles: "Listen, Tommy. I have these chiles stuffed with salmon. Stuffed with bacalao. Stuffed with Chilean bonito. Stuffed with Mexican turtledoves' breasts. Stuffed with turkey meat and mole. . . . But all that's a perversion. Just this long, droop-ing, uninspiring, unstuffed, unpromising old chile with the brown chupango sauce is the best."[53] Elsewhere in Hemingway, the word "perversion" is almost always associated with sexual deviance, especially homosexuality, as when, in *For Whom the Bell Tolls,* Pilar explains to Robert Jordan that her affection for Maria is not sapphic: "I am no *tortillera* but a woman made for men. . . . I do not make perversions."[54] The link between decadent culinary consumption and homosexuality is strengthened later on in the novel when the same Johnny who loves all kinds of chiles describes an upcoming dinner thus: "And yellow rice tonight with plover. Golden plover." To which Hudson's son replies, "You sound like a damned interior decorator."[55]

At other times, though, Hemingway figures aestheticized culinary consumption not as decadent but as participating in a kind of humbled Paterian epiphany. There are for instance the beans and ketchup cooked by Nick Adams in "Big Two-Hearted River": "His tongue was very sensitive. He was very hungry. Across the river in the swamp, in the almost dark, he saw a mist rising. . . . He took a full spoonful from the plate."[56] As John Gaggin notes, Nick acts as both artisan and consumer not just of a plate of beans but of a Paterian "perfect moment."[57]

Hemingwayesque culinary consumption, then, is a continuum in which more cultivated, exotic, or pretentious modes of eating echo a vocabulary of decadence and suspect sexuality, while humbler forms of consumption achieve a kind of chastened, delibidinized Paterianism. Across Hemingway's corpus, however, more cultivated acts of consumption can become inflected by the logic of the humbler ones, even as Hemingway's bare style, which seems the appropriate vehicle for depicting simple foods in spartan circumstances, brings its rhetorical simplicity to bear on relatively lavish foodstuffs. This process is a key part of Hemingway's masculinization of the figure of the dandiacal man-about-town. In *A Moveable Feast,* for example, his description of a typical café meal, tinged by the French language with a certain aura of sophistication, would presumably not merit the slur of sounding like the words of an interior decorator:

> The beer was very cold and wonderful to drink. The *pommes à l'huile* were firm and marinated and the olive oil delicious. I ground black pepper over the potatoes and moistened the bread in the olive oil. After the first heavy draft of beer I drank and ate very slowly. When the *pommes à l'huile* were gone I ordered another serving and a *cervelas.* This was a sausage like a heavy, wide frankfurter split in two and covered with a special mustard sauce.[58]

When it comes to eating, humble foods can take on the intense charge of the kind of decadent gustatory appreciation drawn from models like Huysmans, while unfamiliar foreign foods can be consumed with brisk machismo. Ultimately, the object of consumption becomes relatively unimportant; what matters is that Hemingway has forged a macho discourse of consumption that redeploys aestheticist sensitivity in a toughened rhetoric that partially suppresses the feminized associations of the style of a Huysmans or a Pater. He has not, however, entirely erased the genealogy of this style: his focus on decadence in *Death in the Afternoon* and elsewhere flags its history.

The Style of Reserve and the Code Hero

Henry James, in *A Little Tour in France* (1885), describes a meal thus: "[T]he eggs were so good that I am ashamed to say how many of them I consumed. . . . It was the poetry of butter, and I ate a pound or two of it."[59] I am tempted, glibly, to locate the passage of aestheticized culinary connoisseurship from James to Hemingway in the elimination of that adverb "so"; Hemingway would simply have said "The eggs were good."[60] But Hemingway and James share more substantial continuities and oppositions. While Jimmy, in Connolly's *The Rock Pool*, puts Hemingway and Firbank on the same footing, the narrator, a would-be writer named Naylor, finds himself invested in what Connolly suggests is a contrary tradition: "the dialect of Pater, Proust, and Henry James, the style that is common to mandarin academic circles given over to clique life and introspection."[61] With this lineage in view, Firbank and Hemingway might appear together as artists of the surface, refusing in common the syntax of "introspection," while James's "snobbish, difficultly written shit,"[62] as Hemingway put it, is consigned to the dustbin of the Yellow Nineties.[63]

But Hemingway's agonistic relationship to James is a primary site of his reconstitution of aestheticism.[64] Hemingway carried out his quarrel with James publicly (for instance, in references to James as impotent in *The Sun Also Rises*) and in his correspondence, as Eric Haralson has noted: "More privately, Hemingway went on to demean the drawing room 'fairies' who languished in James's *The Awkward Age*, to scorn his predecessor under the sign of emasculation (James had 'no balls') and effeminacy (one of the 'male old women') . . . and to covet his transatlantic fame."[65] But Hemingway's criticism of Jamesian style in fact indicates a marked sensitivity to an important aspect of the Master's prose: the complex entwinement of Jamesian sexuality and Jamesian syntax.

To the rich perversity of Jamesian syntactical complexity, Hemingway opposes a stripped-down style that, in a letter to Fitzgerald, he celebrates (with what degree of irony is hard to tell) as the linguistic manifestation of heterosexual machismo: "I have to . . . deny myself . . . many of the little comforts like toilet paper, semi-colons, and soles to my shoes. . . . [Otherwise] people begin to shout that old Hem is just a fairy after all and no He man ha ha."[66] (Lest this opposition of semicolons and machismo seem merely idiosyncratic, it is worth noting that it would be repeated—in 2005!—by Kurt Vonnegut, who advised writers, "First rule. Do not use semi-colons. They are transvestite hermaphrodites representing absolutely nothing.")[67]

What Hemingway claimed to object to in James's "difficultly written shit" was, in short, Jamesian style's inheritance of the ambiguous sexuality that would mark late Victorian aestheticism from Pater onward. As James Eli Adams puts it in his indispensable study of Victorian "reserve," Paterian rhetoric would "exert such a profound influence on Wilde—who repeatedly echoed Pater in evoking the fascination of the double life—and on the more diffuse preoccupation with obliquity and obscurity that distinguishes the modernist narratives of Conrad and James."[68] Hemingway had no problem reading such "obliquity and obscurity" as queer and therefore incompatible with the calculated machismo his popular reputation depended on. Rejecting James, then, was in part a tactical strategy by which Hemingway would attempt to distinguish himself from the potentially encompassing influences of Pater and James. In the process, he would turn the dandyish aesthete into the Hemingway hero.

Hemingway's famous "iceberg" theory of writing, in which omission and the apparently simple surface of his sentences gesture toward ambiguous and only partially knowable depths, enacts at the level of prose style a crucial reformulation of Jamesian method. If the endlessly proliferating nested clauses of Jamesian syntax generate epistemological uncertainty and thick textures of concealment, Hemingway's very different prose works toward analogous ends by markedly different means. Hemingway's forceful declarative sentences have always been part of his machismo; indeed, the association of a verbal style with manliness has a long history. In 1862, for instance, James Fitzjames Stephen would write that "the great characteristic of the manners of a gentleman, as we conceive them in England, is plain, downright, frank simplicity . . . the outward and visible sign of the two great cognate virtues—truth and courage."[69] Hemingway would inherit this emphasis on courage and truth, and would maintain the association of a certain kind of style with access to or accurate rendering of the truth. But by making "omission" a central facet of his truth-bearing style, Hemingway manages to invest "plain, downright, frank simplicity" with techniques of obscurity all its own. His statement on *The Old Man and the Sea*, for instance, points toward the potential ambiguity of fictional "truth": "But if I made them good and true enough they would mean many things." Omission works hand in hand with the mysterious polyvalence of the "good and true enough" to give rise to a mysterious richness. Hemingway's slur against Jamesian style should not mask his inheritance of a basic structure analogous to that of the Jamesian secret. Hemingway and James practice twinned techniques for multiplying ambiguities.

Hemingwayesque "omission" should be understood not as rejecting but as continuous with Jamesian obscurity and, therefore, with a whole trajectory of linguistic "reserve" originating, as Adams has shown, in the rhetorical strategies of John Henry Newman and undergoing important transmutations in Pater, Wilde, and James.[70] For Newman, "reserve" involved both a social and a linguistic register. Socially, it required dignified self-control; it was an ethos of self-discipline. Rhetorically, it meant a theological discourse marked by tactical omission and rigorous subtlety when communicating to non-Tractarian religious outsiders. Over the course of the nineteenth century, rhetorical reserve underwent a number of important shifts with regard to the presumed content that its tactical misdirection or obfuscation were meant to conceal. Newman's contemporaries often assumed, for instance, that his emphasis on "reserve" masked a heretical allegiance to the Catholic Church. Later in the century, though, "reserve" was frequently assumed to circle around some unnamable sexual content—hence the "fascination of the double life" in Pater and Wilde becomes a particularly appropriate affect for "reserved" linguistic textures. Newman's own elegant periods, anticipating Pater, were seen by some critics as reserve's formal corollary. As Charles Kingsley, Newman's most vociferous opponent, put it, "No one would have suspected [Newman] to be a dishonest man, if he had not perversely chosen to assume a style which (as he himself confesses) the world always associates with dishonesty."[71]

Importantly, though, "reserve" was also associated with the dignified comportment of the gentleman; it was the outward sign of his authority, of his prerogative to rule, and of his self-mastery. "We may recall," Adams writes, "Kingsley's tribute to the man 'born to rule self, and therefore to rule all he met.'"[72] There is a paradoxical connection, then, between that reserve which indicates a fascinating secret of a presumably sexual nature and that reserve which indicates self-mastery and therefore mastery over others. As Adams notes of the Paterian variety, "such reserve may be a defensive posture, a means of shielding oneself from hostile scrutiny. But Pater presents it throughout his writings as a deeply seductive quality, because reserve is the index of one's powers of self-control—and hence of a power to control others."[73] Reserve performs two apparently incongruous functions: it expresses authority, and it indicates a dangerous secret. For Pater, it does both at the same time: his seductive periphrastic periods seem to indicate some concealed knowledge just underneath or beyond the text, even as the implication of such secret knowledge consolidates his authority as critic.

"Reserve," then, by the end of the century, had become a verbal style with complexly heterogeneous resonances, including nineteenth-century norms of dignified "manliness," overtones of heresy and papism, secret societies, the seductiveness of the well-kept secret, duplicity, and homosexuality. Whatever it was, it was undeniably *interesting*. Hemingway's fiction should be read as part of a long history of literary "reserve" at the level of both style and theme. His practiced "omission"—the way, for example, a sexual wound in *The Sun Also Rises* or abortion in "Hills Like White Elephants" constitutes the unmentionable center around which those texts' affective and libidinal energies swirl—draws on the alignment of "reserve" with sexuality and the double life in Pater, Wilde, and James. The various styles such charisma assumes produce nothing less than modernist interiority itself. As Eve Sedgwick has shown, the nature of this interiority, the secret it is constituted around, would come to be not just sexuality *tout court* but homosexuality, what Sedgwick calls "the condensation of this plurality [of sexual secrets] to *the homosexual topic* that now formed the accusative case of modern processes of personal knowing" around the turn of the century.[74]

But if a certain prose style, marked by the family resemblances that link Newman to Pater to Proust, bears with peculiar formal appropriateness the (sexualized or homosexualized) secret structuring modern interiority, how does Hemingway's minimalism, with its eschewal of fascinating interiority except through implication, stand in relation to this history? Like the protagonists of the classic noir fiction with which they are largely contemporary, Hemingway's heroes have inner lives whose richness we are trained to assume is inversely proportionate to their prolixity. What enabled Hemingway, and his readers, to associate the laconic with the profound? The answer has much to do with the rhetoric of professionalism, intersecting at key points with various rhetorics of reserve, emerging across the nineteenth century. The conventional Hemingway hero represents one culmination of this professional type.[75]

The mixed virtues of the consummately professional Victorian man are best adumbrated by Dickens, whose characterization of professionalism gives an efficient picture of the type inherited and radically reworked by the Hemingway hero. *Great Expectations'* Wemmick and *Bleak House's* Tulkinghorn are both stereotyped professionals, the first representing the type's positive possibilities, the second its risks. With his mouth like a "post-office," indicating his capacity to absorb and retain—but not give out—information, Wemmick exercises the reserve appropriate to the legal profession, but his warm domestic attachments and his friendship with Pip indicate that he has not allowed the strictures of the office to absorb the warmer impulses of his humanity.[76] In *Bleak House's* Tulkinghorn, conversely, Dickens portrays professional reserve cultivated to the exclusion of all other capacities, and the results are monstrous. Tulkinghorn is completely unreadable. He shows "nothing but his shell"; his face is an "expressionless mask—if it be a mask"; he has a "countenance as imperturbable as Death."[77] Tulkinghorn's illegibility suggests to one character not, à la Newman, veiled papism, but a different secret affiliation: "Volumnia is persuaded that he must be a Freemason."[78] Tulkinghorn's cardinal sin, for which Dickens has him murdered, is the eclipse of all empathy by the dictates of a professional duty whose (anti-)affective mode is reserve. The lawyer—professional man par excellence—is the vocational figure most associated with reserve, because his commitment to the interests of his client prohibits the frank openness against which reserve in all of its varieties stands opposed.[79]

Reserve, then, is an affective mode linked, on the one hand, to pejoratively evaluated and often libidinally saturated duplicity and, on the other, to the habits of masculinity normalized and endorsed under the aegis of professionalism. Hemingway's protagonists absorb and synthesize the dual burden of this tradition. The famous Hemingway "code hero," who, in Philip Young's influential definition, "offers up and exemplifies certain principles of honor, courage, and endurance which in a life of tension and pain make a man a man," extends Victorian conventions of masculine professionalism into the twentieth century.[80] The code hero as an exemplar of the special kind of masculine charisma embodied by "reserve" finds its fullest expression in Hemingway's semi- or ex-military figures, who combine a gentlemanly model of soldiery with the mysterious "secret"—the code hero's foundational trauma—to which a "reserved" exterior seems always to point. Jake Barnes, a figure of Hemingwayesque reserve co-originary with Nick Adams, resonates across all of Hemingway's fiction. Barnes is both a consummate professional and a bearer of a very particular sexual secret. As Young puts it, "The rather thin shell of the 'callous' Hemingway hero was painfully drawn over a deep wound as a defense against reopening it."[81] Hemingway's code hero combines contradictory characteristics of Victorian reserve: he is self-disciplined in the approved masculine sense, but also the bearer of a troubling secret.

"[T]he reserve of the Paterian beholder," writes Adams, "fascinates because it seems a public withholding of private experience, which by virtue of being withheld is assumed to be singular, strange, even forbidden."[82] Singular, strange, even forbidden—the reserve appropriate to the gentleman becomes, paradoxically, an index of some buried interior kernel that seems to challenge not just gentlemanliness but, as with Barnes's genital wound, masculinity and even subjective stability itself. In *The Sun Also Rises*, the "secret" regarding Barnes's sexuality is a privative one. His wound is a lack; he is unmanned. By *The Garden of Eden*, Hemingway had reformulated the nature of the "secret" concealed by outward reserve. No longer the privative condition of impotence, it is instead the exciting excess of hermaphrodeity that constitutes the fascinating truth of the Hemingway hero. In tandem with aestheticist culinary connoisseurship, hermaphrodeity signals Hemingway's foundational dandyism. Hemingway has found one possible horizon of the "fascination of the double life": the fascination of double sex. In so doing, he reaches back to Gautier's *Mademoiselle de Maupin*, the foundational text in the tradition of the dandy-as-androgyne.

"The Unreality That Reality Had Become": Hemingway's Aberrant Reveries

Since the publication of *Garden of Eden*, scholars have recognized that its focus on androgyny bears a clear debt to Hemingway's reading of *Mademoiselle de Maupin*, although the implications of this debt remain underdeveloped.[83] One might begin with the shared interest of both in the relationship of impotence to literature. Gautier introduces impotence in the preface to *Mademoiselle de Maupin* as a derogatory figure with which to lambaste reactionary critics: "One thing which is certain and easy of demonstration to those who might doubt its existence, is the natural antipathy of the critic to the poet, of him who makes nothing to him who makes something, of the drone to the bee, of the gelding to the stallion." The critic is compared to a failed poet who "courted the Muse and sought to win her virginity" but "had not sufficient vigor to do so"; he is a "poor eunuch who is obliged to be present at the diversions of the Grand Seignior."[84] Gautier's colorful sexualization of the process of poetic creation cements the alignment of sexual with artistic productivity, and rings the changes on a convention that will continue to resonate, roughly a hundred years later, with the masculine modernisms of Pound and Hemingway. In a letter to Sherwood Anderson, Hemingway called "professional critics" "camp following eunuchs of literature."[85] In the case of Henry James, Hemingway would take comfort in the Master's failure to provide himself with a biological legacy: "Henry James . . . left no descendants . . . and therefore . . . he is as dead as he will ever be."[86] Impotence and infertility, then, become faults so severe as to invalidate or render neutral the force of artistic production—it is as if Hemingway has reversed the priority and structure of Gautier's comparison between the critic and the eunuch. For Gautier, the critic is *like* the eunuch because, unlike the artist, he can produce nothing; for Hemingway, even the highly productive artist, should he actually *be* a eunuch, loses the authority of his art.

But what if, as an alternative to this unacceptable form of impotence, reproductive viability could be circumvented in some other, happier way? For Hemingway, impotence can suggest, beyond the privative, the possibility of a valorized and titillating otherness. If impotence is the negative side of androgyny, then the exciting auto-reproductive capacity of a fantasized hermaphrodeity is impotence's positive obverse. The hermaphrodite becomes the figure for the self-fertilizing creativity of the artist, the ideally creative figure on the androgyne's horizon. This hermaphroditic ideal animates both *Mademoiselle de Maupin* and *Garden of Eden*.

Mademoiselle de Maupin is the story of a love triangle between a man, d'Albert, a woman, Rosette, and the titular Mademoiselle de Maupin, a woman disguised as a man under the name Théodore. Relatively early on, d'Albert articulates a late-Romantic version of the dangerous interior self-investigations—the "auto-vivisection"—that would later be picked up by Huysmans: "I hearken to the throbbing of my arteries, and the beatings of my heart. . . . [W]ith all my reveries and aberrations, I am tremendously afraid of falling into the monstrous or unnatural."[87] One would be hard-pressed to find a style of presenting subjectivity more apparently at odds with Hemingway's, whose world, as Leon Edel put it, can seem one "of superficial action and almost wholly without reflection."[88] But in *Garden of Eden,* deep psychic investigations occur not within the consciousness of a single character, but among the novel's cast. Depth obtains not in the recessed interiority of individual characters but between different characters and within the spatially and temporally closed—even claustrophobic—zone of this metaphorical "garden." Psychic interiority is projected onto the "garden" itself, which becomes the bearer of a kind of subconscious psychosexual truth pertaining to the heterosexual love affairs across much of Hemingway's earlier work.[89]

Garden of Eden's transposition of interiority onto a domestic scene is consistent with what the art historian Marika Knowles, in an analysis of Gautier's short fiction, calls his "vision of a physical interior as a quasi-domestic subversion of the bourgeois home." For Knowles, Gautier's psychologized interiors are sites of hybridity, transformation, and magical segregation from the bourgeois dreariness outside.[90] Not dissimilarly, *Garden of Eden* imagines domesticity as offering possibilities for decadent metamorphosis and enchantment— a twentieth-century recurrence of Williams's fin de siècle "dream worlds." For Hemingway, the negative figure of castration modulates into the efflorescence of hermaphrodeity—embodied in the passage from Jake Barnes to David Bourne. *Garden*'s hermaphrodeity depends on a kind of identity melding and gender swapping between Catherine and David, apparently triggered by Catherine's anal penetration of David ("I'm going to wake up in the night and do something to you that you've never even heard of or imagined").[91] This act inaugurates what the novel repeatedly calls the "change," a change associated both with "corruption"[92] and with the utopian resolution of sexual and subjective difference. "Maybe I'd better go back into our world," Catherine tells David at one point, "your and my world that I made up; we made up I mean."

As Feldman puts it of Gautier—in a statement that might apply just as well to Hemingway—"Thus . . . begins the artist's argument with himself on the subject of gender, an argument that is to characterize the literature of dandyism." Moreover, "In metamorphosis we may seek the etiology of that mythical creature, the dandy, the figure who has transformed himself."[93] Hermaphrodeity for Gautier can be understood as a function of the particular form of interior self-probing that results, in this tradition, from a commitment to nonreproductive sexuality. At first, d'Albert regards his desire to switch sex with deep ambivalence: "I can no longer tell who I am or what others are, I doubt whether I am a man or a woman, I have a horror of myself."[94] Resolving his gender dysphoria by thinking about Greek statues, d'Albert offers an early formulation of the auto-vivisection that would go on to preoccupy decadent protagonists from Baudelaire's Cramer to Wilde's Henry Wotton: he cannot stop "looking at [his] soul through a microscope."[95] Mademoiselle de Maupin likewise seizes fully on the rhetoric of science in describing the motivations behind her own gender transformation, but she applies this rhetoric not to herself but to others: "I wished to study man thoroughly, to anatomize him with inexorable scalpel fibre by fibre, and to have him alive and palpitating on my dissecting table."[96] But she eventually turns her attention to herself, culminating in the profound self-knowledge of her essential androgyneity. This is an early version of the psychological introspection that will appear again in *Dorian Gray* and in Huysmans.

Garden's typically Hemingwayesque avoidance of passages limning its characters' psychological depths couldn't be further from the obsessive self-disclosure performed by d'Albert and Mlle de Maupin. But the sexual role-reversals between David and Catherine do inspire feelings of profound shame in David which seem not to have any equivalent in Catherine (though we are even less privy to Catherine's interiority than to David's; unlike *Mademoiselle de Maupin*, in which d'Albert and Mlle de Maupin take turns narrating, *Garden of Eden's* third person is almost entirely focalized through David). As David thinks at one point, "She changes from a girl into a boy and back to a girl carelessly and happily and she enjoys corrupting me and I enjoy being corrupted. But she's not corrupt."[97] Catherine evinces no such shame: "But now I'm a boy too and I can do anything and anything and anything."[98]

David, as a writer, consciously resists the psychic auto-vivisection marking the tradition of the decadent novel within which Hemingway conceives *Garden of Eden*. This is an irony of literary genre: refusing self-insight, David is somehow stuck in the wrong kind of novel. For David, writing requires perceptiveness about *others*, but it eschews any too-conscious investigations of oneself. As he explains to Marita, "I'm good on other people and on technical things . . . nobody knows about himself when he is really involved. Yourself isn't worth considering. It would be shameful at the time."[99] At one point, David almost provides a theory for Hemingway's recodification of decadent interiority in a hard-boiled idiom: "[I]t is all very well for you to write simply and the simpler the better. But do not start to think so damned simply. Know how complicated it is and then state it simply."[100] The shame attached to self-knowledge is compounded by the destabilizing fluidity of gender and identity, the psychic stresses of which are limned by Hemingway's favorite device for representing interiority, the internal dialogue. Here's David after having his hair cut identically to Catherine's:

> "So that's how it is," he said to himself. "You've done that to your hair and had it cut the same as your girl's and how do you feel?" He asked the mirror. "How do you feel? Say it."
>
> "You like it," he said.
>
> He looked at the mirror and it was someone else he saw but it was less strange now.
>
> "All right. You like it," he said. "Now go through with the rest of it whatever it is and don't say anyone tempted you or that anyone bitched you."[101]

The psychic pressure exerted by David and Catherine's erotic life causes David not to delve into the murky depths of his libidinal interiority in good decadent fashion but rather to actively perform the repression of self-knowledge. "So they were friends, whatever friends are, David thought, and tried not to think but talked and listened in the unreality that reality had become." "Trying not to think" is the terminus of the practice of "omission." The famous reticence of Hemingway's narrative textures is here actively pursued by the protagonist himself, as both a defensive strategy against a self-knowledge he fears and, more interestingly, as a way of increasing to infinity the titillating possibilities of metamorphosis. Once Catherine begins to assume her male identity "in the light . . . there would, it seemed to him, be no end to the change."[102] This "change" may begin as a shared aspect of Catherine and David's psychosexual interiority, but because Hemingway largely eschews descriptions of his characters' interior worlds, the metamorphic intensities that make up David and Catherine's "secret" (David's word) is projected outward, onto the bars, bedrooms, and beaches in which the novel's action occurs. The destabilizing but seductive "change" that d'Albert would locate within himself becomes, in Hemingway's rewriting of Gautier, less an object of interior investigation than the metaphysical principle of David and Catherine's "garden," "the unreality that reality had become."

This dangerous but seductive metamorphic world offers a solution to the problem of impotence Hemingway had begun to explore in the wasteland of *The Sun Also Rises*. In the canonical Hemingway text, as Michael Szalay puts it, "the wound is a threat that writing is meant to alleviate as a surrogate identity. . . . [The text is] an attempt to create forms that are superior alternatives to that body."[103] In a novel like *The Sun Also Rises,* the wounded body achieves a kind of fantasized resolution via a hard-boiled *rhetoric,* a rhetoric that always points back toward textuality itself. "For Hemingway," Szalay says, "literary texts are 'whole, pure, and complete' in a way that actual living organisms can never be."[104] By *Garden of Eden,* this fantasy of a surrogate textuality seems no longer to have been accessible to Hemingway—hence his inability to finish the novel, which would balloon to over two thousand combined manuscript and typescript pages. At one level, then, *Garden's* psychosexual explorations reflect a quest for an alternative form, something with which to supplant the well-crafted, highly economical Hemingway novel or short story.

The wound afflicting Jake Barnes (he's got balls, but no shaft) has been replaced by the suggestion of sterility: David can perform, but might be shooting blanks. The following exchange between David and Catherine suggests that sterility is one context for their bedroom games. Catherine explains, "I thought if I'd be a girl and stay a girl I'd have a baby at least. Not even that." David: "That could be my fault." Catherine: "Don't let's ever talk about faults."[105] But reproduction, in Hemingway, is rarely approved—more often, as in "The Indian Camp" or *A Farewell to Arms,* it is threatening, emasculating, and possibly fatal.[106] What is Edenic, then, about *The Garden of Eden* is the centrality of nonreproductive sexual play, a centrality premised on sterility as a mode of impotence—or as a mode of paradoxical potency.

Furthermore, nonreproductive sexuality becomes the condition of artistic production, insofar as David's experimentation with sexual role reversal permits him to write. There is an explicit connection between "corruption" and writerly production: "Is it possible that the only creation that is a moral act is pro-creation and that is why all other kinds are suspect? . . . All that you know is that you have written better, clearer, and *plus net* he used the French in thinking, as you have deteriorated morally." (As Comley and Scholes point out, the version of the novel published by Scribner's suppresses the link between sexual "corruption" and writerly production.)[107] David may practice repression rather than self-investigation, but, as the "French in thinking" suggests, Hemingway's equation of corruption with creativity reaches back to French models—Huysmans, Baudelaire, Gautier—of auto-vivisection. Too, it amplifies Hemingway's debt to Pater, who also borrowed an aesthetic of hermaphrodeity from the French.[108] Pater looks to Renaissance and classical androgynes for a kind of iconicity composed of equal parts idealization and corruption; his most famous treatment of this androgynous corruption is in the essay on

Leonardo, in which he writes of "the fascination of corruption [which] pene-
trates in every touch its exquisitely finished beauty."[109]

Aestheticized culinary consumption and a valorized hermaphrodeity are
the twin Paterian echoes resonating across Hemingway's garden. *Garden of
Eden* goes even further than Hemingway's earlier novels in insisting on culinary consumption as a form of aesthetic appreciation. At one point in the
manuscript, eating is compared to architecture; at another, Catherine compares eating oysters to Stravinsky, Juan Gris, and Klee.[110] The note of eroticized culinary connoisseurship is struck from the very beginning: "They were
always hungry but they ate very well. They were hungry for breakfast which
they ate at the café, ordering brioche and café au lait and eggs, and the type of
preserve that they chose and the manner in which the eggs were to be cooked
was an excitement."[111] Catherine transposes "hunger" from the culinary to the
aesthetic sphere: "I never wanted to be a painter nor a writer until I came to
this country. Now it's just like being hungry all the time and there's nothing you
can ever do about it." When her meditations turn to mortality, David recommends a Paterian strategy of sensory appreciation: "Look at things and listen
and feel."[112] Later, in an amusingly vernacular echo of Pater on *La Gioconda*
("She is older than the rocks among which she sits"),[113] Catherine, in her early
twenties, says, "I'm older than my mother's old clothes."[114]

The fascinating corruption Pater locates in the *Medusa* and *La Gioconda*
are in both cases products of these paintings' suggestion that their subjects are
caught in midtransformation from female to male, or perhaps from male to female. The fantasy underlying all of *Garden of Eden* is that heterosexual coupling
might produce a kind of hybrid subjectivity, translating the dialogue with oneself Hemingway often resorted to for representing interiority into something
else: a dialogue between self and other in which the other is also oneself. As
Edward Mendelson put it recently, "What Hemingway wanted—both as he-
man and as androgyne—was a lasting intimate connection that did not require
him to be a separate individual person."[115] *Garden of Eden* repeatedly stages this
desire—its successes, rendered at least temporarily possible by the metamorphic world of the garden, but also its failures—as occurring in relation to food.
At one point in the manuscript, for instance, Catherine apologizes to David
for not being able to remember a visit paid by the two of them to the French
bar Lipps'. She then describes instead, in elaborate detail, a meal eaten at another French bar. David, in response, asks her when she began to talk like
Proust.[116]

That Catherine would fail to recall something so important to David represents a fissure in the hybridity he seeks. But her talking like Proust—by which David seems to mean talking with sensual precision, in long sentences, about food and wine—might repair the hermaphroditic bond. In this way, the wound around which the Hemingway code hero constructs his defensive shell is refigured as a space of possibility, in which various pleasures—gustatory, sexual, conversational—might be embraced with the practiced knowledge of the connoisseur. One upshot of this refiguration is the challenge it launches against shame, the "wound" of interiority no longer a source of humiliation but of pride, as when, in the manuscript, Catherine compares her pride in their romantic experimentation to the pride she imagines she would feel if she were wounded.[117]

Considered in view of the long history of a dandyism bifurcated by two competing modes—an emphasis on surface, continence, and power on the one hand and, on the other, a decadent focus on baroque, even pathological, interiority—Hemingway for the bulk of his career would seem most obviously to conform to the first and to eschew the second. His tough guys recover and amplify the machismo always inherent in dandiacal displays of power and control. In such novels as *The Sun Also Rises,* Hemingway's gustatory obsessions point toward, but do not probe, his profound reliance on decadent interiority. In the novels published during his lifetime, decadent interiority is useful mostly as an absence, as a blank center around which to spin the fantasy of the code hero. *The Garden of Eden,* though, pushes the sensual synthesis of food, wine, and androgynous eros in a new direction. The culinary preoccupations, a constant across his career, become an avenue to his far deeper, and far more ambivalent, concern with androgyny. The equation of taste and androgyny would finally liberate Hemingway to resolve his ambivalence, to elevate the kernel of an interiority he feared as pathological to the plane of aestheticist connoisseurship, here figured in the ongoing lovers' dialogue between Catherine and David. Hemingway could not, in his lifetime, bring himself to finish or to publish *The Garden of Eden,* though the manuscript would grow to over two thousand pages: a measure both of the power of his phobia and of the depth of his obsession.

2

RAYMOND CHANDLER'S
DANDIFIED DICK

Wit is absolute social feeling, or fragmentary genius.
—FRIEDRICH SCHLEGEL

Epigrammatic Speech from Wilde to the Private Eye

In 1949, a year after the publication in book form of the Oscar Wilde trial transcripts, Raymond Chandler discussed Wilde's legal troubles in an extraordinary letter to Dale Warren:

> There ought to be a good novel in homosexualism, but this [a novel by Marghanita Laski under discussion] isn't it. . . . What I think would be interesting would be a picture of the peculiar mentality of the homosexualist, his sense of taste, his surface brilliance often, his fundamental inability to finish anything. . . . I can't take the homo seriously as a moral outcast. He's no more than the other rebels against a sanctimonious and hypocritical society. There is no more disgusting spectacle on earth than the business man at a stag smoker, and this is just the type of man who would come down hardest on the abnormal. The difficulty of writing about a homo is the utter impossibility of getting inside his head unless you are one yourself, and then you can't get inside the head of a heterosexual man. If you ever read the cross examination of Wilde by Edward Carson in the suit against Queensberry, I think you are bound to admit that here were two people shouting across oceans

of misunderstanding. The mob impulse to destroy the homo is like the impulse of a wolf pack to turn on the sick wolf and tear him to pieces, or the human impulse to run away from a hopeless disease. This is probably very old and very cruel, but at the bottom of it is a kind of horror, like a woman frightened by a scorpion. All cruelty is a kind of fear. Deep inside us we must realize what fragile bonds hold us to sanity and these bonds are threatened by repulsive insects and repulsive vices. And the vices are repulsive, not in themselves, but because of their effect on us. They threaten us because our own normal vices fill us at times with the same sort of repulsion.[1]

I will return to this ambivalent letter at greater length in a bit; for now I want only to note that, for Chandler, the legally persecuted gay man (here exemplified by Wilde) may or may not be—Chandler really can't decide—a legitimate force of opposition against "a sanctimonious and hypocritical society." His allusion to Wilde and Carson suggests that his reading of the trial transcripts (published as part of a series on famous English court cases) made the rebellious oppositionality of "the homosexualist" newly legible to him. Chandler's charged indecisiveness regarding this subject should be understood, as I will discuss below, to have important ramifications for another rebel—Philip Marlowe—and the strange role of the notorious "pansies" in Chandler's early novels. Wilde and his trials can tell us a great deal about "rebel[ling] against a sanctimonious and hypocritical society." And the way that Wilde spoke while under legal examination can tell us a great deal about the speech—witty, condensed, aggressive—of the hard-boiled private eye. The transformation of dandiacal bon mots into wisecracking tough talk brings dandyism directly into popular literature and mass consciousness, where the private eye remains the most recognizable of dandiacal types.

"I do not know what Queensberry rules are, but the Oscar Wilde rule is to shoot at sight."[2] Thus did Wilde threaten his lover's famously belligerent father, the Marquess of Queensberry, an enthusiastic pugilist whose "Queensberry rules" inform professional boxing to this day. Wilde and Queensberry, of course, never came to blows; their intense antagonism played out instead in the verbal medium of the courts. Wilde's legal troubles began when he himself brought a libel action against the Marquess of Queensberry for accusing him on a calling card of "posing as a somdomite" [sic].[3] In his defense, Queensberry set out to prove, first, that his claim regarding Wilde was true, and, second, that his saying so was for the public good. Wilde withdrew his initial charge, but it was too late; he was now facing public prosecution for homosexual behavior. The story of Wilde's trials and resultant imprisonment has been told elsewhere.[4] For my part, I want only to emphasize those aspects of the trial record that demonstrate Wilde's use of his vaunted verbal wit as an actual strategy of legal defense, a strategy not unrelated to wit's deployment in terms of physical defense in the "shoot at sight" anecdote. As Wilde's quippy threat demonstrates, epigrammatic speech can encode a great deal of violence, though usually of a more implicit kind than here. In threatening to shoot, Wilde laid bare an underlying feature of his epigrammatism: its efficacy in contests of masculine mastery.

If the Wildean epigram is a practice of masculine mastery, then the trial of Oscar Wilde is both its apotheosis and its death knell. With the commencement of the first court date, the Wilde trials entered on a process of entextualization that began in breathless tabloid coverage and culminated in H. Montgomery Hyde's book-length account and record *The Trials of Oscar Wilde* (1948). Wilde's verbal facility was a major emphasis both in the coverage of Wilde's contemporaries during the trials and in accounts looking back at the trials as, already, history. As Ed Cohen puts it of Hyde's book, "*The Trials of Oscar Wilde* seemed to celebrate the audacity and intelligence of a man who publicly tried to keep the monologic forces of law and state at bay armed only with the blades of his wit and witticism."[5] As the martial emphasis of Cohen's language suggests, the symbolic significance of Wilde's comportment during his trials inheres in the implicit violence of epigrammatizing, here captured in the figure of a weaponized Wilde wielding blades at all comers. The trials are the epigram's apotheosis because in them the epigram becomes the tool par excellence of an oppositional masculinity positioned against the state. They are its death knell because Wilde lost and went to prison, cementing an association between dandiacal epigrammatizing and powerless, persecuted homosexuality that would continue far into the new century.

Epigrammatic speech is a primary formal marker for the hard-boiled novel, but it could only become so as a result of a radical reconstitution in terms of its relation to sexuality, gender, and class. Epigrammatic speech, from Wilde to the private dick, is both charismatic and oppositional; indeed, charisma and oppositionality are, for both, mutually reinforcing and all but inextricable.[6] What can succeed as popularly legible charismatic oppositionality, however, changes radically after the Wilde trials. I take as axiomatic Alan Sinfield's thesis that it was only *after* his trials that the brand of dandiacal aestheticism associated with Wilde could signify as "gay."[7] It is in the context of this epochal transformation in the signifying potential of a particular type of recognizable personality—the aesthete with his polished epigrammatism—that noir tough talk must in part be understood. Furthermore, epigrammatic tough talk could be easily grafted onto the pared down idiom—broadly legible as a signature of machismo—made so appealing by Hemingway. Chandler, during his apprenticeship phase in the early 1930s, practiced his craft by pastiching other writers, including Hemingway, whom he thought "the greatest living American novelist."[8] As with the suggestive economy of Hemingwayesque omission, the noir epigram often indicates—and forms a protective fence around—depths it cannot dwell on.

For the hard-boiled hero, wisecracking becomes a mode of masculine quippiness and antidomestic oppositionality distinctively *not* gay. As any number of theorists of noir have noted, the noir hero must simultaneously signal his difference from both organization-man style white-collar domesticity and blue-collar drudgery, from feminized spheres of commodity consumption, and from the definitionally nondomestic male homosexual (this last being important because the private dick's rejection of feminized domesticity raises the suspicion that he might be gay).[9] Marlowe himself frequently articulates the noir hero's resistance to any work structure save self-employment, as when, for instance, he explains in *Farewell, My Lovely* that he became a private eye after being fired from the D.A.'s office "for talking back."[10] Talking back is one among many modes of talking tough, a habit of speech proper to the private eye but with roots in a tradition of clever speech of which the mythologized figure of the aristocratic dandy is, for the hard-boiled private eye, a determinative proximate context. As the onscreen text in the trailer for the 1941 film version of Dashiell Hammett's *The Maltese Falcon* says of Humphrey Bogart's Sam Spade, "He's as *fast* on the draw—as he is in the drawing room."[11] Insofar as the noir novel is built around the wisecracking of the private dick, it is a descendant not only of the American naturalism with which it shares so much but also of the Victorian social comedy. The noir hero himself, then, is the self-composed dandy at the center of the comedy, dispatching his interlocutors with practiced verbal sallies.

Formally, I mean "epigrammatic speech" broadly to denote any instance of condensed, memorable, or witty dialogue. "Epigrammatic speech" encompasses jokes, paradoxes, bon mots, one-liners, witticisms, and wisecracks or "talking wise." A partial heritage for epigrammatic speech can be found, of course, in the Renaissance poetic form of the "epigram" and, perhaps more directly, in the self-contained witticisms of the eighteenth-century heroic couplet.[12] But unlike, say, the rhymed couplet, "epigrammatic speech" does not lend itself to a conclusive taxonomic definition. While I will highlight certain tendencies of epigrammatic speech, I will not attempt to impose on it the security of a generic stability it does not in fact possess. This instability reflects the historical instability of the definition of the epigram itself. Barbara Herrnstein Smith underscores the challenges of defining the epigram with adequate precision:

> It is difficult to make general observations on the epigram without engaging in the treacherous sport of definition stalking. The problem of finding for any literary term defining properties that will be both broad enough to accommodate historical usage and specific enough to be interesting is particularly harassing with regard to the epigram, for the range and diversity of its moods and subjects are enormous. . . . It may be that as a potential subject for formal definition, "the epigram" must remain an elusive or even chimerical animal.[13]

While advisedly avoiding "definition stalking," I would suggest that one aspect of epigrammatic speech—if not the sine qua non at least an extremely prominent tendency—is its usefulness in jockeying for social dominance, which it does by indexing its speaker's superior "presence of mind," a phrase I take, following Erving Goffman, to denote "mental calmness and alertness." In *Interaction Ritual*, Goffman analyzes "composure" (a mode of "presence of mind") in these terms: "This kind of presence of mind is what people known as wits have and the self-conscious person does not. Books of famous *mots*, brilliant statements of tact, and effective 'squelches' and 'put-downs' attest to the general interest in this mindedness."[14] "Epigrammatic speech," I would suggest, is a central line of formal organization linking the composure of an Oscar Wilde (frequently collected in "books of famous *mots*") to that of the hardboiled detective (good at "effective 'squelches' and 'put-downs,'" certainly). Goffman goes on to observe that "[c]omposure in all its different dimensions has traditionally been associated with the aristocratic ethic [but that] in recent years . . . a version of this quality has been strongly touted by raffish urban elements under the label 'coolness.'"[15] While "coolness"[16] is not part of the lexicon of classic noir, a downwardly mobile aristocratic composure is very much a feature of the hard-boiled detective's compelling iconicity.[17]

Another frequent feature of epigrammatic speech, as Goffman's "books of famous *mots*" suggests, is its portability—such speech lends itself to being detached from its dramatic context and repeated "for its own sake." In this respect, the epigram's portability places it at the center of a long trajectory that might include, for instance, commonplace books designed for public consumption, in which the primary principles of organization are wit, pithiness, and an emphasis on homiletic wisdom. Wilde's epigrams bring to perfection this tradition of portability. "[T]he epigram," as Amanda Anderson notes regarding Wilde's comedies, "seems always to pull away from the text, and from the context of the action, announcing itself as quotable, transferable, and indifferent."[18] In such publications as his 1894 "Phrases and Philosophies for the Use of the Young" (from which came the title for a 1909 volume of selected Wilde called *Epigrams, Phrases and Philosophies for the Use of the Young*), Wilde could produce epigrams for later use. This plundering works because, in the plays, the epigrams never really depend on their dramatic context anyway.[19] A line from "Phrases and Philosophies"—"In all important matters style, not sincerity, is the essential"—might get lifted by Gwendolen in *The Importance of Being Earnest*, but it is in some sense more at home as an item in a list.[20]

Philip Marlowe's fantastic similes ("He looked about as inconspicuous as a tarantula on a slice of angel food") are Chandler's most recognizable contribution to the tough guy idiom, and true to the tradition of epigrammatic detachability, Marlowe's fans are fond of compiling lists of the most striking (C, 143). Though Chandler's similes do fulfill a number of specific contextual purposes (atmospheric evocation, pithy characterization, and so on), they are ultimately as arbitrary as the epigram in a Wilde comedy; they are always extractable, and the websites devoted to enumerating the best ones are correctly executing the logic of the form.[21] Decontextualized lists of Marlowe's "greatest hits" exist in a parasitic relation to Chandler's novels, just as Wilde's *Phrases and Philosophies* does to Wilde's comedies and other writings. Or perhaps in both cases this parasitism actually runs the other way. Perhaps the stand-alone lists should, in fact, be considered aesthetically primary; Chandler's novels and Wilde's plays are the convenient vehicles for transporting the epigram to an audience.

Furthermore, the Chandlerian simile and the Wildean epigram (specifically, that species of epigram contemporaneously termed "paradox") share a similar structure. Jonathan Freedman has defined "the formal structure of the Wildean epigram" as one that "mimics the binary form of conventional moral sentiments and then simply (one might also say elegantly) reverses one of those terms in order to subvert that sentiment's original intention."[22] (Think of "The Decay of Lying": "Lying, the telling of beautiful untrue things, is the proper aim of art.")[23] Similarly, Marlowe's similes often depend on the surprising appearance of a term we didn't expect; as one critic puts it, "Most often Chandler yokes two incongruous subjects to achieve a startling and fresh observation."[24] The Wildean paradox relies on the scandalous reversal of the terms organizing the prescriptions of social convention; the Chandlerian simile relies on the scandalous proximity of subjects not normally associable. In both cases, incongruity, unexpectedness, and a certain violation of good taste contribute to the pungent memorability, and citability, of the phrase.

The Chandlerian simile (which almost always occurs in Marlowe's first-person narrative voice, not in direct speech) is one kind of tough talk, but it exists alongside another, very different kind—the wisecrack as deployed by the private dick in dialogue with his adversarial interlocutors (criminals, femmes fatales, or intellectually dense police). Like Marlowe's similes, tough-guy dialogue in some sense precedes the novelistic context in which it occurs, as Chandler himself confirmed: "How could I possibly care a button about the detective story as form? All I'm looking for is an excuse for certain experiments in dramatic dialogue . . . all I really care about is what Errol Flynn calls 'the music,' the lines he has to speak."[25] But Marlowe's dialogue, as opposed to his first-person similes, has concrete efficacy in his dramatic world; indeed, it is his principal weapon. As James Guetti notes, "[E]ven in situations where Marlowe himself resorts to physical violence, and wins, it is still his words that really count."[26] At the beginning of *The Big Sleep* (1939), his first novel, Chandler wastes no time establishing Marlowe's verbal dexterity, here deployed (as so often after) to extract information from a recalcitrant woman, in this case the duplicitous Mrs. Regan:

> I didn't ask to see you. You sent for me. I don't mind your ritzing me or drinking your lunch out of a Scotch bottle. I don't mind your showing me your legs. They're very swell legs and it's a pleasure to make their acquaintance. I don't mind if you don't like my manners. They're pretty

bad. I grieve over them during the long winter evenings. But don't waste your time trying to cross-examine me. (C, 12)

The conclusion of this little speech ("don't waste your time trying to cross-examine me") establishes the generic contours for just about every conversational exchange in Chandler's fiction: all talk takes place under the sign of the cross-examination. The aristocratic Mrs. Regan, unused to playing under this set of rules, tries to reject them: "'People don't talk like that to me,' she said thickly" ("thickly," here, reflecting the reduced verbal power always effected by successful instances of Marlovian speech) (C, 13). What gives Marlowe the consistent upper hand in such exchanges, though, are the flourishes of style that, though they might seem gratuitous, in fact establish the rhetorical core of his tough talk: here, the comically incongruous "I grieve over them during the long winter evenings." "Manners," and the world of polite intelligence to which they are proper, are never far from Marlowe's mind, and in this respect Marlovian talk represents a real departure from its ostensible model in Hammett.[27] In *Farewell, My Lovely* (1940), Marlowe proposes an ostensible opposition between "getting tough" and good manners: "'Don't make me get tough,' I whined. 'Don't make me lose my beautiful manners and my flawless English. Just tell me how I got here'" (C, 248). In fact, as these two examples suggest, a prominent strategy in Marlowe's tough talk consists in demonstrating a capacity for or knowledge of good manners alongside a willingness to disavow them when necessary (which is to say, all of the time). As John T. Irwin remarks in a reading of another exchange between Marlowe and Mrs. Regan, the private eye "gives Vivian a lesson in manners"—a lesson he can only impart because he does indeed possess the "beautiful manners" registered with a sarcasm only apparent.[28] Marlowe works hard, though, to feign an incapacity for politeness. "All I need," as he says in *Farewell*, "is a silver tongue and the one I have is like a lizard's back" (C, 294). The alleged opposition this phrase formulates between manners and tough talk is constantly undone by the actual rhetorical work of Marlovian speech. Tough talk and "beautiful manners" occur in the same medium of effortless verbal dexterity, in which, when practiced by the private dick, the drawing room is always collapsing into the draw.

In Marlowe's world, then, there are two distinct levels of epigrammatic speech: first-person similes and the instrumental "wisecracks" deployed in dramatic dialogue.[29] The similes are primarily ornamental, while the wisecrack is both ornamental and aggressive.[30] The aggressive epigram, though, is hardly an original product of the noir novel. In the case of Wilde's plays, Anderson helpfully distinguishes between the inconsequential or "flirtatious" use of the epigram (in a sense, the epigram's default position) and other, more "freighted" deployments: "Once lives have become entangled through extended relationships that have generated expectations, obligations, or shared suffering, then the epigram becomes a freighted speech act that necessarily does more than announce the heightened postconventionality of the ironic critic." Such speech acts lead to "the staging of successful instances of seizing the moment, or what we might call heroic dandyism."[31] For Anderson, the epigram is a distinctly masculine mode of speech, and heroic dandyism rhetorically ratifies male dominance. Useful epigrammatizing gets "promoted alongside and by means of a traditional conception of female subordination, adapted to underwrite its pragmatically inflected ethics."[32] While an epigram in its default position succeeds if it becomes quotable and fails if it cannot, the pragmatic epigram can instead fail or succeed in terms of the dramatic diegesis in which it occurs. Pragmatic—or heroic—epigrammatizing propels the dandy and the private dick alike through fraught and hostile environments.

In the noir novel, the link between epigrammatic aggressivity and masculine dominance assumes a marked thematic centrality. As Mrs. Regan goes on in the exchange with Marlowe discussed above, "I loathe masterful men . . . I simply loathe them" (C, 13). In *Farewell, My Lovely*, Anne Riordan frustratedly responds to Marlowe's smart talk with an indictment of maleness as such:

> "Do you always have to say things like that?" She flushed bitterly. "Sometimes I hate men. Old men, young men, football players, opera tenors, smart millionaires, beautiful men who are gigolos and almost heels who are—private detectives."
>
> I grinned at her sadly. "I know I talk too smart. It's in the air nowadays." (C, 223)

Here, Anne posits "say[ing] things like that" as a constitutive feature of objectionable maleness generally, but the way the litany winds up, with "private detectives" after that dramatic dash, situates the private dick in a position of priority in terms of the rest of the series. His profession is the ground, and paradigm, of irritating masculine mastery. The gendered structure of verbal mastery is so central to Chandler's novels that, by *The Lady in the Lake* (1943), it can be referenced almost as an aside, as in this exchange, irrelevant for plot purposes, between Marlowe and a telephone operator: "The bell rang immediately and the long distance operator told me sharply I had put in five cents too much money. I said the sort of thing I would be likely to put into an opening like that. She didn't like it" (C, 512). Chandler, here, doesn't even bother to reproduce Marlowe's wisecrack for us, nor the operator's objection—he simply summarizes structures noir readers have already been trained to recognize. The double entendre is a meta-epigrammatic summary of a basic noir formula, which might (admittedly sacrificing the Marlovian ring) be further reduced thus: *Masculine verbal mastery provokes feminine irritation; sexual tension abounds.*

But a worry that epigrammatism is primarily ornamental haunts the private dick and the hard-boiled genre. The usefulness of wisecracking must be constantly reinforced. For the quick-tongued private eye, there's always the risk that he might become *merely* a man of words, that the very speech meant to generate his mastery might render him instead an empty talker. As one adversarial police officer says to Marlowe in *Farewell, My Lovely,* "You could get too smart. . . . You could get so smart you couldn't think about anything but bein' smart" (C, 279). Or as a savvy client says to the Continental Op in Hammett's *Red Harvest,* "You're a great talker. . . . A two-fisted, you-be-damned man with your words. But have you got anything else? Have you got the guts to match your gall? Or is it just the language you've got?"[33]

For Marlowe, the fear that wisecracking might constitute not mastery but a mask for powerlessness and impotence finds expression in his frequently reiterated observations (projections) regarding the tough-guy poses of his adversaries, poses Marlowe interprets, importantly, as lifted from Hollywood movies. "His voice," Marlowe narrates of Brody in *The Big Sleep,* "was the elaborately casual voice of the tough guy in pictures. Pictures have made them all like that" (C, 48). The threat of the commodified tough-guy act haunts Marlowe; what, after all, separates him from his own cutting representation of the two-bit gangster Morny in *The High Window,* whose "[e]very motion, every gesture, [is] right out of the catalogue" (C, 398)? By calling attention to the norms of the hard-boiled genre in which he is a character, Marlowe's anxious criticism of other people's tough talk occasionally produces moments of amusing metafiction, as in this exchange with a police officer in *The High Window:*

"We used a wop on him," Breeze said. "A wop named Palermo."

"Oh. You know something?"

"What?" Breeze asked.

"I just thought of what is the matter with policeman's dialogue."
"What?"
"They think every line is a punch line." (C, 419)

Tellingly, Chandler himself ascribed his propensity for one-liners to "that nox-ious habit of writing lines for actors which are overpointed for effect, so that the line is really said to the audience rather than to the character in the play."[34] In blaming (not entirely ingenuously) his penchant for writing epigrammati-cally on the vulgarizing influence of Hollywood, Chandler acknowledges the hard-boiled detective's overt theatricality, a theatricality indeed so obvious that Marlowe's (or Chandler's) anxious disavowal of the "voice of the tough guy in pictures" serves not so much to create distance between Marlowe and the movies as to knowingly underscore their collusion.

No matter how dramatically aggressive, the wisecrack, like the Wildean paradox, always pulls away from its context, gravitating toward an audience for whom it will become memorable and quotable. But are aggressivity and ornamental quotability necessarily at odds? Before the advent of the hard-boiled noir novel, perhaps no novelist understood the aggressivity of epigram-matic speech better than George Meredith. In *The Egoist* (1879), Meredith's great ironic, tragicomic masterpiece, the wheels of the plot are practically set in motion by the force of an epigram. The novel treats the betrothal and pain-ful, protracted falling out of the arrogant Sir Willoughby, the "egoist" of the title, and the initially naive and then powerfully disillusioned Clara Middleton. Though both Sir Willoughby and Clara are resourceful rhetorical opponents, their verbal sparring is not marked by epigrammaticality as it is understood in the novel. The wielding of epigram is left to Mrs. Mounstuart Jenkins, a middle-aged widow whose friendship with Sir Willoughby makes her a priv-ileged observer of the drama. Mrs. Mounstuart's claim to fame rests on her powerful capacity for memorable speech:[35]

> Mrs. Mounstuart was a lady certain to say the remembered, if not the right, thing. Again and again was it confirmed on days of high cele-bration, days of birth or bridal, how sure she was to hit the mark that rang the bell; and away her word went over the county: and had she been an uncharitable woman she could have ruled the county with an iron rod of caricature, so sharp was her touch. A grain of malice would have sent county faces and characters awry into the currency. . . . Her

words sprang out of her. She looked at you, and forth it came: and it stuck to you, as nothing laboured or literary could have adhered. Her saying of Laetitia Dale: "Here she comes, with a romantic tale on her eyelashes," was a portrait of Laetitia. And that of Vernon Whitford: "He is a Phoebus Apollo turned fasting friar," painted the sunken brilliancy of the lean long-walker and scholar at a stroke.[36]

Mrs. Mounstuart's epigrammatism inheres in her capacity to capture a person's social essence in a phrase. (Meredith not infrequently gives his women characters dandiacal traits—an aspect of both his feminism and his formal radicalism.) This is, incidentally, also an occasional function of noir wisecracking, as when Marlowe describes "a charming middle-aged lady with a face like a bucket of mud and if she has washed her hair since Coolidge's second term I'll eat my spare tire, rim and all," to which his interlocutor replies, "Skip the wisecracks" (C, 163). Unlike Marlowe's pejorative portraiture, though, Mrs. Mounstuart's "word" is like a superpower used for good; it limns her social world with accuracy, but gently. She marries poetry to epistemology, and the poetry becomes quotable. Her speech successfully defines Laetitia and Vernon Whitford and then travels "over the country" by virtue of its citable poetic rightness. Its work is chiefly descriptive—it doesn't *do* anything other than describe well. But alongside this benign function of Mrs. Mounstuart's word, Meredith articulates another, darker possibility: "had she been an uncharitable woman she could have ruled the county with an iron rod of caricature, so sharp was her touch." Apt description, it seems, might confer actual, which is to say abusable, power. This sinister power is also ascribable to the easy citability of Mrs. Mounstuart's word; the ease with which she might (if she chose) send a caricatural or malicious characterization "into the currency" means that her rhetorical skill could allow her to dictate social reality.

The potentially dangerous aspect of Mrs. Mounstuart's word becomes apparent when she labels the newly betrothed Clara a "dainty rogue in porcelain," which Sir Willoughby finds ominous out of all apparent proportion. "For once Mrs. Mounstuart Jenkinson was unsuccessful. Her 'dainty rogue in porcelain' displeased Sir Willoughby. 'Why rogue?' he said. The lady's fame for hitting the mark fretted him . . . the more he thought of the epigram launched at her, the more he grew displeased."[37] Across two pages of anxious dialogue, Sir Willoughby interrogates Mrs. Mounstuart about her phrase, as if parsing the esoteric prophecies of a sibyl:

"I am persuaded I shall never comprehend it!" [Sir Willoughby]

"I cannot help you one bit further."

"The word rogue!"

"It was dainty rogue."

"Brittle, would you say?"

"I am quite unable to say."

"An innocent naughtiness?"

"Prettily moulded in a delicate substance."

"You are thinking of some piece of Dresden you suppose her to resemble."

"I dare say."

"Artificial?"

"You would not have her natural?"

"I am heartily satisfied with her from head to foot, my dear Mrs. Mounstuart."[38]

Willoughby's insistence on decomposing Mrs. Mounstuart's epigram and examining its component parts violates the logic of the form, whose inherent rightness depends on its being received as a seamless unit. Mrs. Mounstuart understands this. "Like all rapid phrasers, Mrs. Mounstuart detested the analysis of her sentence. It had an outline in vagueness, and was flung out to be apprehended, not dissected."[39] Willoughby's "dissection" is a defensive maneuver, designed to strip the epigram of its force. There are truths we don't want to know, and the wit which would reveal them against our wishes is an enemy.

As Clara puts it, "I must avoid [Mrs. Mounstuart]. The thought of her leaves me no choice. . . . She could tattoo me with epigrams."[40] Crowning a series of verbs attached to Mrs. Mounstuart's speech that includes "hit," "sprang out," "launch," and "flung out," the word "tattoo" (with its simultaneous signification of "rhythmic tapping or drumming" and permanently marking the skin) encapsulates the violence behind Mrs. Mounstuart's verbal power, its incursion on one's consciousness against one's will.[41] These words are needles, and they leave permanent marks.

That her epigrams might actually generate the social world they purport merely to describe invests Mrs. Mounstuart with tremendous power, and in this she resembles the noir private dick, one end of whose tough talk is the aggressive construction of a manageable reality. As Guetti puts it, "[T]he detective takes aggressive action upon his case by means of a certain kind of talk. The case confronts him as a welter of strange fragments, and he attacks it by verbally recomposing it, by rephrasing it."[42] In detective fiction, naturally, this construction frequently occurs in a juridical context—the private dick must defend himself against the legal assaults of the police or convincingly make the case for the apparently implausible guilt of the perpetrator. I said before that, in Chandler, all talk takes place under the sign of the cross-examination. I want to turn, now, to the record of actual cross-examinations, those of Oscar Wilde on trial for sodomy. Nowhere else does the pragmatic applicability inherent in epigrammatic speech become so clear.

Toward the beginning of the first trial, Wilde's witty tone called down a rebuke from the questioning magistrate: "Only answer the questions, please."[43] By attempting to close the gap between only answering the questions and the marked speech of a famously clever dandy, Wilde meant to impose his personality on the bureaucratic machinery of the law, although at least one friend warned him of the insufficiency of this approach. As Frank Harris told Wilde, "You don't realize what is going to happen to you. It is not going to be a question of clever talk about your books" (*T*, 44). In fact, much of the trials *was* a matter of clever talk about Wilde's books and other writing—the prosecution's case often hinged on suspicious readings of both *The Picture of Dorian Gray* and an extravagant love letter written to Alfred Douglas. But Wilde's handling of these portions of the trial largely redounded to his benefit. As H. Montgomery Hyde remarks regarding his "sparkling answers to the questions put to him about *Dorian Gray* and other of his writings," Wilde "scored off Carson heavily. His spontaneous quips were every bit as good as those he had put into the mouths of the characters in *An Ideal Husband* and *The Importance of Being Earnest*. This was indeed as good as a play—and a Wilde play at that!" (*T*, 50). When, for instance, Wilde is asked about his admission of "adoration" in a letter to Douglas, he responded, "I have never given adoration to anybody except myself" (*T*, 129). The general thrust of Wilde's answers to these portions of cross-examination was clearly meant to establish his uniqueness, his self-possession, and his intellectual superiority to the examiner.

But the façade does eventually break down. Wilde, asked whether he had ever kissed one Walter Grainger, responds thus: "Oh dear no. He was a peculiarly plain boy. He was, unfortunately, extremely ugly. I pitied him for it" (*T*, 150). Wilde meant this as yet another instance of his self-possessed wit, but it backfired badly. The prosecutor refused to let this apparent admission of homosexuality go, eventually forcing Wilde to abandon his trademark style of speech. As Hyde recounts, "[T]he witness began several answers almost inarticulately, and none of them he finished. His efforts to collect his ideas were not aided by Mr. Carson's sharp staccato repetition: 'Why? Why?' . . . At last the witness answered: You sting me and insult me and try to unnerve me; and at times one says things flippantly when one ought to speak more seriously" (*T*, 25). This exchange is almost unbearably painful, not only because of the atmosphere of homophobic persecution it evokes, but because the image of a mute and stuttering Wilde attempting semi-articulately to retreat from his preferred style has the poignancy of any representation of the wounded hero. Within the rhetorical economy of the transcripts, a direct line can be drawn from this episode to the conclusion of the final trial, after sentence has been handed down: "'OSCAR WILDE—And I? May I say nothing, my lord?' [His lordship made no reply beyond a wave of the hand to the warders, who hurried the prisoners out of sight]" (*T*, 339). If, following Anderson, the heroic dandy wields his epigrams in pragmatically driven contests of will in which the stakes involve "ethical interventions that will benefit others," Wilde's failures of speech, or the denial by the court of his very right to speak, constitute beyond even his imprisonment the terms of his martyrdom.[44]

On trial, all Wildean epigrammatizing is heroic, in the sense that it is always pragmatically driven, and the stakes are high indeed. In his own discussion of the Wilde trials, Cohen cites M. M. Bakhtin's famous treatment of the legal trial and its relationship to the modern novel in *The Dialogic Imagination*:

> [T]he testing of a strong personality who opposes himself, on one ground or another, to the community, who seeks to attain a complete self-sufficiency and a proud isolation, or who aspires to the role of a chosen leader; the testing of the moral reformer or amoralist, the trial of the Nietzschean man or the emancipated woman and so forth—these are all very widespread organizing ideas in the European novel of the nineteenth and early twentieth century.[45]

We can now recognize Wilde fulfilling almost all the functions Bakhtin enumerates. An entirely appropriate icon for the "strong personality" whose representation becomes so central to modernity's narratives about itself, Wilde expressed his own "complete self-sufficiency" by his commitment throughout the trial to his famous epigrammatic persona, a strategy of dubious legal utility but of undoubted value in terms of cementing for his contemporaries and for

history his charismatic oppositionality. The simultaneously attractive and coercive force of charismatic oppositionality was at the end of the nineteenth
century—and remains today—the most readily available vector for narrativiz-
ing Wilde's trials, and surely informs Anderson's reading of "the several modes
of the [Wildean] dandy [as] epigrammatic irony, pragmatic transvaluation,
and heroic intervention."[46] As Wilde wrote in an 1898 letter to an early activist
for what we would now call gay rights, "I have no doubt we shall win, but the
road is long, and red with monstrous martyrdoms."[47] Martyrdom, here, is oppositionality's bloodiest horizon.

Chandler's Dandies

The private dick inherits a mode of epigrammatic speech from Wilde, but he
submits this mode to systematic alterations that serve both to signal a difference from the dandiacal and to covertly, complexly, mark affiliation. Like the
dandified aristocrat, the hard-boiled private eye must disaffiliate from feminized domesticity and normal work structures, but he must *also* (or conse-
quently) indicate his distance from the threatening specter of the oppositional
homosexual with whom his rejection of married domesticity might all too
easily lump him. Leslie Fiedler writes that, unlike Sherlock Holmes, the American private eye "is not the dandy turned sleuth; he is the cowboy adapted to
life on the city streets"—"cowboy" here being shorthand for the self-employed,
the extradomestic, the unmarried, the rough, and understood to be at odds
with the refined sensitivity marking the dandy.[48] As Perry Meisel reminds us,
though, in *The Cowboy and the Dandy*, it is not impossible to be both at the
same time. Recalling Wilde's 1882 visit to the mining town of Leadville, Col-
orado, Meisel recounts the unlikely fellowship that sprang up between Wilde
and the "miners and cowboys" he met there. "Such an unlikely affection," Meisel writes, "between the most famous dandy of the day and a bunch of rugged
Westerners is unsettling."[49] Understood in terms of valorized masculine oppositionality, though, it is also perfectly explicable.[50]

But it is not enough simply to mark or stage disaffiliation from the dandiacal. In Chandler, "talking tough" slides into dandiacal epigrammatizing according to flickering codes of identification and disidentification—the hard-boiled
hero's shtick is always predicated on a fascination with the dandiacal that is
nevertheless shot through with phobia and distaste. His tough talk is *always*
a covert form of dandiacal epigrammatizing. Though Chandler's trademark

witty dialogue and epigrammatic similes occupy all of his novels, *The Big Sleep* and *Farewell, My Lovely* are unique in their focus on homosexuality, which they understand in terms of a decidedly nineteenth-century emphasis on dandiacal bohemia. *Farewell, My Lovely* contains the most dandiacal figure in the Chandler oeuvre, the flamboyantly named Lindsay Marriott. Before turning to these novels, though, I want to recall Chandler's letter to Warren, written in 1949. Though this letter postdates the first two novels by a decade, it is continuous with them in terms of its interest in "the homosexualist" and in the valorized rebelliousness to which he may or may not be linked. Chandler's allusion to the Wilde trials within a larger discussion of "homosexualism" can tell us a great deal about the psychosexual economy underlying the world of Philip Marlowe. The letter is notable above all for its extreme ambiguity. Chandler can't seem to decide whether he wants to diagnose homosexuality (the homosexual is "sick," suffers from a "fundamental inability to finish anything," is likened to "a scorpion" and "repulsive insects") or whether, instead, he means to diagnose homophobia ("All cruelty is a kind of fear"). Most tellingly, Chandler cannot decide how to assess the homosexual in terms of the rebellious oppositionality he would otherwise endorse: "He's no more than the other rebels against a sanctimonious and hypocritical society." No more, but no less either. Chandler's contempt for the homophobic "business man at a stag smoker" seems to undo his assertion, two sentences earlier, that he "can't take the homo seriously as a moral outcast." By referring to the Wilde trials in terms of "the mob impulse to destroy the homo," Chandler admits his sympathy for Wildean oppositionality even as he goes on immediately to cancel it (Wilde/the homosexual is a "sick wolf" victimized by the presumably healthy pack). Indeed, in *The Big Sleep* the private eye, that exemplar of a style of masculine oppositionality that signifies powerfully to this day, must continually define himself against the homosexual, whose persecuted and illegal subjectivity represents a competing model of the "rebel against a sanctimonious and hypocritical society."

Very early on in *The Big Sleep*, Marlowe describes himself this way to General Sternwood: "I'm thirty-three years old, went to college once and can still speak English if there's any demand for it. There isn't much in my trade. I worked for Mr. Wilde, the District Attorney, as an investigator once" (*C*, 7). Unlike his old boss's namesake, Marlowe claims no sparkling conversation. The name "Wilde" is a little joke, although it inaugurates a broader pattern. In *The Big Sleep* and to some extent in the other Marlowe novels, Chandler systematically disaffiliates his hero from various signifiers marked as aestheticist, decadent, and homosexual.[51] The allusions involved in this process of disaffiliation—or, more precisely, of ironic affiliation under the sign of disaffiliation—constitute something of a running gag. And Wilde's isn't the only literary name to make an appearance:

> [Vivian Regan]: "I was beginning to think perhaps you worked in bed, like Marcel Proust."
>
> "Who's he?" I put a cigarette in my mouth and stared at her. She looked a little pale and strained, but she looked like a girl who could function under a strain.
>
> "A French writer, a connoisseur in degenerates. You wouldn't know him."
>
> "Tut, tut," I said. "Come into my boudoir." (C, 34)

Strictly speaking, a boudoir is a woman's bedroom; in inviting Vivian into his, Marlowe activates the model of homosexual gender inversion central to the *Recherche*—a little joke for the Proustians among Chandler's readership. "Boudoir," here, has something of the charge of a naughty word, though its naughtiness is vertiginously multifaceted. To name it is to advance a sexual proposition, but in such a way as to undo the offer even as it is spoken. The boudoir is a curiously queered space in which the tension between Marlowe and Vivian might be—in some other kind of novel—resolved sexually. The joke depends on what we are meant to take as the obvious unsuitability of the boudoir to a tough guy like Philip Marlowe, as if the comic spectacle of Marlowe playing the Baron de Charlus ought to render self-evident the absurdity of any such association. But the ironic camouflage with which Marlowe dons his Proust drag shouldn't conceal the possibility that, in fact, Marlowe is never so in earnest as when he's tut-tutting.

Are we to believe Marlowe's ignorance of the name "Marcel Proust"? In 1949's *The Little Sister*, the Philip Marlowe who "went to college once" knows enough literature to quote Browning ("The poet, not the automatic") at one baffled femme fatale.[52] By 1953's *The Long Goodbye* Marlowe famously discusses T. S. Eliot, though this knowledge can't necessarily be read back into the earlier novels.[53] As early as *Farewell, My Lovely*, Marlowe recognizes a calendar reproduction of a Rembrandt self-portrait, "rather smeary . . . due to an imperfectly registered color plate"; he evaluates the portrait in the tough-guy aesthete idiom familiar from Hemingway: "His face was aging, saggy, full of the disgust of life and the thickening effects of liquor. But it had a hard cheerfulness that I liked, and the eyes were as bright as drops of dew" (*C*, 165). All of which is to say that, from *Farewell* onward, Chandler takes some care to provide Marlowe with evident conversancy in high culture. It hardly matters, though, whether the Marlowe of *The Big Sleep* knows Proust or not; the point is that Vivian thinks he doesn't ("You wouldn't know him,") and that, though she means this assertion to be snobbish, in fact his ostensible ignorance, or the performance of that ignorance, distances him from "degenerates" and degeneracy. Vivian tropes aesthetic sophistication in terms of class, and Marlowe responds by troping both in terms of pathologized sexuality.

A similar class divide animates Marlowe's tense exchanges with the entitled Lindsay Marriott in *Farewell, My Lovely*, a divide signaled first and foremost through qualities of voice and speech. Marriott calls Marlowe hoping to hire him for a job; Marlowe asks whether the job is legitimate:

> The voice grew icicles. "I should not have called you, if it were not."
> A Harvard boy. Nice use of the subjunctive mood. The end of my foot itched, but my bank account was still trying to crawl under a duck. I put honey in my voice and said: "Many thanks for calling me, Mr. Marriott. I'll be there." (*C*, 166)

No Ivy Leaguer Marlowe, and broke to boot, but endowed by Chandler (himself an English public school boy) with the specific kinds of knowledge that mark the educated.[54] (There are many things a smart man without formal education might know; the subjunctive mood is not likely to be one of them.) Marlowe's authority vis-à-vis rich clients like Marriott depends on the gap between his intellectual and cultural equality (or superiority) on the one hand and his inferior polish, not to mention his straitened finances, on the other. This tension animates his relationship with Marriott throughout *Farewell*, but especially at the scene of their first meeting. Here is how Marlowe describes this "tall blond man in a white flannel suit with a violet satin scarf around his neck":

> There was a cornflower in the lapel of his white coat and his pale blue eyes looked faded out by comparison. The violet scarf was loose enough to show that he wore no tie and that he had a thick, soft brown neck, like the neck of a strong woman. His features were a little on the heavy side, but handsome, he had an inch more of height than I had, which made him six feet one. His blond hair was arranged, by art or nature, in three precise blond ledges which reminded me of steps, so

that I didn't like them. I wouldn't have liked them anyway. Apart from all this he had the general appearance of a lad who would wear a white flannel suit with a violet scarf around his neck and a cornflower in his lapel. (*C*, 170)

Marriott is a consummate dandy, replete with every overdetermined dandiacal signifier Chandler could stuff into a brief description. (Indeed, except for the blond hair, this tall, somewhat heavy, thick-featured but handsome man could be modeled on Wilde.) He leads Marlowe into "the kind of room where people sit with their feet in their laps and sip absinthe through lumps of sugar and talk with high affected voices and sometimes just squeak. It was a world where anything could happen except work" (*C*, 170). Marlowe is peculiarly out of place here because, we are meant to understand, he most certainly *works*, a fact accented because otherwise the reader might misconstrue his routine—moving through various picturesquely decrepit Southern Californian settings, drinking whiskey, saying clever things, and fending off the advances of women—as flagrant *flaneurie*. As the scene continues, Chandler lays it on thicker; the depiction of the mismatch between Marriott's pretentious cultured leisure and Marlowe's tough-guy act becomes so exaggerated as almost to violate the hard-boiled genre's (always rather thinly sustained) claims to naturalism, to slip into cartoonish satire:[55]

> Mr. Lindsay Marriott arranged himself in the curve of the grand piano, leaned over to sniff at the yellow rose, then opened a French enamel cigarette case and lit a long brown cigarette with a gold tip. I sat down on a pink chair and hoped I wouldn't leave a mark on it. I lit a Camel, blew smoke through my nose and looked at a piece of black shiny metal on a stand. It showed a full, smooth curve with a shallow fold in it and two protuberances on the curve. I stared at it. Marriott saw me staring at it.
>
> "An interesting bit," he said negligently. "I picked it up just the other day. Asta Dial's *Spirit of Dawn*."
>
> "I though it was Klopstein's *Two Warts on a Fanny*."
>
> Mr. Lindsay Marriott's face looked as if he had swallowed a bee. He smoothed it out with an effort. (*C*, 170)

Marriott's dandyism is languid and ineffectual, precisely because the privilege of epigrammatic speech has been wrested from him and given, instead, to Marlowe. Marriott may look something like a (blond) Wilde, but he can't manage to talk like one; Marlowe gets the good lines, while Marriott suffers facial contortions. This is a burlesqued version of the Proust exchange in *The Big Sleep*; once again, cultural and economic capital are pointedly aligned against Marlowe, who nevertheless gains the upper hand by riffing on the forms through which the leisured demonstrate their cultural sophistication to one another. Unlike Geiger in *The Big Sleep,* Marriott is never unequivocally identified as gay, but his costume, his casual art collecting, his gait ("He moved away like a dancer, his body almost motionless from the waist up" [C, 175]), his laugh ("rather boyish, but not a very young boy" [C, 173]) are all stereotyped marks of the "homosexualist," and legible to Chandler's audience as such. Marlowe almost renders his suspicion of Marriott's gayness explicit when he asks him whether this job is "a matter of blackmail":

> [Marriott] frowned. "Certainly not. I'm not in the habit of giving people grounds for blackmail."
> "It happens to the nicest people. I might say particularly to the nicest people."
> He waved a cigarette. His aquamarine eyes had a faintly thoughtful expression, but his lips smiled. The kind of smile that goes with a silk noose. (C, 171)

It is not, though, until the fatal explosion of violence in the desert that Marlowe, in the form of a slur, will remark upon the sexuality for which all the marks of dandyism have been signs. Marriott and Marlowe drive into the desert for the ostensible purpose of handing off money for some stolen jewels (the reason Marriott gives for hiring Marlowe); leaving Marriott in the car, Marlowe heads out into the darkness to do recon, finds nothing, and returns to the car only to be knocked unconscious. Waking up, he realizes that the bad guys must have taken care of Marriott in the brief period during which he himself left the car. "They must have moved quick and quiet. He didn't even let out a yell. . . . The guy scared easily. They must have thrown a small light in his face and he passed out—just from panic. The pansy" (C, 178). In fact, as Marlowe and the suddenly materialized Anne Riordan learn a few pages later, Marriott has not passed out but passed on. Marlowe confirms this when he borrows a flashlight from Anne and shines it onto Marriot's head: "His hair was dark with blood, the beautiful blond ledges were tangled with blood and some thick grayish ooze, like primeval slime" (C, 183). The revelation by flashlight of

Marriott's death replays, with a brutal difference, Marlowe's earlier surmise that "[t]hey must have thrown a small light in his face and he passed out." Marriott, "the pansy," never had a chance, because—as Marlowe says of Geiger's boyfriend in *The Big Sleep*—"a pansy has no iron in his bones" (*C*, 61).

As in the Wilde trials, decadent domestic interiors in Chandler's novels are charged with suspicious meaning; like Wilde's cross-examiner, Marlowe enumerates these rooms' paraphernalia with phobic obsessiveness, though with a good deal more style. In *The Big Sleep*, the gay rare books dealer and pornographer Geiger's "place was horrible by daylight. The Chinese junk on the walls, the rug, the fussy lamps, the teakwood stuff, the sticky riot of colors, the totem pole, the flagon of ether and laudanum—all this in the day time had a stealthy nastiness, like a fag party" (*C*, 39). As with Marriot's den of leisure, Marlowe finds himself intruding on zones of decadent consumption (laudanum, absinthe, ether, sugar), not himself to consume, but to do a job.

Part of this job involves apprehending Geiger's boyfriend, a would-be tough guy named Carol Lundgren who lives in "a nice clean manly little room" of his own at Geiger's place and has mistakenly shot Joe Brody in revenge for Geiger's killing. Lundgren's manly room is pointedly distinguished from Geiger's decadent digs, and his willingness to fight back presumably reflects his sturdy taste in interior decorating. When Marlowe demands a key from Lundgren to access Geiger's house, he denies having one. Marlowe: "Don't kid me, son. The fag gave you one. . . . He shooed you out and locked it up when he had lady visitors. He was like Caesar, a husband to women and a wife to men. Think I can't figure people like him and you out?" (*C*, 61). Lundgren throws a punch and a brief struggle ensues, with Marlowe predictably triumphant (iron, bones). But Marlowe's description of their fight is informed throughout by a barely sublimated erotics:

> I twisted him around and heaved him a little higher. I took hold of my right wrist with my left hand and turned my right hipbone into him and for a moment it was a balance of weights. We seemed to hang there in the misty moonlight, two grotesque creatures whose feet scraped on the road and whose breath panted with effort. . . .
>
> "Go —— yourself," he said with a soft stricken sigh.
>
> "You're going to cop a plea, brother, don't ever think you're not. And you're going to say just what we want you to say and nothing we don't want you to say."

"Go —— yourself."

"Say that again and I'll put a pillow under your head." (C, 61–62)

This is a fistfight as courtship dance, and its interest lies less in its potential decoding by a clever critic than in the evident superfluity of any such decoding: Chandler has laid it all out for us. Importantly, the flourishing of erotic possibility animating this scene occurs in a fight *not* with a dandified homosexual like Geiger, but with a gay tough guy conspicuously lacking any decadent or dandified signifiers (that "manly little room"). A language of dandyism, though, comes in subtly; Lundgren's "soft stricken sigh" at the moment of a defeat nearly indistinguishable from sexual conquest inscribes him in a kind of decadent poem. Swinburne, for one, has written of a butterfly "soft as a long low sigh" and of a tide "[s]oft and listless as the slumber-stricken air"; Chandler could have read both of these quotations (shorn of their context) in Frank J. Wilstach's 1916 *A Dictionary of Similes,* in which they are listed adjacently.[56] Whatever its provenance, Lundgren's "soft stricken sigh" represents something like the return of the feminized, decadent repressed assumed to mark the homosexual in Marlowe's world.

Marlowe's erotic investment in tough guys will be replayed, in a different key, in *Farewell, My Lovely,* in which he falls in love with a big ex-cop named Red Norgaard.[57] Marlowe runs into Norgaard on the docks while trying to get passage to an offshore gambling boat. Norgaard provides this passage, and the two men share an intimacy unrivaled elsewhere in Chandler, an intimacy apparently enabled by Norgaard's striking combination of hypermasculine traits and a gentleness coded by Marlowe as feminine. Norgaard is described as a "big redheaded roughneck in dirty sneakers and tarry pants," but "[h]is voice was soft, dreamy, so delicate for a big man that it was startling":

> I looked at him again. He had the eyes you never see, that you only read about. Violet eyes. Almost purple. Eyes like a girl, a lovely girl. His skin was as soft as silk. Lightly reddened, but it would never tan. It was too delicate. . . . His hair was that shade of red that glints with gold. But except for the eyes he had a plain farmer face, with no stagy kind of handsomeness. (C, 287, 288)

Norgaard's intense physicality, compounded of masculine bigness and feminine gentleness, enchants Marlowe more successfully than any femme fatale, rendering him uncharacteristically confessional: "I told him a great deal more than I intended. It must have been his eyes" (C, 291).

Part of Norgaard's appeal for Marlowe depends, clearly, on what one critic has called the "entanglement of masculine and feminine signifiers" with which he is depicted.[58] But the quality of Marlowe's attraction to Norgaard can be clarified in light of his aversion to Lindsay Marriott in the same novel. Marriott, too, embodies an entanglement of the masculine and the feminine, but he does so under the explicit sign of dandyism. Norgaard, on the other hand, is an androgynous anti-dandy, with his messy, unkempt clothes and his "plain farmer face, with no stagy kind of handsomeness." Norgaard's androgynous appeal is constituted in contradistinction to Marriott, just as Lundgren with his "manly little room" is contrasted with the decadent Geiger. Chandler, it seems, wants to rescue both androgyny and male-male eroticism from dandyism, a gambit having finally more to do with class than with sexuality—Marlowe can fall for Norgaard with his farmer's face, while Marriott, with his aristocratic clothes and his Harvard voice, must die in the desert.

Class tensions within Chandler's novels should be understood in terms of his attempt to forge a serious popular literary style against the background of a difficult high modernism ratified by the intelligentsia. The dialectic between the hard-boiled and the dandiacal reflects at the level of character type Chandler's commitment to forging a style at once popular (distanced from contemporary high modernism) and serious (more aesthetically ambitious than mere pulps). In his Gumshoe America (2000), Sean McCann has convincingly traced the terms of this dialectic as it relates to larger patterns of political thought during the twenties, thirties, and forties. McCann argues that the New Deal is "the absent center of Chandler's literary imagination" and that his "fascination with an evanescent vernacular spirit mirrored the demand for popular representation that echoed through the American thirties."[59] According to McCann, Chandler's role of "sentimental populist" involved renouncing the pretentious claims of high art, which he considered "effete," in favor of a vernacular literature whose promise inheres in no small part in its self-evident masculinity.[60] The point is not that Chandler's novels in fact depict or endorse the need for a New Deal–style politics, but that Marlowe's corrupt and disintegrating Los Angeles represents a critique whose implicit but never stated corrective is the New Deal. More: the articulation of the need for such a corrective assumes its immanent aesthetic in the tough, popular style Chandler adapts from his *Black Mask* cohort. This corrective, in noir, is always deferred, horizonal; its realization would involve the absorption and containment of the oppositional private eye by a collective labor–based sociality in which the hard-boiled outsider would have no continued function.[61]

Marlowe's joke about "Klopstein's *Two Warts on a Fanny*" (a joke predicated on the presumed nonrepresentational nature of Asta Dial's sculpture) sums up Chandler's insistent opposition to contemporary trends in modernist abstraction and hermetic difficulty, traits implicitly linked (through Lindsay Marriott's proud ownership of the sculpture) to the effete and the dandiacal. The link between high-modern abstraction and dandiacal effeteness becomes even clearer in light of Marlowe's sensitivity to the Rembrandt self-portrait. Marlowe's take on the Rembrandt—"aging, saggy, full of the disgust of life and the thickening effects of liquor"—might be said to "frame" Rembrandt within the parameters of Marlowe's own idiom; representational high art, at least, is shown to be potentially commensurate with the honest approach to debased modernity best reflected by the popular noir novel. Rembrandt's alcohol-ravaged mug, unlike the Proustian boudoir, represents aesthetic seriousness distinctly *not* tethered to the effete, the feminine, or the dandiacal.

But Chandler's masculinist populism is complicated by his deep ambivalence regarding the popular, an ambivalence that McCann shows to be the rule among midcentury crime novelists.[62] When, in *The Big Sleep*, Marlowe apes what he imagines is the language of a "French . . . connoisseur in degenerates" ("Tut tut. Come into my boudoir") we are meant to chuckle at the wide difference between our hero and whatever we imagine of the boudoir-dwelling connoisseur. But the force of Vivian's jest, of her hypothetically likening Marlowe to Proust—"I was beginning to think you worked in bed, like Marcel Proust"—cannot be so neatly undone. As Peter Conrad notes in a perceptive 1978 *TLS* review essay entitled "The Private Dick as Dandy," Chandler's "is a fugitive and self-distrustful aestheticism which needs the alibi of filth and meanness; he is a dandy on the defensive," and "Marlowe is a neurasthenic weakling pretending to be hardboiled."[63] Authorizing this skepticism regarding Marlowe-as-tough-guy is Chandler's own highly ambivalent relationship to *Black Mask* and popular writing.[64] Indeed, the tension between dandiacal elegance and the approved masculinity of the tough guy plays itself out with comic explicitness in Chandler's notebooks, as Conrad observes: "In the notebooks a set of fashion tips, comprising such exquisite items as a 'gazelle leather sports coat nutmeg brown,' another such garment of 'creamy white Shetland wool,' and alligator shoes, is abruptly censored by a penciled exclamation: 'Oh my God.' Chandler has caught himself unawares, and recoils in alarm."[65]

The tough guy, then, must distance himself from the dandy even when (especially when) his own erotic investment in other men seems clearest, but there is always the risk that the dandiacal will return, that Marlowe will in fact become the boudoir-dwelling dandy he sarcastically apes. At the level of the broader literary field, the intrusion of the dandiacal into the precincts of a tough masculinity presumably excluding it becomes structurally necessitated by Chandler's ambivalent relationship both to high modernism (which he codes as pretentious, aristocratic, and effete) and to *Black Mask*–style genre fiction, which he alternately embraces and scorns. On all fronts, Chandler wants to have it both ways: he wants a popular modernism; he wants macho male-male erotics at a time when homosexuality was popularly legible as effeminate; and he wants to preserve dandiacal epigrammatism without its aristocratic class affiliations.

Which brings us back to talking tough, that mode of epigrammatic speech proper to the noir novel. Tough talk does a lot of things in hard-boiled fiction, but it is perhaps above all the verbal signature whose deployment indicates opposition: to the careless greed of the professional criminal class, to the police, to the inanities of an encroaching consumer culture, to the law itself. An emblematic scene at the center of Hammett's *The Maltese Falcon* (1929), from which Chandler learned a great deal about the wisecracking hard-boiled dick, illustrates tough talk's valuable role as a mode of resistance to state power, here represented by a meddling district attorney. Like the Continental Op, *The Maltese Falcon*'s Sam Spade is a good talker, but whereas the Op's verbal facility is overtly aggressive (a "two-fisted, you-be-damned man with your words"), Spade's is a bit more polished. "You have always," Joel Cairo says at one point, "a smooth explanation ready." Spade: "What do you want me to do? Learn to stutter?"[66] When Spade is called in to meet with the district attorney and his assistant—with a court stenographer present—he defuses a potentially threatening scenario through his constitutive inability to falter or stutter:

> Spade glanced his way, chuckled, and asked [D.A.] Bryan: "Anything I say will be used against me?"
>
> The District Attorney smiled. "That always holds good." He took his glasses off, looked at them, and set them on his nose again. He looked through them at Spade and asked: "Who killed Thursby?"

Spade said: "I don't know."

Bryan rubbed his black eyeglass-ribbon between thumb and fingers and said knowingly: "Perhaps you don't, but you certainly could make an excellent guess."

"Maybe, but I wouldn't."

The District Attorney raised his eyebrows.

"I wouldn't," Spade repeated. He was serene. "My guess might be excellent, or it might be crummy, but Mrs. Spade didn't raise any children dippy enough to make guesses in front of a district attorney, an assistant district attorney, and a stenographer."

"Why shouldn't you, if you have nothing to conceal?"

"Everybody," Spade responded mildly, "has something to conceal."

"And you have—?"

"My guesses, for one thing."

The District Attorney looked down at his desk and then up at Spade. He settled his glasses more firmly on his nose. He said: "If you'd prefer not having the stenographer here we can dismiss him. It is simply as a matter of convenience that I brought him in."

"I don't mind him a damned bit," Spade replied. "I'm willing to have anything I say put down and I'm willing to sign it."[67]

"He was serene." Like the Hemingway hero, the private eye is unthinkable without this carapace of composure, reserve. The most salient feature of this passage is Spade's refusal to allow the D.A. to dismiss the stenographer. At the level of the plot, this is an expression of Spade's self-confidence, of his refusal to be seen as cornered or compromised. But it's also a metafictional nod to the requirements of the genre. The fast talk of the private eye should be recorded. The courtroom stenographer, as Spade and Oscar Wilde each understands, is the whole point. If no one's taking notes, why talk so well?

The hard-boiled private eye remains a touchstone in the popular imagination, an inexhaustible archetype for film in particular. But he can no longer exercise his mastery, verbal or otherwise, with quite the impressive force wielded in the hard-boiled noir of the thirties, forties, and fifties. He comes wrapped in the gauze of nostalgia, a figure of conscious anachronism; more recent treatments emphasize and heighten the contradictions that were contained and only partially resolved by a Philip Marlowe or a Sam Spade. The theatricality of his particular brand of dapper machismo is too obvious, now, to pass without comment or to unfold without challenge. Robert Altman's 1973 film version of Chandler's *The Long Goodbye* formalizes the hard-boiled hero's inadequacy to changed historical conditions. Its hapless Marlowe (Elliot Gould) can't seem to figure out how to crack wise. In the 1970s in which Altman sets his homage to the film noir classics of Hollywood's golden age, the wisecracking verbal wit—the epigrammatic dandyism—associated with the private eye no longer seems to work. Not that Gould doesn't try. "I only see hoods by appointment," he at one point tells a roomful of unimpressed gangsters. One responds: "Is that supposed to be some kind of smart crack?" Gould, lamely: "I'm sorry, it was the only thing I could come up with." The gangsters kick Gould's ass all over the room, effectively in punishment for his failure to crack wise successfully.

Altman's revisionist noir is a clever demonstration of the generic impossibility of the hard-boiled dick in the disenchanted 1970s. His suspicion of the epigrammatic mastery exalted by his film's antecedents would obtain into the twenty-first century. The 2005 neo-noir comedy *Kiss Kiss Bang Bang* (dir. Shane Black), for instance, is an overt Chandler homage, right down to the titles of its onscreen "chapters," all of which are taken from Chandler texts ("Trouble Is My Business," "The Lady in the Lake," "The Little Sister," "The Simple Art of Murder," "The Long Goodbye"). But unlike Chandler proper, it needn't be coy about the sexuality of its private eye, "Gay" Perry (Val Kilmer), whose entirely out gayness is the subject of extended jovial remark. (Already dated, much of this humor seems tone-deaf and offensive now, though it's clearly well-intentioned.) Like Philip Marlowe before him, "Gay" Perry is aware of the potential for the commodification of the detective's shtick; unlike Marlowe, he makes a business of it, giving "detective lessons" to actors aspiring to play noirish movie roles. And, in a kind of reversal of Marlowe's eroticized combat with characters like Carol Lundgren, Perry exploits his adversaries' homophobia to defeat them. In other words, *Kiss Kiss Bang Bang* cannily demystifies the hard-boiled detective's sexuality; out of the closet, he's charming and effective and, in this film at least, not at all tormented. But he never really "cracks wise" in the old-fashioned noir manner—a conspicuous formal choice for a film so consciously rooted in the longer history of the genre. It's as if without the need for elaborate coding, without the pressure of sexual subterfuge, without the dizzying maneuvers of identification and dis-identification animating the classical hard-boiled hero, the peculiar verbal formation that is hard-boiled tough talk no longer seems like an essential part of the detective's armature. Toward the film's end, Perry roughs up a major villain, now a bedridden elderly man. "An old man who can't defend himself," the victim says. "Big tough guy." "Yeah, that's right," Perry replies, in a tone of rueful resignation. "Big, tough guy." This is the reduced afterlife of hard-boiled wisecracking, all ornament stripped away—just an uncertain assertion of toughness, an attitude so conscious of its own exhaustion that it can no longer find the words or remember the tune.

Kiss Kiss Bang Bang notwithstanding, an openly gay noir idiom needn't sacrifice the formal pressure of Chandlerian rhetoric, as William S. Burroughs will show in the next chapter. Just as Chandler had practiced his chops imitating Hemingway, so Burroughs's earliest writing imitated Chandler—an influence that would resonate across his whole career, with its pastiched hard-boiled style and its "private asshole," Burroughs's answer to the private dick. In reconstituting noir talk for his experimental fantasias, Burroughs would both absorb and subvert noir's reliance on a fetishized machismo and its opposed, threatening interiority. And while the epigram was always detachable from its context, aspiring to a kind of autonomy, Burroughs's "cut-up" writing would push this autonomy to its limit.

PART II

DECADENT DANDIES

3

WILLIAM S. BURROUGHS'S
MODERNIST GENRE DECADENCE

The only difference between symbol and symptom is that between advocacy
and analysis.
  —PHILIP RIEFF, *The Triumph of the Therapeutic*

Preliminary: Dandies and Drudges from Carlyle to Burroughs

In Thomas Carlyle's *Sartor Resartus* (1836), the satirical sartorial philosopher
Diogenes Teufelsdrockh predicts an apocalyptic future in which all of England
has been drawn off into two opposed poles: a "Dandiacal Sect," lounging around
in elaborate and expensive clothing, and a "Drudge Sect," "Poor-Slaves" who
live in "dark dwellings" and can afford no better food than potatoes and salted
herring. "To me it seems probable that these two Sects will one day part England between them," Teufelsdrockh explains. Carlyle expresses anxiety about
the extremes produced by a rapidly industrializing England by likening his
sects to two great "Electric Machines," one positively and the other negatively
charged. These opposed bodies will come to thunderous conflict:

> Hitherto you see only partial transient sparkles and sputters: but wait
> a little, till the entire nation is in an electric state: till your whole vital
> Electricity, no longer healthfully Neutral, is cut into two isolated por-
> tions of Positive and Negative (of Money and of Hunger); and stands
> there bottled up in two World-Batteries! The stirring of a child's fin-
> ger brings the two together; and then—What then? The Earth is but

shivered into impalpable smoke by that Doom's thunder-peal; the Sun misses one of his Planets in Space, and thenceforth there are no eclipses of the Moon.[1]

In *The Time Machine* (1895), H. G. Wells would give Carlyle's conflict between dandies and drudges a scientific twist. Drawing on the pseudo-Darwinian discourse of degeneration theory, Wells imagines a future in which Carlyle's bifurcated society has become biologized in the conflict between the Eloi and the Morlocks. The effete Eloi are upper-class decadent dandies gone slack, lassitude their one remaining posture. "These exquisite creatures" have a "Dresden china type of prettiness"; they adorn themselves and the Time Traveler with the "delicate and wonderful flowers countless years of culture had created."[2] The first Eloi encountered by the Time Traveler still displays—here in the year 802,701—the decadent's ancestry in the type of the romantic sufferer of tuberculosis: "His flushed face reminded me of the more beautiful kind of consumptive—that hectic beauty of which we used to hear so much." In this futuristic decadence—"The ruddy sunset set me thinking of the sunset of mankind"—apparent if not actual hermaphrodeity has become the norm: "Then, in a flash, I perceived that all had the same form of costume, the same soft hairless visage, and the same girlish rotundity of limb. . . . In costume, and in all the differences of texture and bearing that now mark off the sexes from each other, these people of the future were alike." And, just as it would for Hemingway in *Garden of Eden*, hermaphrodeity requires a garden: "There were no hedges, no signs of proprietary rights, no evidences of agriculture; the whole earth had become a garden."[3] The underground Morlocks, conversely, are a drudge sect turned feral, feeding on the Eloi, their onetime masters.

At first, the Time Traveler fails to discern the relationship between the Morlocks and the Eloi. "But gradually the real truth dawned upon me; that man had not remained one species, but had differentiated into two distinct animals."[4] The Time Traveler concludes that both the Eloi and the Morlocks are "heir to our age," a formulation emphasizing the metaphorical power of hereditary thinking:

> But at first, starting from the problems of our own age, it seemed as clear as daylight to me that the gradual widening of the present merely temporary and social difference of the capitalist and the laborer was the key to the explanation. No doubt it will seem grotesque enough to you

and wildly incredible, and yet even now there are circumstances that point in the way things have gone. . . . Even now, an East End worker lives in such artificial conditions as practically to be cut off from the natural surface of the earth and the clear sky altogether.[5]

The temporal telescoping of Wells's urban present into the distant future, achieved most succinctly in the deployment of the perfect tense ("circumstances that point in the way things have gone"), positions these creatures as both biological heirs of nineteenth-century humanity and, in Wells's monitory sci-fi allegory, the symbolic climax of the income inequalities attendant on industrialization. Class has become species. The Time Traveler, having absorbed both Wells's socialism and his admiration for Carlyle, attempts to console himself for the grisly fate of the Eloi by "regarding it as a rigorous punishment of human selfishness. . . . I tried even a Carlyle-like scorn of these wretched aristocrats in decline."[6]

William S. Burroughs had been thinking about *The Time Machine* since at least 1953 when, in a letter to Ginsberg, he discussed his career-long fascination with time travel: "H. G. Wells in *The Time Machine* speaks of undescribable vertigo of space time travel. He is much underrated."[7] Thirty years later, Burroughs would incorporate aspects of *The Time Machine* in *Cities of the Red Night* (1981), the first volume of his second trilogy, which also includes *The Place of Dead Roads* (1983) and *The Western Lands* (1987). At one point in *Cities* a young boy named Toby is reading *The Time Machine;* a passage of Wells's prose describing the construction of the machine is excerpted at length.[8] And a key episode in that novel replays the species war between the Morlocks and the Eloi: "The inhabitants [of the cities of the red night] were divided into an elite minority known as the Transmigrants and a majority known as the Receptacles."[9] In this radically bifurcated, metempsychotic society, Transmigrants exploit Receptacles as vessels they can inhabit when their own bodies weaken. Because Transmigrants have access to an endless series of Receptacles, they can jump from body to body indefinitely. Just as the decadent Eloi subjugated the animalistic Morlocks, so have "the Transmigrants reduced the Receptacle class to a condition of virtual idiocy." Like good dandies, the Transmigrants develop a cult of youth, committing suicide "at the age of eighteen to spare themselves the coarsening experience of middle age and the deterioration of senescence," only to be reborn again, still young, via a subjugated Receptacle. In something of an ironic understatement, the narrator observes that "[t]here was a basic conflict of interest" between the two groups, and rumors of Receptacle rebellion.[10]

From Carlyle to Burroughs, these apocalyptic scenarios of biologized class antagonism are remarkably consistent. Carlyle's "Electric Machine" conceit—an imaginative spasm both partaking of and reacting against the transformative energies of the Industrial Revolution—might be thought of as an instance of dystopian science fiction *avant la lettre*. It is no coincidence that anxieties about world-ending class warfare should take such a form. At the very heart of the impulse toward such speculative fantasizing lie the twinned figures of the dandy and his abject opponent, the drudge, the weird, unprecedented creatures generated by a terrifyingly unfamiliar and rapidly unfolding modernity.

I begin with the conjunction of speculative fiction and the dandy to show that Burroughs, more than any other heir to modernism, recognized that formal experimentation was grounded in the convergence of two strands of the fin de siècle imagination not obviously interconnected: dandyism and Darwinian science fiction. Critics such as Peter Nicholls and Andrew Goldstone have observed the centrality of the dandy to modernism's imagination of formal autonomy, while Helen Sword and Leon Surette have reconstructed modernism's reliance on occult technologies such as the Ouija board. Burroughs's oeuvre, with its decadent dandies, its "cut-up" techniques for semirandomized textual production, and its elaborate Darwinian mythologies, represents the most radical extension in postwar American letters of modernism's weirder tendencies. For Burroughs, formal techniques like the cut-up find their thematic corollary in his novels' fictional world, obsessed as it is with such Wellsian scenarios as time travel and surgical experimentation. Burroughs's dandiacal self-fashioning is the indispensable ground for his literary experiments, partially because the dandy's "voice" is one of the earliest Burroughs knew how to sample, but more importantly because the dandy, as the personality corresponding most readily to an aesthetic practice understood as "autonomous," would constitute for Burroughs the reigning model of the artist.

Accordingly, the first part of this chapter will examine the role of the "dandy" in Burroughs's fiction—particularly insofar as Burroughs uses him to harness aestheticism and decadence, tendencies associated with the fin de siècle and with major stakes for modernism proper—alongside his plundering of such "genre" forms as science fiction. In the second part, I will discuss Burroughs's cut-up technique alongside H. G. Wells's *The Island of Dr. Moreau* and the Dadaism of Tristan Tzara in order to explicate Burroughs's reformation of modernist formal precedent in the crucible of science fiction. By showing us how modernist formal experimentation depends on converting into formal terms the thematic preoccupations of fin de siècle science fiction, Burroughs can help make modernism itself seem strange again.

William Burroughs's (In)continent Dandies

Burroughs was one of the great dandiacal literary celebrities of the twentieth century. His influence on the group of considerably younger men who became the Beats hinged on his anachronistic identification with an aristocratic composure fascinating precisely for its inconsistency with the grimy marginality glorified by students like Ginsberg and Kerouac. Ginsberg would later recall "the strange Burroughs that Kerouac and I knew, the gentle melancholy blue boy, the proud elegant sissy, the old charmer, the intelligent dear."[11] As Elisa Glick points out in her discussion of Burroughs's "gutter dandyism," Ginsberg's characterization of his friend "creates an image of Burroughs as an effete, costumed dandy whose hyperrefinement is the very antithesis of his image as a cool and cantankerous tough guy."[12]

But the "tough guy" and the "dandy" were never really antitheses at all—they were instead entwined complementarities, and Burroughs understood their shared logic better than any writer before him. Burroughs's extraordinarily risky drug abuse represents the terminus of a trajectory of decadent consumption encompassing Des Esseintes's experiments with his "mouth organ" or Dorian Gray's drift into the opium dens. Burroughs was a late explorer of pathological interiority, and his insistence that language is a virus literalized familiar metaphors of psychical illness. Burroughs's fiction oscillates between the two constitutive poles of late dandyism: Oscar Wilde's cool surfaces and the baroque interiority of the fin de siècle sufferer.

Further, Burroughs's iconic role in the beat movement might be understood as part of the legacy of a dandiacal-decadent counterculture, particularly if we read the Beats as the postwar American resurgence of the fin de siècle "demimonde." Emily Apter describes the long afterlife of the "eminently recyclable" codes of 1890s decadence that constitute the "demimonde as a subcultural style" signifying through modernism and beyond.[13] For Apter, "decadence" continues to signify within subcultural sites that might be broadly described as queer, and which certainly resonate with the underworlds associated both with Burroughs's biography and with his fiction. If, historically, "decadence" is legible as a cluster of period features contemporary with and subtending modernism, Apter suggests that this apparently quaint set of codes continues to reverberate in more recent countercultures.[14] Apter's description of the "half-worlds" symptomatic of "demimonde decadence" sounds acutely Burroughsian: "the shadowy visuality of nightworlds in extramural locations; the pathos of codependency (including the 'queerly' familiar spaces of sexuality-by-half: bisexed, third-sexed, cross, and transgendered); half-steps on the ladder of social hierarchy (blurred distinctions of race, ethnicity, and class); and the poetics of psychosexual splitting."[15] Burroughs's own preoccupations with "splitting"—in, for instance, his likening the page to the two halves of the human body—resonate powerfully with this characterization of decadence. Not for nothing, as I'll discuss below, does the year "1890" recur with totemic prevalence across Burroughs's oeuvre.

Like the beat undergrounds of New York, Burroughs's Tangier, with its cast of Americans and Europeans on the run from Cold War conformity, constitutes just such a decadent demimonde. *Naked Lunch*'s Interzone (so called after Tangier's status as an "international zone") emblematizes the shift from nineteenth-century decadence to postwar genre decadence, terrain exuberantly explored by all of Burroughs's fiction. I mean "genre" in the sense of "genre fiction," those traditions of popular fiction (the detective story, science fiction, the western) that might broadly be considered as opposed to or dialectically engaged with the development of the modernist art-novel out of realism. By "genre decadence," I want to suggest two related narratives: first, the process by which both decadence and degeneration theory not infrequently served as the thematic motor of important early instances of genre fiction, from *The Time Machine* to *Dracula* to the Sherlock Holmes stories; and, second, the way Burroughs's own turn to genre fiction involves decadent period borrowings that occasion a distinctly Burroughsian disintegration and re-scripting of genre codes. Murray G. H. Pittock has observed that fin de siècle decadence's most durable legacy obtains in the long afterlife of the "fantastic tale" in twentieth-century genre fiction.[16] As in decadence proper, the dandy is at the center of genre decadence, albeit a dandy who, in keeping with the fantastic Darwinism of so much science fiction, has undergone some startling mutations.

About two-thirds of the way through Burroughs's 1983 novel *The Place of Dead Roads*, the Regency-era dandy Beau Brummell himself makes an appearance. Kim Carsons, the novel's young, queer, gun-slinging hero, is thinking with displeasure about "the risk of being trapped by old age in a soiled idiot body like Somerset Maugham's." From the subject of Maugham's decay the narrator pivots to a consideration of Brummell, whose deterioration is figured as the archetypal instance of unfortunate aging:

> Like Beau Brummell, [Maugham's] rigid mask was cracking to reveal a horrible nothingness beneath.
>
> "Brummell would rush upon his plate and gulp down a roast in such a revolting manner that the other guests complained they were nauseated and Brummell had to be fed in his room . . ."
>
> And here is the mask in place. When Beau Brummell was exiled to Calais by his debts and Princely displeasure, a local lady sent him an invitation to dinner and he sent back the message:
>
> "I am not accustomed to *feed* at that hour."
>
> Toward the end of the month when his allowance ran out, Brummell would rush into a sweet shop and cram into his mouth everything he could reach [. . .]
>
> A friend who took care of Brummell in his last years wrote, "His condition is indescribable. No matter what I do it is impossible to keep him *clean*."[17]

Brummell, the first dandy, was an icon of self-control and rigorously disciplined self-presentation, and the tragic irony of his geriatric decline depends on the faltering, the failure, of this self, what Burroughs calls the "rigid mask . . . cracking to reveal a horrible nothingness beneath." Burroughs's conception of this mask—and what it conceals—partakes heavily of the fin de siècle's decadent dandy, particularly as (dis)embodied in Dorian Gray. As the division of Dorian between his youthful body and his ghastly portrait suggests, the decadent dandy is a split creature. The "nothingness" beneath the mask is not a blank; it is the excessive efflorescence of decay—like the hideousness of Dorian's portrait— a hideousness sometimes associated by Burroughs as by Wilde with the symptoms of aging. The decay of aging had occupied Burroughs as early as *Junky* (1953), the final paragraph of which provides a melancholy appreciation of the "kick" (drug-induced or otherwise) that understands it as a defense against aging: "Kick is momentary freedom from the claims of the aging, cautious, nagging, frightened flesh."[18]

At the center of his work is a paradox Burroughs recognized from the start. Drug taking doesn't only accelerate the deterioration against which it's meant as buffer, it grants putative refuge from the claims of the flesh by raising appetite to the level of transcendence. To cathect consumption as the drug user must is always to soil oneself. Beau Brumell's grotesque pursuit of candy produces his terminal filthiness as surely as, in *Junky*, William Lee's near-suicidal drinking produces the "incipient uremia" that makes his entire body smell like urine: "Bill, it's you smells like piss!"[19] From the beginning, Burroughs's fiction was obsessed by the specter of decay, and by the acts of consumption, notoriously chemical, which might allay the burdens of embodiment. The appearance of an elderly Maugham/Brummell encapsulates a pattern of tension found throughout Burroughs's work, a pattern organized around such binarisms as surface and interiority, youth and age, smoothness and decay, and control and incontinence. All of these pairs inform dandiacal decadence as a master category concerned with the way surfaces both protect against and betray a pathological interiority.

Burroughs's ornate grotesqueries depend on the eruption of interior rottenness, an eruption always becoming general, exploding infinitely. The terms of the problem are earliest articulated in *Junky*:

> I got drunk on the fifty pesos. About nine that night, I ran out of money and went back to my apartment. I lay down and tried to sleep. When I closed my eyes I saw an Oriental face, the lips and nose eaten away by disease. The disease spread, melting the face into an amoeboid mass in which the eyes floated, dull crustacean eyes. Slowly, a new face formed around the eyes. A series of faces, hieroglyphs, distorted and leading to their final place where the human road ends, where the human form can no longer contain the crustacean horror that has grown inside it.[20]

The gothic horror of a De Quincey opium reverie lies behind this passage, and, just as De Quincey's hallucinations threaten to overwhelm the real world in the *Confessions*, Burroughs's own figures—hieroglyphs, amoebas, crustacean forms—will take on a life of their own as Burroughs moves from the realist reportage of *Junky* to the symbolist fantasias of *Naked Lunch* onward. The "crustacean horror that has grown inside" is Burroughs's earliest formulation of the horror against which the masks of human sociality are constructed in defense.

Burroughs presents the discovery of Oscar Wilde as one pivotal event in his development as a writer, and his interest in the hard-boiled detective story as another. Burroughsian genre decadence is the result of a particular network of influences, a mixed genealogy to which Burroughs himself often referred.

In *The Adding Machine,* he presents a narrative of writerly development that moves from dandiacal identification to Wildean imitation to the fateful discovery of the hard-boiled. "As a young child I wanted to be a writer because writers were rich and famous. They lounged around Singapore and Rangoon smoking opium in a yellow pongee silk suit. . . . languidly caressing a pet gazelle."[21] From this childhood fantasy of the writer as Orientalist adventurer Burroughs would go on, as a teenager, to write short westerns, an interest to which he would return much later, in the second trilogy. His western juvenilia was interrupted by his reading of Oscar Wilde, which would inspire such characters as "Reggie" and "Lord Cheshire," "a mawkishly sentimental Lord Henry." Burroughs then describes a long period of writer's block occasioned by rereading his diary, which dwelt upon a childhood crush. "The act of writing had become embarrassing, disgusting, and above all *false.* It was not the sex in the diary that embarrassed me, it was the terrible falsity of the emotions expressed. I guess Lord Cheshire and Reggie were too much for me."[22] Burroughs breaks his yearlong aversion to writing by working on a collaborative story "in the Dashiell Hammett/Raymond Chandler line." He attributes overcoming his block—what he calls "the curse of the diary"—to "the act of collaboration."[23] But, as the hard-boiled style of *Junky* attests, the adoption of the "Dashiell Hammett/Raymond Chandler line" was just as important.

The Hammett/Chandler line is depicted as a way out of the dead end of Wildean imitation and, simultaneously, out of the emotionally false homosexual confessionalism of his diary. But in the preface to *Junky,* Burroughs's dandiacal reading, homosexuality, and attraction to the underworld form part of the same logical series. Unlike Raymond Chandler, Burroughs had no need to erect the hard-boiled in opposition to a dandyism queered since the Wilde trials—he could, on the contrary, assert the obvious queerness of the tough-guy pose and of tough-guy prose. Burroughs was especially attracted by the outsider status conferred by homosexuality and the hard-boiled alike. Burroughs recalls that after his discharge from the army ("This man is never to be recalled or reclassified"), "I worked as a private detective, an exterminator, a bartender . . . I played around the edges of crime."[24]

Burroughs will repeatedly deploy the tough postures drawn from genre fiction in antihomophobic set pieces across his work, a strategy whose ambiguous origins can be found in *Junky,* in which a tough queer style is effeminophobically juxtaposed with an effete one. Despite William Lee's unabashed homosexuality (which was largely redacted by Ace Books upon first release, but restored in later editions), *Junky* presents caricatural "fags" with as much vigorous phobia as anything in Chandler:

> In the French Quarter there are several queer bars so full every night the fags spill out on to the sidewalk. A room full of fags gives me the horrors. They jerk around like puppets on invisible strings, galvanized into hideous activity that is the negation of everything living and spontaneous. The live human being has moved out of these bodies long ago. But something moved in when the original tenant moved out. Fags are ventriloquists' dummies who have moved in and taken over the ventriloquist. The dummy sits in a queer bar nursing his beer, and uncontrollably yapping out of a rigid doll face.[25]

What to make of the bravura toxicity of this passage? In Elisa Glick's account of Burroughs's "gutter dandyism," Burroughs's "hard-boiled style aims to purge the queer junky from dandyism, aestheticism, and the taint of femininity." These hard-boiled tactics borrow more than just style from Raymond Chandler: they also borrow his homophobia. According to this account, the abject "fag" bears the brunt of Burroughs's macho "refusal of the feminine and effeminacy," a refusal that "does not result in a productive tension, but halts and stalls."[26] Burroughs explicitly articulates his investment in a dichotomy between the approved, macho "queer" and the denigrated, effeminate "fag" in a letter to Ginsberg regarding Ace Books' initial intention to title Burroughs's second novel *Fag* (Burroughs preferred *Queer*, under which title the book finally appeared, in 1985):

> Now look you tell Solomon I don't mind being called a queer. T. E. Lawrence and all manner of right Joes (boy can I turn a phrase) was queer. But I'll see him castrated before I'll be called a Fag. That's just what I been trying to put down uh I mean *over*, is the distinction between us strong, manly, noble types and the leaping, jumping, window dressing, cock-sucker. Furthechrissakes a girl's gotta draw the line somewhere or publishers will swarm all over her sticking their nasty old biographical prefaces up her ass.[27]

According to Glick, Burroughs here "attempts to elevate and masculinize the queer by invoking cold war culture's cruel cliché of the fag as horrifyingly effeminate, perverse, and sexually unrestrained." The "campy bit of gender inversion" with which Burroughs concludes this letter reflects his "ambivalent relationship to femininity . . . revealed in the contradictions of the queer junky, whose gutter dandyism bears more than a passing resemblance to the figure of the nineteenth-century European dandy."[28]

While I find Glick's account broadly convincing, I think it a mistake to read Burroughs's abjection of the "fag" as a thoroughly sincere bit of vitriol. To do so requires that one accept at face value Burroughs's celebration of the "strong, manly, noble types" with whom he purports to identify. But the Burroughsian butch, in the above letter to Ginsberg as in the novels, is always ironized, dependent on the sampled and ventriloquized machismo of "right Joes." Burroughs's self-mocking parenthetical—"boy can I turn a phrase"—acknowledges that this particular masculine construction draws on widely available clichés. It is no less "campy" than the gender inversion with which the letter concludes.[29]

Lee's discussion of his homosexuality in one of *Queer*'s many "routines" rings all the changes in Burroughs's arsenal of parodic rhetoric. Lee's elaborate "routines" are extended comic monologues presented for the benefit of one Allerton, whom he wants to seduce:

> A curse. Been in our family for generations. The Lees have always been perverts. I shall never forget the unspeakable horror that froze the lymph in my glands—the lymph glands that is, of course—when the baneful word seared my reeling brain: **I was a homosexual.** I thought of the painted, simpering female impersonators I had seen in a Baltimore nightclub. Could it be possible that I was one of those sub-human things? . . . It was a wise old queen—Bobo, we called her—who taught me that I had a duty to live and to bear my burden proudly for all to see, to conquer prejudice and ignorance and hate with knowledge and sincerity and love. Whenever you are threatened by a hostile presence, you emit a thick cloud of love like an octopus squirts out ink . . .[30]

Lee presents the typographically boldfaced fact of his homosexuality surrounded by a barely controlled burlesque always threatening to collapse into unconstrained mania. Beginning with the gothic (and degenerationist) language of the "curse," Burroughs moves from one parodied discursive model to another.[31] The "unspeakable horror" of the gothic secret gives way to the recollection of Bobo's crucial tutelage, her lessons of self-acceptance and "sincerity and love" toward others. Does the figure of the "wise old queen" mitigate Lee's distaste—presumably exemplary of the misogyny with which even his fondest readers have charged him—for the "painted, simpering female impersonators" of the Baltimore nightclub? And does the preposterous but oddly affecting comparison to the ink-squirting octopus increase or cancel the sincerity with which Bobo's lessons are remembered by Lee? Perhaps most importantly, how are we to take Bobo's lesson of nonviolence? Burroughs's parodic and satiric tonalities are so thoroughgoing and comprehensive that it is usually impossible, in my view, to see around them or to recognize an approved norm whose nonfulfillment they are meant to highlight. In the above passage, a certain kind of nonviolent activism is being either proposed or found wanting, perhaps both at once.

But images of love-dispensing octopi are not typical of Burroughs's emblems of gay liberation. Violence, not love, is the more frequent focus. An aging Burroughs's drunken rambling as captured in Howard Brookner's 1985 documentary *Burroughs* is representative: "We'll have an organization with false passports, weapons on arrival. . . . If anybody says anything against gays, we'll find 'em, track 'em down, and kill 'em."[32] In his second trilogy, Burroughs filters this frankly revolutionary program through sustained engagements with popular genre forms, most pointedly crime fiction and the western. The result is a weirdly destabilized novelistic landscape, complete with campily cartoonish explosions of violence whose viciousness nevertheless lingers like a strange odor.[33] Burroughs's butch personae are comedic fantasies of macho reaction, reveling in representations of vengeance without really believing in them. *Junky*'s preface provides an early, very dry example of this pattern: "I was timid with the other children and afraid of physical violence. One aggressive little Lesbian would pull my hair whenever she saw me. I would like to shove her face in right now, but she fell off a horse and broke her neck years ago."[34] This sardonic piece of disproportionate cruelty, chilling, pathetic, and amusing all at once, gives us the core structure of vengeance in Burroughs's novels, stripped of the hallucinatory and cartoonish trappings that will attach to it as Burroughs moves away from realism.

By *The Place of Dead Roads*, the bullied, Oscar Wilde–reading child of *Junky* will have been transformed into the cowboy Kim Carsons. Kim begins not as a gunslinger but as a radically exaggerated version of the autobiographical William Lee of *Junky*'s preface. He is a figure of Yellow Nineties grotesquerie with undertones of Dorian Gray's "strange joys and stranger sins" and Des Esseintes's practiced perversities:

Kim is a slimy, morbid youth of unwholesome proclivities with an in-
satiable appetite for the extreme and the sensational. His mother had
been into table-tapping and Kim adores ectoplasm, crystal balls, spirit
guides and auras. He wallows in abominations, unspeakable rites, diseased demon lovers, loathsome secrets imparted in a thick slimy whis-
per, ancient ruined cities under a purple sky, the smell of unknown
excrements, the musky sweet rotten reek of the terrible Red Fever,
erogenous sores suppurating in the idiot giggling flesh. In short, Kim
is everything a normal American boy is taught to *detest*.[35]

Kim is a parodically distended decadent dandy, characterized by all the hallmarks of the type—outsider status, aestheticized pathology, heretically appropriated Catholic imagery. Not just the content of the passage but its very
syntax and rhythm—the list of "abominations" unfurling in increasingly swol-
len clauses set off by commas, each clause a bit more drawn out and a bit
more disgusting—recognizably mimics the standard idiom for decadent excess in the canonical novels of decadence. Those suppurating sores perform
a hallmark mission of decadent literature itself: they break down the opposition between surface and interior. "There were a number of medical books,
which Kim read avidly. He loved to read about disease, rolling and savoring
the names on his tongue . . . the poisonous pinks and greens and yellows and
purples of skin diseases, rather like the objects in those Catholic stores that sell
shrines and Madonnas and crucifixes and religious pictures. There was one
skin disease where the skin swells into a red wheal and you can *write* on it."[36]
The fin de siècle topos of the forbidden book—most familiar from *Dorian Gray*,
in which a French novel usually presumed to be *À Rebours* exerts a mysterious
corrupting influence on Dorian—has been startlingly literalized, as the act of
writing converges with infectious pus. Interest in the forbidden book is extended when Clem Snide, *Cities of the Red Night*'s private detective, or "private
asshole,"[37] must track down a set of rare volumes containing the history of a
radioactive virus, books which operate on a principle of contagious synesthe-
sia, "a mutating virus, a *color* virus, as if the colors themselves were possessed
of a purposeful and sinister life . . . the purples, reds, and pinks of diseased
skin—rising from the books palpable as a haze, a poisonous miasma of color."[38]
These books are a magical version of Burroughs's own oeuvre, an ideally defil-
ing viral text whose redundancies, obsessive repetitions, endlessly elaborated

sexual fantasies, ritually developed scenes of violence, are all part of the infectious, subversive, contaminating possibility of the book not just as forbidden but as weaponized. Kim Carson's "first experiment with biologic warfare," for instance, involves sending "free illustrated Bibles impregnated with smallpox virus" to a group of antivaccinationist Christian cultists.[39] Dorian Gray's "poisonous book" takes on new meaning.

Kim starts out a "slimy, morbid youth" writing his disease against the regime of normal American boyhood—this is Burroughs's version of Beat oppositionality, more French *poète maudit* than Kerouacian *picaro*. But there's a twist. He might begin like some satirically nightmarish footnote to Max Nordau's *Degeneration*, but Kim quickly walks into another genre altogether. He becomes a gun-slinging cowboy. How else to respond to the ostracizing pressures of being "everything a normal American boy is taught to *detest*"? "Kim decides to go west and become a shootist. If anyone doesn't like the way Kim looks and acts and smells, he can fill his grubby peasant paw." As this threatening line suggests, the conversion from decadent to cowboy involves demonstrations of a surprising adeptness at killing. Strobe, in *Cities of the Red Night*, impresses his fellow sailors by handily dispatching a group of pirates: "They had . . . conceived contempt for Strobe as an effeminate dandy. After he had killed five of the ringleaders they were forced to revise this opinion." Kim, likewise, responds to a couple of homophobes in a saloon ("Now I don't like drinkin' in the same room with a fairy") by shooting both. "As Kim looks down at the two bodies crumpled there, spilling blood and brains on the floor, he feels good—safer."[40] *Junky*'s fag/queer dichotomy, with its effeminophobic abjection of the "fag," has been left behind in favor of figures like Kim and Strobe, who might read to adversaries as effeminate dandies or fairies but who nevertheless have recourse to the toughness of *Junky*'s valorized "queers."[41]

The fag/queer dichotomy reworks the dandiacal dialectic between surfaces and pathologized depths, and depends therefore above all on how the Burroughsian "gutter dandy" inherits discourses drawn from the decadent aestheticism of the 1890s. The phrase "the 1890s" appears across Burroughs's fiction as shorthand for the whole problem of decadent interiority and the aestheticist surfaces with which the decadent dandy makes an atmosphere for himself.[42] "1890" is above all an atmosphere word, and what it captures is the back-and-forth between the polished surfaces of the boudoir and the pathologized interiority of the decadent sitting in it. Burroughs's cartoonish cowboy, his Kim Carsons riding off into the sunset, has vanquished that interiority, which plagued his youth but which, by adulthood, has been overcome via the fantasy-pastiche of the western adventure story. Kim is a dandy beyond decadence, supremely continent, all surface—and, unlike the cowboys of adventure fiction and Hollywood film whom he inherits and parodies, still gay. Kim's fixation on an aging Brummell demonstrates the risk to be avoided: the appetites indicated by dandiacal consumption result in a disgusting old codger—"it is impossible to keep him *clean.*"

Burroughs was famously a master of the nauseatingly evocative, but the incontinent eruptions of body fluids in the second trilogy only occasionally achieve the power to disgust. Rather, as above, the "blood and brains" often seem somewhat lackadaisically dispensed with. This has everything to do with genre, with the conversion of Kim from adolescent degenerate at the constant mercy of his nastily excessive insides to the cool, continent cowboy of the weird, pop-parodic Burroughsian western. I want "pop" to indicate not just Burroughs's debt to the popular fiction of his youth but also the Warholian *flatness* of Burroughs's play with genre, the way genre fiction is used to produce fascinating but impenetrable surfaces, screens across which Burroughs moves his hauntingly pathos-laden cartoons. Steven Shaviro, in a discussion of *Cities,* refers to the late fiction's "lack of a consistent self-identity" which generates "no inside, no interiority."[43] I am reminded of Benjamin Buchloch's discussion of Warhol's "one-dimensional art," a formulation that takes over from Warhol's own insistence that "there's nothing behind" the surfaces of his work.[44] Much of the haunting fascination of Burroughs's late work stems from the impenetrability of his generic pastiche, the melancholy cancellation of all of the "insides" associated with the conventional, that is to say psychological, novel.[45]

But insides return, not as psychology but as the decadent putrefaction I have been tracking throughout. In *The Place of Dead Roads,* the dialectic between insides and outsides is explicitly played out in Kim's exchange of his "old plague cloak" with its "sweet diarrhea smells from cholera wards" for what he calls an "M-5 suit." The plague cloak—an external garment that perversely advertises its wearer's insides—will no longer do. "Something inconspicuous, sir?" the salesman asks Kim. Kim replies, "Exactly. The well-dressed man is the one whose clothes you never notice. . . . That's what you English say, isn't it?"[46] The source of the maxim is Beau Brummell, who supposedly advised the budding dandy thus: "If people turn to look at you in the street, you are not well dressed." Accessorizing Kim's suit? A "blade, fashioned by a Japanese craftsman" and "tempered in [the] human blood [of] an insolent peasant who called my ancestor a Dishdigger . . . that's medieval slang for 'queer'. . . . Intolerable, was it not?"[47] Burroughs brings to the surface the violence implicit in dandiacal self-assertion. This armed Brummell kills homophobes.

The Cut-Up and the Larynx: Wells, Tzara, Burroughs

In Burroughs, the dialectic between surface-oriented dandyism and a decadent focus on pathologized interiors gets expressed most clearly in an obsession with cleanliness, a preoccupation that is the compulsive obverse of the deliberate obscenity of much of his work. The obscene, decadent half of this dialectic is, in Burroughs, explicitly Darwinian—this is his most obvious borrowing from Victorian science fiction. Most famously, there is the "talking asshole" routine in *Naked Lunch,* in which a carnival performer "who taught his asshole to talk" ends up being taken over, literally engulfed, by that newly articulate organ. With the asshole's "teeth-like little raspy incurving hooks" and "jelly like a tadpole's tail," Burroughs offers a hyperbolic literalization of an imaginative metaphysic predicated on Darwinesque imagery of organic change over time.[48] The passage is a riff on a familiar science-fictional set piece in which an amoral mad scientist plays, God-like, with the fundamental codes of organic life. (*Frankenstein* is of course the Romantic urtext of this genre, but its modern form depends on the transformations wrought by the influence of Darwin on the late Victorian imagination.)[49] As Benway, the story's narrator, puts it: "We're scientists . . . Pure scientists. Disinterested research and damned be him who cries, 'Hold, *too much!*'"[50] For Burroughs, *The Island of Dr. Moreau* (1896) is the most proximate model for the treatment of this convention and the host of questions it summons up: How might evolutionary theory provide a tool for shaping man anew? Can the line between man and animal be crossed in either direction? Where does speech come from? Finally, how should psychic interiority be understood after the ascendance of materialistic explanations for human psychology? Burroughs's cut-up technique, itself a demented sort of surgery, provided the means for testing all of these questions, a textual laboratory where his most outlandish thematic and his most radical formal concerns meet. If, as the "talking asshole" routine suggests, articulacy and filth are inextricable, cleanliness will finally require a total escape from words.

In a 1966 interview, Burroughs expatiates on a favorite topic: literature without or after the word, narrative proceeding in the space left after one follows his injunction to "rub out the words." "Try this," he recommends:

"Carefully memorize the meaning of a passage, then read it; you'll find you can actually read it without the words' making any sound whatever in the mind's ear. . . . When you start thinking in images, without words, you're well on the way."[51] Burroughs's desire to think in images rhymed with his fascination with Egyptian hieroglyphics, the pictorial representativeness of which reminds him that, as he puts it in *The Book of Breeething*, "a written word *is an image* and that written words are images in sequence that is to say *moving pictures*," truths suppressed by alphabetic scripts. In *The Book of Breeething*, Burroughs even produced his own hieroglyphic system, which he hoped "would constitute a workable international means of communication" because of the hieroglyph's cross-cultural legibility as "a picture of what it represents." A glyph of an owl followed by a glyph of an ejaculating phallus, for instance, would mean "in the presence of."[52] (Why this should mean "in the presence of" rather than "masturbating on an owl" is unclear, at least to me.)

We might think of Burroughs's fascination with nonalphabetic scripts and the poetic possibilities they represent as a late-modernist extension of Ezra Pound's interest in Chinese ideography. Burroughs's own interest in Chinese typifies his blending of modernist approaches to language with his brand of science fiction: "A far-reaching biologic weapon can be forged from a new language. In fact such a language already exists. It exists as Chinese, a total [*sic*, tonal?] language closer to the multi-level structure of experience, with a script derived from hieroglyphs, more closely related to the objects and areas described."[53] Even Burroughs's cinema-inspired designation of written words as "*moving pictures*" seems derived from Pound and Fenollosa's conviction that Chinese preserves adjectives and nouns' roots in the verb more actively than do Indo-European languages. And Burroughs's distrust of the copula is clearly continuous with Pound and Fenollosa's directive regarding the Chinese "substratum of verbal meaning," which, they write, "We should try to render . . . in translation, not be content with some bloodless adjectival abstraction plus 'is.'"[54] Or, as Burroughs puts it, "The is of identity is rarely used in Egyptian pictorial writing. Instead of saying he is my servant they say he (is omitted) *as* my servant: a statement of relationship not identity."[55]

But overemphasizing these modernist continuities risks domesticating Burroughs's project. True, Burroughs sounds like an *imagiste* when he endorses a poetics that will return to the poet a kind of primal clarity, so that he can see like a "farmer [who] really sees his cows, he really sees what's in front of him quite clearly," but even Pound's grandiose sense of his poetic's political potential does not anticipate Burroughs's insistence that studying hieroglyphs can "break down" the "automatic reactions to words themselves that enable those who manipulate words to control thought on a mass scale."[56] This is why language can be a "biologic weapon." Modernist interest in ideography is finally epistemological; a language rooted in active verbs and written in hieroglyphically originated ideograms can, the thinking goes, more accurately describe the phenomenal world. Pound's politicization of this epistemology insists that a right relation between language and the world it describes will ensure a properly run polis.[57] Burroughs biologizes this epistemology, which is to say he ontologizes it: "In the beginning was the Word [. . .] and the word was flesh . . . human flesh . . ."[58]

Burroughs believed formal experimentation of the sort he shared with modernist precursors like Pound might facilitate the flight from the prisons of word and body. His cut-up writing—by which he produced new material through cutting up and recombining his own and others' texts—produces heightened media awareness, and it is no coincidence that such a technique would find appropriate content in the fantastic speculations of science fiction. As John Guillory has pointed out, the emergence of a "media concept" is a ripe site for "science-fictional resonance."[59] In Burroughs's case, such resonance will depend on his literalization of the organic metaphors behind the cut-up and its modernist ancestors, a literalization that, at the level of literary genre, will demand a return to Wellsian sci-fi, which has more to do with the figures of the decadent and the dandy than one might first assume. The *Island of Dr. Moreau* was, according to Wells's preface to the 1924 edition, prompted in part by "a scandalous trial about that time, the graceless and pitiful downfall of a man of genius."[60] As Wells scholar Simon J. James notes, this "man of genius" is "usually presumed to be Oscar Wilde."[61]

It's far from obvious why Wells's nightmarish Darwinian fable should have been inspired by Wilde's trials, though James suggests a reading of the "Victor Hugo-quoting" Dr. Moreau himself as an "irresponsible aesthete . . . who describes the human vivisection that was the Spanish inquisition as 'aesthetic torture.'"[62] This seems right, though "vivisection" as a figure for decadent self-investigation seems equally important. As *Dorian Gray* puts it of Henry Wotton, the supreme dandy, "[He] had always been enthralled by the methods of natural science, but the ordinary subject-matter of that science had seemed to him trivial and of no import. And so he had begun by vivisecting himself, and he had ended by vivisecting others."[63] Wells recasts the auto-vivisection

preoccupying *Dorian Gray* and the decadent novel more generally by returning it to its origins in physical medicine. The novel's narrator, Prendick, finds
himself trapped on a remote island overseen by Dr. Moreau—notorious to
Prendick from remembered newspaper reports detailing his experiments in
vivisection—and peopled by extraordinary, bestial humans. A locked room
in Moreau's compound, from which animal cries can be heard to issue, piques
Prendick's fascinated horror: "What could it all mean? A locked enclosure on a
lonely island, a notorious vivisector, and these crippled and distorted men?"[64]
In the key of gothic adventure fiction, Wells recombines the basic elements of
The Picture of Dorian Gray: a notorious vivisector, a locked enclosure, the hid-
eous physical transformations wrought by inappropriate investigations. The
magical transformation of Dorian's portrait collapses the figurative into the literal in the manner of a fairy tale, but Wells's treatment of forbidden knowledge
and Faustian bargains proceeds according to the generic rules he played such
a major role in inventing: the science-fiction allegory.

In *Dr. Moreau*, medical experimentation is introduced in terms deliberately
reminiscent of the aura of dandiacal ennui and the aestheticist delectation
meant to ward it off. Having been saved from shipwreck by Dr. Moreau's assistant, Montgomery, Prendick thanks his rescuer. Montgomery responds, "I
injected and fed you much as I might have collected a specimen. I was bored,
and wanted something to do. If I'd been jaded that day, or hadn't liked your
face, well—it's a curious question where you would have been now!"[65] Montgomery's construal of his actions as amoral specimen collection collapses the
physician into the dandy. And unlike the properly professional physician,
Moreau's experiments are not oriented toward any discernible goals: they are,
like Des Esseintes's sensory devices and the art for art's sake which they em-
blematize, an end in themselves. "Had Moreau any intelligible object," Prendick says, "I could have sympathised at least a little with him. I am not so
squeamish about pain as that. I could have forgiven him a little even, had his
motive been only hate. But he was so irresponsible, so utterly careless!
His curiosity, his mad, aimless investigations, drove him on."[66]

Initially Prendick mistakes Dr. Moreau's scientific practice; he assumes
that the bestial people of the island are the broken results of vivisected human
beings, rather than recognizing them as animals who have been transformed
into something human. "Could it be possible, I thought, that such a thing as
the vivisection of men was carried on here?" Resolved to escape this grisly
fate himself, Prendick runs away from Moreau's compound and plans to drown

himself. But he reverses course at the last minute, and in the process shifts the valence of a quite literal vivisection back to the figurative auto-vivisection absorbed from Wilde: "I had half a mind to drown myself then; but an odd wish to see the whole adventure out, a queer, impersonal, spectacular interest in myself, restrained me."[67] Prendick, faced with actual vivisection—a fate worse than death—finds refuge in the generic precursor to his story: he converts the scalpel and the bone saw to the subtler tools of psychological self-investigation.

Once Prendick discovers what Moreau's actually up to—not vivisecting men into beasts but vice versa—he judges the work immoral but nevertheless credits him with having discovered nothing less than the foundational boundary between man and animal. "[T]he great difference," Moreau explains, "between man and monkey is in the larynx . . . in the incapacity to frame delicately different sound-symbols by which thought could be sustained."[68] Moreau has discovered how to turn beasts into men by manipulating the larynx, but he cannot quite get it right. Here's how Prendick describes some ritualistic chanting by three of Moreau's creatures, one "evidently a female; the other two were men . . . naked, save for swathings of scarlet cloth about the middle":

> They were talking, or at least one of the men was talking to the other two, and all three had been too closely interested to heed the rustling of my approach. They swayed their heads and shoulders from side to side. The speaker's words came thick and sloppy, and though I could hear them distinctly I could not distinguish what he said. He seemed to me to be reciting some complicated gibberish. . . . Their eyes began to sparkle, and their ugly faces to brighten, with an expression of strange pleasure. Saliva dripped from their lipless mouths.[69]

Moreau's naked creatures participate in an unintelligible chant with strong sexual overtones, perhaps a mating dance. Prendick doesn't wait to find out. Disgusted by "these foul beings" and their "grotesque and unaccountable gestures" in which he recognizes "the unmistakable mark of the beast," he turns and flees.

This scene, in which primitive protospeech orchestrates some kind of ritual activity, rhymes with a central passage in Burroughs's 1961 cut-up novel *The Soft Machine* describing the foul acquisition of "the muttering sickness." In a passage of lyrical Beckettian abjection, Burroughs offers an origin myth:

> In the pass the muttering sickness leaped into our throats, coughing and spitting in the silver morning. frost on our bones. Most of the ape forms

died there on the treeless slopes. dumb animal eyes on "me" brought the sickness from white time caves frozen in my throat to hatch in the warm steamlands spitting song of scarlet bursts in egg flesh. beyond the pass, limestone slopes down into a high green savanna and the grass-wind on our genitals. came to a swamp fed by hot springs and mountain ice. and fell in flesh heaps. sick apes spitting blood laugh. sound bubbling in throats torn with the talk sickness. faces and bodies covered with pus foam. animal hair thru the purple sex-flesh. sick sound twisted thru body. underwater music bubbling in blood beds. human faces tentative flicker in and out of focus. We waded into the warm mud-water. hair and ape flesh off in screaming strips. stood naked human bodies covered with phosphorescent green jelly. soft tentative flesh cut with ape wounds. peeling other genitals. fingers and tongues rubbing off the jelly-cover. body melting pleasure-sounds in the warm mud. till the sun went and a blue wind of silence touched human faces and hair. When we came out of the mud we had names.[70]

In this remarkable fable, the movement into and then out of the mud recalls pivotal moments in a longer evolutionary narrative, namely the transition from sea to land and the rise of the vertebrates, here organized around the contracting of the language virus. On the "high green savanna" evolutionary psychologists love to invoke—that remote savanna whose features are supposedly responsible for shaping all of mankind's mental structures—the language virus hatches in the throat and ape becomes man: "When we came out of the mud we had names." In a large-scale recapitulation of the psychoanalytic subject's passage from the prelinguistic to the linguistic stage, insistent alliteration ("underwater music bubbling in blood beds") codes the decisive passage from muteness to a sonically patterned "music" still inarticulately somatic to, finally, the disenchanted realm of human speech. The "underwater music" becomes a "sick sound." Fluids that might be associated with physiological interiority erupt from or are imposed upon the body and, importantly, the face: those "faces and bodies covered with pus foam" suggest that the process of individuation requires the abject immersion in "the jelly-cover," as if the eclipse of the most symbolically resonant human surface—the face—by goo is a paradoxical precondition of the emergence of the human individual possessed of language.

But the movement is precisely *into* and *then* out of the mud, as if symbolic communication and human individuation required first an immersion in the resolutely pre- or nonsymbolic. The journey into the mud might be thought of as a headfirst dive into one's own asshole, so that language acquisition depends on the undoing of the apparent opposition between mouth and anus, the obscene conjunction of which is the subject of *Naked Lunch*'s "talking asshole" routine. And while Burroughs hadn't yet thought up the genitalized larynxes found in *The Place of Dead Roads*, the rapid cutting between images of "throats torn with the talk sickness" on the one hand and "egg flesh," "genitals," and "sex-flesh" on the other suggests the imaginative proximity of speech and sexual reproduction. Burroughs's primordial sexed larynxes are the de-evolutionary correlative to his oft-repeated assertion that language is a virus. But despite Burroughs's well-known obscenity, the fantasy toward which all his writing tends is one of purity beyond the body. As an early cut-up has it, "Surgical dynamite this is else you don't go, subject ape. Man, come float clean terms past hi-thing story."[71] Burroughs's innovative writing techniques are a kind of surgery meant to convert the simian subject into a higher being whose "clean terms"—uncontaminated by corrupting corporeality—permit him to transcend the kind of narrative ("hi-thing story") still tethered to the animal body.

And like Wells's Dr. Moreau, this surgery will focus on the larynx. In *The Job*, Burroughs quotes the theory of another of his fictional medical men, the Teutonic Dr. Kurt Unruh von Steinplatz, "that alterations in inner throat structure were occasioned by a virus illness. And vot an occasion! [. . .] *Ach, Junge*, what a scene is here . . . the apes are molting fur, steaming off, the females whimpering and slobbering over the dying males like cows with aftosa, and so a stink—musky, sweet, rotten-metal stink of the forbidden fruit in the Garden of Eden . . ."[72] Dr. Steinplatz is describing the contracting of the Word Virus, the evolutionary primal scene of Burroughs's whole mythology, the dire consequences of which the cut-up method will purportedly correct. From medial experimentation to medical experimentation, then, Burroughs's late fiction and theory occupy a distorted territory of Darwinian nightmare in which "the laboratory experiments undertaken with Brion Gysin"[73]—namely, the cut-up technique as applied to tape, film, and printed page—might liberate man's word from its shameful origin in the wet, mucosal throat.

The first cut-up trilogy is an agonized encounter with the cut-up method's failure to decouple the word from the flesh. The reader is exhorted to resist the word virus thus: "Try halting your sub-vocal speech. Try to achieve even ten seconds of inner silence. You will encounter a resisting organism that *forces you to* talk."[74] Here, Burroughs enjoins the reader to discover the fact of laryngeal subvocalization for herself. In other words, the cut-up trilogy is something like a guide to practice, with textual illustrations. (As he wrote in *Naked Lunch*, "The Naked Lunch is a blueprint, a How-To book.")[75] Burroughs's cult appeal has always depended on the possibility that he is more guru than novelist. And like any guru, his teachings might turn out to be incoherent. It's "time to look beyond this animal body," Burroughs says in *The Job*,[76] but over and over again his discussions of the cut-up return to the core fantasy of splicing together the animal and the human, of in fact rendering the human *even more* animal. In *Electronic Revolution*, he describes the cut-up as "the magic that turns men into swine. To be an animal: a lone pig grunts, shits, squeals, and slobbers down garbage." It's as if Prendick's initial suspicion were correct: Moreau's methods don't turn animals into humans but the other way around. The cut-up fails in its dematerializing mission—it fails to liberate man from the body and the word virus. Instead, like the researches of Dr. Moreau, it produces composite, potentially obscene creatures. Not "a mold filled with light, a mold that will soon be empty,"[77] but textual monsters result.

The first trilogy was written between 1961 and 1964. Twenty years later, the second trilogy would abandon the cut-up as technique but reabsorb it, along with its attendant mythology, as plot material. In *The Place of Dead Roads*, for instance, the "resisting organism" prohibiting the suppression of laryngeal sub-vocalization would reappear as part of a "missing link" narrative. Kim Carsons is sent by a certain Language Institute to "the highlands of Yemen . . . where the original link between ape and man that led to speech may still survive. These beings are called 'smouners.'" Smouners "use the larynx as a sexual organ" but can also use it as a weapon. Kim's task is to penetrate the smouners' habitat and transcribe their primordial speech for the benefit of the linguists.

Burroughs borrows more from H. G. Wells than just the larynx as the focal point for the "missing link."[78] *Dead Roads'* rewriting of Moreau also rewrites the history of the cut-up as technique. With the Language Institute's focus on the larynx, Burroughs provides the generic lineage of a formal innovation: he roots the cut-up in nineteenth-century Darwinian sci-fi and its fascinated anxiety about demented surgery—"vivisection"—run amok. Like Wells, Burroughs's imaginative repertoire for describing primordial language draws on late Victorian degeneration theory as well as on a version of fin de siècle decadence crucially interested in the science of philology.[79] Burroughs's "viral" theory of language extended and biologized the fragmentation of language into its material component parts seized on in decadent style.

Through Brion Gysin and Victorian science fiction, Burroughs revisited the most radical tactics of modernism and the historical avant-garde in order to remake their experiments in his own image: the cut-up became a dandiacal form par excellence. When Burroughs adapted the cut-up method from his friend the painter Brion Gysin, chance procedures and varieties of randomized text generation had been available to writers for forty years. There was, for instance, Tristan Tzara's 1920 "Dada Manifesto for Feeble Love and Bitter Love," as Burroughs acknowledges in a 1960 letter: "The Possibility of literary creation by random? cutting and rearranging of material was indicated when Tzara at a Dada meeting in the 1920s proposed to create a poem on the spot by pulling words out of a hat."[80] (Burroughs, as it happens, met with Tzara, Duchamp, and Man Ray in Paris, in 1958.)[81] "The poem," Tzara wrote in his list of instructions for producing a cut-up, "will resemble you," despite its aleatoric, foreign origins.[82] Tzara's cut-up technique complements the Surrealists' roughly contemporaneous exquisite corpse (*cadavre exquis*) games, which underlined, in name and often in result, the organic metaphor underpinning these avant-garde strategies. The scissor becomes a kind of surgical instrument, and the text a Frankenstein's monster. The cut-up method emphasizes the materiality, indeed the organicity, of the text. As Tzara puts it earlier in the manifesto, "Must we no longer believe in words? Since when do they express the contrary of what the organ that utters them thinks and wants? Herein lies the great secret: thought is made in the mouth."[83] The scissors are an instrument by which the words of others can be made in one's own mouth. Like the collage, the cut-up brings media to the fore, in the process exposing the human body itself as medium. For Burroughs, the theory of the cut-up and the material conditions of its practice were inseparable—and the "scissors" involved become, according to the logic of the organic text, a scalpel. This equivalence crops up, for instance, in the postscript to a 1963 letter to Gysin: "Do you know that Anatole France 'wrote with a pair of scissors'? cutting out sentences and pasting them together? That perhaps he rather than Tzara is the original cut up? Perhaps it is time to exhume this cadaver and perform the indicated autopsy."[84] To deploy the cut-up method is to *be* the cut-up, to have a (textual) body upon which surgery can be performed. To "exhume" France's "cadaver"—his *cadavre exquis*—is to cut up a cut-up.

The importance of decadent science fiction to Burroughs's formal experimentation supplements this more familiar, and more obvious, lineage of modernist and avant-garde experimentation. Robin Lydenberg has criticized others for "focus[ing] on Burroughs's mythology" and ignoring his "repeated reminders that content is irrelevant, that what must be attended to in all linguistic formulations is the structure of the discourse itself."[85] But Burroughs's fascination with science fiction and body horror (a serviceable if anachronistic label for much of the Burroughsian grotesque) takes his experimentation in a direction impossible to imagine from the perspective of Poundian modernism. Burroughs believed that "[w]ords—at least the way we use them—can stand in the way of what I call nonbody experience. It's time we thought about leaving the body behind," and this fantasy of disembodied posthumanity occupies both his fiction and his theoretical writings on medial experimentation.[86] Burroughs's formal innovations are inseparable from his thematic preoccupations. The flipside of this theoretical focus on dematerialization is the fiction's obsessive interest in bodily excess, breakdown, waste, corruption, death. For Burroughs, the word stands at a critical crossroads between its tendency towards disembodiment (pure concept, most closely approximated in hieroglyphic image writing) and its fall into corrupted materiality.[87]

The cut-up's rootedness in Victorian science fiction resonates with the metaphors of embodiment articulated from Tzara onward. In this, it is a direct descendant of fin de siècle theories of literary form which posit an analogy between the decadence (later, more scientistically, the degeneration) of the organism and the decadence of cultural products. The most famous pronouncement here is that of the French poet and novelist Paul Bourget (1852–1935): "The same law [as governs the animal organism] governs the development and decadence of that other organism, language. The style of decadence is one where the unity of the book decomposes to give way to the independence of the page, where the page decomposes to give way to the independence of the sentence, and where the sentence decomposes to give way to the independence of the word."[88] The cut-up method, with its necessarily fetishistic decoupling of the sentence from the paragraph and the word from the sentence, achieves precisely the "decomposition" described by Bourget. Gérard-Georges Lemair seemed to recognize as much when, in his contribution to Burroughs and Gysin's collaborative collection *The Third Mind*, he writes that "[t]he main intention of Brion Burroughs and William Gysin [*sic*] has been to free the text from the page, to free the word from the surrounding matrix."[89] Or, as Burroughs himself says, "Carried further we can break the page down into smaller and smaller units in altered sequence."[90] This textual decomposition finds its organic expression as early as *Junky*, for instance when Lee, in an asylum taking the cure, describes a fellow patient thus: "He did not have the concentration of energy necessary to hold himself together and his organism was always on the point of disintegrating into its component parts."[91]

Thus, while Burroughs's cut-up practice can obviously be understood as a descendant of modernist collage, we should avoid reducing it to a late-modernist footnote. The modernist Burroughs didn't simply impose his esoteric beliefs about possession and the dematerialization of the word onto modernist formal practice. Far more interestingly, his shamanic science fiction develops strands integral to "modernism" itself, which, as scholars have in recent years begun to demonstrate, depended on weird brews of mysticism and magical belief, on materially manifested spirit worlds and ectoplasmic eruptions at séances, on hauntings and ghosts and fairies and visitations from beyond. Lawrence Rainey has observed, for instance, that Marinetti's futurism depends on "mediums and automatic writing,"[92] a method of occult access famously favored by Yeats's wife, Georgie. *Ghostwriting Modernism* (2002), Helen Sword's definitive study of the subject, shows that modernist fascination with posthumous mediumistic communication was hardly the exclusive preserve of such acknowledged mystics as Yeats; even professed skeptics like André Breton could offer at least "metaphorical approbation to spirit mediums." Breton, for instance, "recognized and even highlighted similarities between surrealist writers' 'automatisme physique' and the spiritualist phenomenon of automatic writing."[93] Modernist innovation, in other words, was surprisingly indebted to the popular spiritualism animating the mediumistic receipt of the words of the dead—in séances or before audiences of the public—common from the late Victorian period through World War II. In this context, Burroughs's claim about *The Place of Dead Roads'* stylistic borrowings from the English writer Denton Welch (1915–48) takes on added force: "It's table tapping. . . . [Welch is] writing beyond the grave."[94]

At the heart of modernist mediumism lies a contradiction that will be familiar to readers of Burroughs, what Sword calls "its paradoxical proclivity to materialize the spirit world even while trying to spiritualize the material one."[95] Sword locates spiritualism's most durable legacy in T. S. Eliot. As modernism's most important collage poem, the bravura ventriloquism of *The Waste Land* (with its mediumistic *clairvoyante* Mme Sosostris at the center) "validates the methods and forms, perhaps even the abject corporeality, of mediumistic discourse."[96] As Eliot's example suggests, the paradoxes of modernist spiritualism were formally very productive. And point for point, they have their analogue in the career of Burroughs. Not at all coincidentally, we might begin to trace Burroughs's mediumistic modernism in his relationship to Eliot, the literary precursor whose lines show up most frequently in his cut-ups. Burroughs saw the cut-up as a means of absorbing prior poets into his own body, of, to recall Tzara's phrase, making their meaning in his mouth: "So forth anybody can be Rimbaud if he will cut up Rimbaud's words and learn Rimbaud language talk think Rimbaud . . . And supply reasonably appropriate meat. All dead poets and writers can be reincarnate in different hosts."[97]

Like mediumistic spiritualism, the cut-up is constituted by a central paradox. On the one hand, the cut-up ushers in the dematerialization of the word. It facilitates the detachment of language from the physicality of speech. On the other hand, it roots poetic production in a body understood in terms of its "meat." Just as, for Eliot, the resources of the canon could be plundered for haunting fragments, so for Burroughs the "meat" of past poets might be reanimated on the page of the cut-up artist. But Burroughs's "meat" puts a heavy accent on the materiality of this "reincarnation." If modernism makes formal use of a metaphorized mediumistic logic, Burroughs puts pressure on the metaphor. The cut-up, for him, is less a question of the Eliotic collage's uncanny summoning of the ghostly traces of a poetic past than it is a disturbing eruption of the "ectoplasmic evulsions so popular in late-nineteenth-century mediumship."[98] In other words, *he might actually mean it.*

The central paradox formalized and mythologized by Burroughs's cut-up practice is drawn from the long history of the dandy, who has always been a creature constitutively split. The dandy, from the beginning, has been engaged in "an asceticism that equals the most mortifying mystical techniques," techniques with which "he constantly cancels from himself any trace of personality," as Agamben puts it of Beau Brummell.[99] Drawing on modernist experiment, the cut-up technique is one end point for such radical asceticism, a technology for total depersonalization. But the dandy's body always returns, in the decadent pathologies dwelt on by writers like Huysmans, or in the decay suffered by Dorian Gray's portrait. In characteristically extreme form, Burroughs—who "had the physician's unflinching attentiveness to the material realities of the body"[100]—converts decadent embodiment into a grotesque image system in which the dematerializing cut-up collapses into a bestiary.

Like the dandy himself, the cut-up cannot achieve immateriality; instead, it risks a kind of terminal putrescence.

Fading Out: Overcoming the Cut-Up

In an introductory prologue at the beginning of *The Western Lands* (1987), the final novel of the second trilogy, Burroughs describes an "old writer" who "lived in a boxcar by the river." Washed-up, no longer writing, this ex-author has succumbed to "a disgust for his words" that "choked him."[101] A qualified inspiration continues to visit him. "Often in the morning he would lie in bed and watch grids of typewritten words in front of his eyes that moved and shifted as he tried to read the words, but he never could. He thought if he could just copy these words down, which were not his own words, he might be able to put together another book and then . . . yes, and then what?"[102] The model of composition here described—a kind of alien inspiration that collapses the distinction between "writing" and "copying"—of course resembles the cut-up, and the grids are reminiscent of Gysin's many grid-based visual and textual collages. The old writer's visions suggest that another cut-up novel might be possible—but not necessarily worth it: "yes, and then what?"

The Western Lands, like the rest of the second trilogy, contains almost no actual cut-up writing, but the technique's melancholy enshrinement in the opening depiction of an aging, indigent writer grants the cut-up a sort of compromised priority. The technique is explicitly yoked to science fiction, via an allusion to Stanley Kubrick's *2001: A Space Odyssey.* One of the words appearing to the old writer is "2001," which he recalls "was the name of a movie about space travel and a computer called HAL that got out of control."[103] We learn that the old man is William Seward Hall, a Burroughs stand-in from earlier in the trilogy (Seward was Burroughs's middle name), and that he has vowed "to write his way out of death." The prologue ends with a Goethe couplet, in German and then in English: "When you don't have this dying and becoming, / You are only a sad guest on the dark Earth."[104] It is as if the cut-up has been wistfully replaced by the melancholic plenitude of these rhymed lines, with their Romantic-humanist resignation in the face of a vanishing myth.

Burroughs, as mentioned above, explains that he wrote much of the second trilogy "in the style of Denton Welch," although he did not actually cut up Welch's texts: "It's table tapping. . . . He's writing beyond the grave."[105] While the cut-up had all along inherited the contradictions of mediumistic modernism, in this case Burroughs's explicit alignment of the late non-cut-up work with mediumism accents the dematerializing side of his practice. The shift from the surgical cut-up method to the spiritualized figure of the Ouija board suggests that Burroughs abandoned the cut-up because, finally, it was too rooted in metaphors of surgery and laryngeal grafting to overcome solidity, to "create [the] land of dreams"[106] that Burroughs's late program demanded. The cut-up could not alleviate the old writer's "disgust for words"—it may even have exacerbated that disgust. Michael Clune has written of postmodern experimentation as the "invent[ion of] virtual techniques, imaginary forms for arresting neurobiological time by overcoming the brain's stubborn boundaries."[107] The cut-up should be thought of as one such technique—a failed one.

The cut-up "fails" not because it could no longer produce interesting work but *because of the mythology in which it was always embedded.* What does it mean for the cut-up to fail in terms of its own myth? In his recent study *Fictions of Autonomy* (2013), Andrew Goldstone has described how modernist claims to autonomy are always socially embedded, and often quite self-consciously so. For Goldstone, the articulation of this historicized autonomy involves "emphasizing a basic continuity between modernism and late-nineteenth-century aestheticism," from which autonomy's founding "fictions" are drawn.[108] Burroughs's cut-up practice revolves around two of the signal pivots of modernist autonomy Goldstone identifies: autonomy from the person (exemplified by Eliotic impersonality and objectivity) and autonomy from reference (exemplified in Goldstone's account by Stevensian tautology, but one might also add Steinian play and Mallarmé's ideal of "pure" poetry). In the escape it provides from the body, the cut-up literalizes some of the autonomy claims modernism would cluster around "impersonality"—or, to shuffle terms somewhat, it *mythologizes* what for modernism proper was merely a serviceable "fiction." Goldstone's reminder that autonomy was always rooted in nineteenth-century aestheticism and art for art's sake should alert us to the whole mythos of the dandy underlying the autonomy claims of the next century. From Carlyle's "dandiacal body" through to Wilde and beyond, the dandy is always mythologically emplotted. Burroughs's authorial persona takes up this myth wholesale by transforming its component parts—its aestheticist emphasis on autonomy and its decadent preoccupation with pathological psychology—into an elaborate, science-fictional myth world.

In the process, it translates modernist autonomy into the realm of literary *fantasy*—a mode which, as Lance Olsen has observed, is a signally postmodern one, "hovering between the marvelous and the mimetic."[109] The Burroughsian cut-up would seem to exemplify what Olsen calls one "consummation of post-modern art," "a kind of self-consumption, a decreation . . . through an impulse toward silence."[110] But Burroughs's guru status, and the continuity between his claims for the real-world efficacy of the cut-up in his critical writings and inter-views on the one hand and his fiction on the other, propel his fiction beyond "fantasy" into some other, wilder realm: perhaps the fertile delusions of the outsider artist. It is these delusions that the second trilogy abandons—thereby announcing the "failure" of the cut-up. The old writer of *The Western Lands* puts hieropraxis behind him. He proposes instead, with a certain bathos and romantic naïveté the sincerity of which is difficult to gauge, that the solution to the problem of the body lies in art, with which we can "make ourselves less solid":

> Well, that's what art is all about, isn't it? All creative thought, actually. A bid for immortality. So long as sloppy, stupid, so-called democra-cies live, the ghosts of various boring people who escape my mind still stalk about in the mess they have made.
>
> We poets and writers are tidier, fade out in firefly evenings, a Prom and a distant train whistle, we live in a maid opening a boiled egg for a long-ago convalescent, we live in the snow on Michael's grave falling softly like the descent of their last end on all the living and the dead, we live in the green light at the end of Daisy's dock, in the last and greatest of human dreams. . . .[111]

By sampling such favorites of his as "The Dead" and *The Great Gatsby*, Bur-roughs alludes to the cut-up method that the second trilogy has left behind (both texts were frequent sources of cut-ups in earlier work), but refrains from subjecting these lines to experimental mangling. The implication is clear: the cut-up has nothing further to offer.

In *The Western Lands*, with its lament for the failure of the cut-up, "modern-ism" as a period style will come to serve not as a spring to further experiment but as a nostalgic retreat from a "virtual technique" that has failed to produce the liberation it seemed to promise. (As always with nostalgia in Burroughs, a certain mawkishness is knowingly courted.) He finds "tidiness" not so much in the writers themselves, who may personally have quit this world with as little grace as the aging Beau Brummell, but with the echoes of their prose, floating on the air like strains of half-remembered music. If the cut-up was once thought capable of achieving freedom from the flesh by "dismember[ing] and explod[ing]" the "'soft machine' of the body," as Lydenberg has it,[112] that particular technique for achieving immateriality has been found wanting in *The Western Lands*. A different, gentler form of fragmentation is preferred: the humanist fragmentation that results from an aging man of letters haphazardly recalling a life's reading, and, as the final passage of *The Western Lands* makes clear, the modernist fragmentation of Eliot, no longer radically disorienting but instead inspiring a comforting wistfulness. *The Western Lands* lovingly revisits that characteristically decadent stylistic territory dubbed by Vincent Sherry the "dying fall that goes on dying."[113] *The Waste Land*, always implicit in Burroughs's title, gets the last word:

> The old writer couldn't write anymore because he had reached the end of words, the end of what can be done with words. And then? "British we are, British we stay." How long can one hang on in Gibraltar, with the tapestries where mustached riders with scimitars hunt tigers, the ivory balls one inside the other, bare seams showing, the long tearoom with mirrors on both sides and the tired fuchsia and rubber plants, the shops selling English marmalade and Fortnum & Mason's tea . . . clinging to their Rock like the rock apes, clinging always to less and less.
>
> In Tangier the Parade Bar is closed. Shadows are falling on the Mountain.
>
> "Hurry up, please. It's time."[114]

The aggressive disruptions of the cut-up have here been replaced with a milder sort of bricolage; *The Waste Land* has been defanged, its dissonance resolved. Of all the authors discussed in this book, the gutter dandy William Burroughs goes furthest in reconciling dandyism's competing master modes, the tough-guy continence of surfaces and the decadent grotesqueries of a pathologized psychic interiority. The cut-up itself is the dandiacal form that most explicitly achieves, or hopes to achieve, this reconciliation. Its failure occasions a retreat to an altogether different sort of dandyism: the artful sentimentality of the aged aesthete, living among fragments of an artistic past that, hauntingly, seem more real to him than the current chaos. Despite his reputation, toward the end of his career, as a punk-rock godfather notating the anarchic effusions of the present, Burroughs's dandyism offered, finally, an idiom not of rebellion but of artful quietism among the tapestries, the marmalade, the Fortnum & Mason's tea.

4

DJUNA BARNES'S CROSS-GENDERED CONCEITS

A broken heart have you! I have fallen arches, flying dandruff, a floating kidney, shattered nerves *and* a broken heart.
—DR. MATTHEW DANTE O'CONNOR, in *Nightwood*

Coco Chanel vs. Djuna Barnes

Well before William Burroughs attempted to resolve the risks of decadent interiority with the cut-up, Djuna Barnes (of whom Burroughs was a great fan) attacked the problem in a similarly experimental fashion—although she was less interested in escaping decadence than in finding a new form for it, a special language all its own. In all her work and especially in *Nightwood* (1937), she would give the chaotic, threatening morass of decadent interiority shape and form through a poetic practice that granted uncanny autonomy to metaphor. And like Burroughs, Barnes understood decadent interiority as opposed to an ethos of continence, an opposition that emerges most clearly in her 1931 media interview with Coco Chanel. Barnes would go on to set herself up as the anti-Chanel: the two offer rival models for how to be a woman dandy in the age of modernism.

The fashion designer, a famously early riser, offers rather stern advice in her interview with Barnes:

> You cannot maintain two destinies, that of the fool or the intemperate and that of the wise and the temperate. You cannot keep up a nightlife

and amount to anything in the day. You cannot indulge in those foods and liquors that destroy the physique and still hope to have a physique that functions with the minimum of destruction to itself. A candle burnt at both ends may shed a brighter light, but the darkness that follows is for a longer time.[1]

Chanel's insistence on clean living amounts to a repudiation of those habits of consumption associated with decadent dandyism. This is a particularly pointed rejection, insofar as Chanel herself was, as the Fashion Institute of Technology's Valerie Steele puts it, "the first female dandy."[2] If, as I have been insisting, dandyism has been constituted all along by a certain tension between decadent interiority and cool, controlled surfaces, then Chanel, here, hopes polemically to identify herself with those controlled surfaces, to claim for herself a dandyism purged of all traces of decadence (as Lisa Chaney puts it, Chanel "concentrated on the silhouette, the structure and architecture of clothes").[3] Her aesthetic is attended by a homiletic moralism: "What have you heard after midnight that you count worth sitting up for?"[4] This sounds less like Wilde than like Thoreau—"Have you knowledge of the morning? Are you abroad early, brushing the dews aside? . . . [I]f you are not acquainted with the morning star, what relation have you to wisdom and purity?"—but its dandiacal thrust, its thirst for control, cannot be missed.[5] (Chanel was famous for her epigrammatic "maxims," offered in fashion magazines and interviews.)[6] She favored an androgynous style ("I hate breasts that show. . . . [Women] can have hips, that's all right, but in the front and back, they should be flat like men") achieved via the sartorial discipline of breast-binding garments.[7] The suppression of secondary sex characteristics was part of a larger distaste for bodily expression *tout court;* as Linda Simon, one of her biographers, puts it, she had "a fetish for cleanliness that she would forever equate with virtue. . . . One of [her] highest compliments was that a woman hid her 'personal odor'" successfully.[8]

Ideally—as her famous perfume Chanel No. 5 would demonstrate—one could hide one's "personal odor" with a scent resembling something entirely inorganic. "Chanel did not want her perfume to be identified with any particular flower, but instead, she insisted, to be something completely artificial."[9] Chanel's preoccupation with bodily control, and her distaste for the organic, made her notorious for barely eating.[10] Simon writes that camellias were Chanel's favorite flower, "no matter that in France the flower was associated with courtesans and dandies; in China, the camellia was a symbol of purity."[11]

But this is to see a contradiction where none exists: the camellia was Chanel's flower not despite its association with dandies but because Chanel's variety of dandyism involved the relentless pursuit of bodily purification.

Barnes characterized Chanel's "philosophy"—"the cause of her success and her fame"—as, in essence, a disciplined relationship to the appetites:

> She believes in being natural, and when she uses the word "natural" she does not use it as it is customarily used, to denote things ugly, uncouth, untrained. To her that thing is natural which is the most complete and coordinated. If you say that your way of being natural is to sit up until dawn, drink everything in sight, dress so that you are conspicuous, eat so that you are gorged, she will say, "Very well, but what a *bad* nature you have!"[12]

The definitions of "natural" that Barnes attributes to Chanel are not entirely consistent. While at first it appears that the "natural" simply *is* that which is "complete and coordinated," by the end of the passage completeness and co-ordination would appear to be the desirable traits of a *good* nature; a "*bad* nature" is, contrarily, that of a gluttonous, alcoholic, loudly dressed night owl. Such all-too-human messiness, like Burroughs's portrayal of a Maugham whom it is "impossible to keep clean," represents one avenue for denigrating decadence—for downgrading its subversive romanticism into mere sloppiness. Conversely, as Barnes implies, Chanel's idiosyncratic use of the word "natural" as entailing "completeness and coordination" aligns the Chanelian dandy with the machine, and therefore with those terminal cases of macho modernism discussed in my introduction. (Indeed, Chanel is evidence that such a modernism can accommodate a variety of gender styles—femininity is no necessary bar to it.) As Burstein says, Chanel's "bead necklaces made of metals like steel and platinum" are "representative of a mechanistic aesthetic"; her sartorial innovation "turns on a rendering of the human body as mechanized and reproducible."[13] "Natural"—at least when its valence is positive—is, for Chanel, paradoxically equivalent to the "mechanical": efficient, functional, and without appetite.

That the "natural" as "complete and coordinated"—as "good"—is not Barnes's ideal is suggested not only by her decadent fiction but by her 1920 *Vanity Fair* article "Against Nature," in which she celebrates "intricacy, falsity, perfidy—anything that is a step removed from this eternal simplicity that everyone seems to like."[14] As the Huysmans nod in the title indicates, Barnes is interested in resisting "the natural" according to a rather different pattern than Chanel's machine aesthetic. As Robin Blyn puts it of *Nightwood*'s "decadent and trans-gendered . . . freak dandies," "their will to Aestheticism becomes the measure of their freakishness."[15] While Chanel (in Barnes's paraphrase) rejects conspic-uous dress, Barnes's antinaturalism embraces "freakishness" in all its blatancy.

Chanel and Barnes, then, offer competing models for modernist female dandyism, although transvestism and androgyny are central to both. The dandy may be a member of that archetypically male family including the fop and the rake, but, as the trajectory of aestheticist androgyny running from Pater through Hemingway makes clear, dandyism's gender is not a simple quantity. Chanel's dandyism resonates with the surface-oriented machismo of Wyndham Lewis. (After all, the *BLAST* manifesto blesses "the hairdresser," indicating Vorticism's consonance with the arena of fashion in which Chanel operated.) Barnes's dandyism, on the other hand, descends into the abysses of interiority I have throughout this book shown to be associated with "deca-dence," and which, insofar as it is gendered, favors androgyny and hermaph-roditism. To recur, as a thumbnail heuristic, to those binarisms sketched in my introduction, Chanel's dandyism is "aestheticist" (or "cold" in Burstein's phrase, or "classical" in Hulme's), while Barnes's is "decadent" (or "hot" or "romantic").

But just as, in the case of Hemingway, such binarisms prove unstable or ultimately descriptively inadequate, the neat schematic I've offered—Chanel vs. Barnes—cannot hold. This is especially the case with respect to the gender affiliations of the female dandy, which are dizzyingly involved. If the dandy is a primarily male social type associated with effeminacy, the *female* dandy is at once parasitic on this type and, in her constitutive androgyny, some-how a more primary instance of it.[16] While Barnes offers what Blyn calls "transgendered . . . freak dandies," Chanel's originality in the fashion world involved making women's dress more like men's, a transformation premised on personal experimentation. As Douglas Messerli recounts, Chanel "caused a small sensation" in the years before her career began by wearing bespoke jodh-purs and other conventionally male attire, some of it lent to her by her then lover Etienne Balsan. "The style she created over the next decades—more tailored and trimmer than the clothes women had worn for centuries—helped change the course of fashion."[17] In other words, Chanel's fashion innovations—the par-ticular brand of female dandyism she helped market and codify—depend for force and originality on cross-gendering.

Chanel's dandyish cross-dressing inhabits a French tradition that stretches well back into the nineteenth century. We might start with George Sand, whose own penchant for male clothing, for which a contemporary referred to her as "the illustrious hermaphrodite," began, like Chanel's, with the ostensibly merely practical need for appropriate horseback riding attire.[18] Similarly, the pioneering French artist Rosa Bonheur was granted a *Permission de Travestissement*, "for reasons of health."[19] Despite their allegedly practical motivations, such female transvestism would prove, as Daniel Cottom puts it, "an iconic image of bohemian provocation."[20] "Like Sand," Cottom goes on to say, "the dandy was a kind of transvestite, an 'Androgyne,' as Barbey said, in his stereotypically feminine care for his appearance and exquisite behavior."[21] But there is a large cultural difference between a woman dressed as a man and the effeminate coding of a man's attention to dress and display. This latter is the nexus of male dandyism's originary androgyny, which much of the modernist dandiacal writing I have discussed so far has been concerned with transforming, sometimes even repudiating. In this tradition, dandiacal habits of outward display are indices of a complex androgynous psychic interior. With this in mind, we might see the dandyism Chanel expressed in her interview with Barnes as either a variety of modernist *masculinity*—like Lewis, Hemingway, or Chandler, her transvestism involves a fetishism of surfaces—or a specifically feminine version of the surface-oriented aesthetics associated most immediately with macho modernism.

For Chanel, as for Wyndham Lewis, valorized aesthetic experimentation is oriented toward the external and the inorganic. Barnes's own model of female cross-gendering inverts and complements Chanel's. For Barnes, the radical revelations made available by transvestism are decidedly organic—hence her (semiparodic but, as we will see, transformative) interest in degeneration theory. Michael Davidson insists that Barnes's "non-sequiturs, baroque rhetoric, and elaborate hyperbole force attention on to the surface of language rather than elucidating some interior psychological state"; *Nightwood* is therefore "the antithesis of the modernist interior monologue that attempts to render some subterranean, unchanging bottom nature or core personality."[22] The reality is somewhat more complicated. It is true that Barnesian prose, in its elaborate artificiality and allusiveness, does something quite different from the various psychologisms associated most readily with the label "stream of consciousness." But Barnes is in fact profoundly invested in laying bare the animal substrate of human sociality. At its most extreme, this investment reduces consciousness to a kind of muscle, sheer flesh: as *Nightwood*'s Doctor O'Connor says, "[I]f one gave birth to a heart on a plate, it would say 'Love' and twitch like the lopped leg of a frog."[23] While imagery like this eschews the modernist promise of rich interiority, its orientation is not exactly toward "the surface," either. Rather, it proposes that psychological substrates are no more than the reflex actions of the viscera. What Davidson describes Barnes resisting is Burstein's "hot" modernism, a modernism of interiority, psychology, and depth. But Barnes is not a cold modernist—she has not, like Lewis or Chanel, abandoned psychological interiority in favor of the shell or the machine. Rather, she has abandoned it for a conception of the human not as Pascal's thinking reed but as a muscle that mutely feels. This is indeed an "elucidati[on of] some interior psychological state," albeit by means crucially different than had been normalized by the stream of consciousness. It offers an antihumanism quite distinct from cold modernism's, and a vision of interiority separate from the more familiar trajectory Davidson refers to under the sign of "stream of consciousness." As we will see, Barnes's antihumanism depends on two linked thematic focuses, transvestism and Darwinesque degeneration theory, which she yokes together and routes through parody.

Nightwood's Transvestism

The transvestite female dandy makes an early English appearance (the first, as far as I know) in Meredith's *The Ordeal of Richard Feverel* (1857), when the eponymous hero, Dick Feverel, is tempted away from lawful marriage by the seductions of one Mrs. Mount (Bella), whose "man-like conversation, which he took for honesty, was a refreshing change on fair lips."[24] In a kind of prevision of the enchanted androgynous dialogism that Hemingway would explore in *Garden of Eden*, Bella's cross-dressing—she likes to dress as a man in "outrageous affectation of the supreme dandy"—will awaken hitherto unsuspected erotic possibilities for Dick: "He began to conceive romance in that sort of fun." Bella and Dick christen Bella's masculine alter ego—her "dandy's attire"—"Sir Julius."[25] Bella/Sir Julius's transformations, however comically presented, occupy some of the same uncanny, metamorphic territory explored earlier by Gautier and later by Hemingway. Dick's tender flirting with Sir Julius even approaches the kind of identity melding fantasized about by David and Catherine in *Garden of Eden*. Dick tells Sir Julius that she "must grow more" (to be taller, to be more like a man) and then demonstrates how: "'I'll show you how,' and he lifted Sir Julius lightly, and bore the fair gentleman to the looking-glass, holding him there exactly on a level with his head. 'Will that do?'" As in those filmic dramas of identity merger from *Persona* to *Mulholland Drive*, the mirror offers a space in which the difference between people gets magically dissolved, however tentatively. From *Mademoiselle de Maupin* on, this fantasized resolution of difference as such is routed through the figure of the dandiacal androgyne. And, while Sir Julius's dandyism is a mask, something assumed and cast off, certain core features of dandyism mark Bella in her uncostumed state as well. Specifically, Bella (Mrs. Mount) is master of the kind of verbal power possessed elsewhere in Meredith by *The Egoist's* Mrs. Mountstuart, discussed in my second chapter. In Bella's case, such power has, as the dandy's always does, the disturbing capacity to dismantle the symbolic hold of the most cherished social institutions. She takes particular aim at the institution of marriage: "Imputations upon wives: horrible exultation at the universal peccancy of husbands. This lovely outcast almost made him think she had the right on her side, so keenly her Parthian arrows pierced the holy centres of society, and exposed its rottenness."[26]

Decadent dandyism's twinned fascination with and repulsion toward women provides the female decadent with, at best, a pointedly ambiguous model for imitation. The canonical representations of female decadence in the nineteenth century by a woman author are Rachilde's *Monsieur Vénus* (1884) and *La Marquise de Sade* (1887), both of which can only tolerate the contempt for women that is so large a part of decadence by reinscribing this contempt in a parodic key.[27] As it happens, such reinscription is an especially available avenue for decadence, because decadence is *already* a discourse with a strong tendency toward the parodic. Decadence exploits transvestism's formal affinity with parody. As Judith Butler has influentially put it, "In imitating gender, drag implicitly reveals the imitative structure of gender itself."[28] Transvestism might be *locally* parodic insofar as it imitates (appreciatively or contemptuously as the case may be) the contemporaneous conventions by which gender is performed, but its parody always points toward a much broader destabilization of the sex/gender system. As early as *Richard Feverel*, such destabilizations offer, thrillingly or threateningly, to dissolve the very boundaries of selfhood.

In *Nightwood*, Djuna Barnes's masterpiece, the central appearance of transvestism is male-to-female, although its dynamics are profoundly indebted to the possibilities of female-to-male cross-gendering offered by decadence from Gautier onward. In what Marjorie Garber calls "one of the most disquieting cross-dressing scenes in all of twentieth-century literature,"[29] Nora comes across Dr. Matthew O'Connor, in bed, "in a woman's flannel nightgown":

> The doctor's head, with its over-large black eyes, its full gun-metal cheeks and chin, was framed in the golden semi-circle of a wig with long pendent curls that touched his shoulders, and falling back against the pillow, turned up the shadowy interior of their cylinders. He was heavily rouged and his lashes painted. It flashed into Nora's head: "God, children know something they can't tell; they like Red Riding Hood and the wolf in bed!"[30]

What makes this scene so "disquieting" for Garber? She reads its culminating revelation as imbricated, formally and thematically, with the Freudian primal scene, particularly as developed in *The Wolfman*—a comparison enabled in part by Freud's own discussion of "Little Red Riding Hood" in that case study.[31] The implication seems to be that this "primal scene of cross-dressing" confronts Nora with the contingent enculturation of biological sex.[32] If, as Butler says of drag, "part of the pleasure, the giddiness of the performance is in the recognition of a radical contingency in the relation between sex and gender,"[33] Barnes's "disquieting" scene proposes that the converse of such liberating giddiness is a frightening encounter with the biological raw material that culture transforms into social legibility, an encounter decadence stages over and over again.

In the doctor's case, as in the sci-fi fantasias of H. G. Wells and William Burroughs discussed in the previous chapter, amorphous, decadent interiority is framed by the tools and symbols of the medical trade—in particular, the scalpel. Here's the doctor's room as perceived by Nora immediately before she discovers him in bed:

> A pile of medical books, and volumes of miscellaneous order, reached almost to the ceiling. . . . Just above them was a very small barred window, the only ventilation. On a maple dresser, certainly not of European make, lay a rusty pair of forceps, a broken scalpel, half a dozen odd instruments that she could not place, a catheter, some twenty perfume bottles, almost empty, pomades, creams, rouges, powder, boxes and puffs.[34]

By enumerating surgical instruments alongside items of feminine beautification, Barnes proposes a troubling continuity between the body as an object of medical intervention on the one hand and of aestheticizing improvements on the other. This is a typically decadent assemblage, and it prepares the way for the revelation of the doctor's transvestism in the following paragraph. If, following Garber, this is a "primal scene," it can only become so because, by highlighting the cultural contingency of gendered costume, it brings forcefully to consciousness the unmarked flesh beneath *all* costume—not just the skin beneath the dress but the meat too, the Nietzschean "human being under the skin." This is what it means for cross-dressing to be, as Garber says, "constitutive of culture"—the transvestite primal scene allegorizes the repressions and constructions of enculturation as such.[35]

Such primal scenes do not happen just anywhere, in modernist literature at least. They require the decadent atmosphere, the right sort of interior decorating. As Barnes goes on to describe Dr. O'Connor's bedroom, "There was something appallingly degraded about the room, like the rooms in brothels, which give even the most innocent a sensation of having been accomplice."[36] Barnes's evocation of this degraded interior partakes of some of the ambivalent moralizing with which decadent texts in the modernist period so often frame their queer figures of fascination.

Or, more accurately, it *imitates* such moralizing without, perhaps, really participating in it. Symptomatically, older feminist readings of *Nightwood* are unsure how to handle the "degradation" Barnes associates with transvestism, because they are not sufficiently sensitive to the dynamics of parody at work. Sandra Gilbert, for instance, wants to insist that unlike such representations of androgyny as *The Waste Land*'s Tiresias—a "fever dream of the hermaphrodite, the nightmare of gender disorder"—female modernists including Barnes offer a "kind of utopian ceremonial androgyny whose purpose is very different from the ritual transvestism" depicted by Joyce or Eliot.[37] Susan Gubar, likewise, insists that "[u]nlike the grotesque transvestities [*sic*] in modernist literature by men, both of the inverts of *Nightwood* [Robin Vote and Dr. O'Connor] are closely identified with heroic attempts to get back to prehistory."[38] Leaving aside the question whether "male modernists" are quite as one-sidedly reactionary in their engagement with transvestism, androgyny, and hermaphroditism as these accounts suggest, I believe that such optimistic or politically positive readings miss the extreme ambivalence, the real horror at the materiality of the flesh, which *Nightwood* presents.[39] This is not to suggest that Gubar and Gilbert are wrong to see in *Nightwood* celebrations of the queer, but to insist that such celebrations unfold in rhetorical complicity with, not in contradistinction to, discourses which find in decadence precisely the "*Walpurgisnacht* of misplaced sexuality" which Gilbert ascribes, pejoratively, to Eliot.[40] As I hope will become clear in what follows, Barnes's felicity with stylistic parody is the key to her ambivalent articulation of decadent interiority, an articulation that exploits above all the toxic tropes of degeneration theory.

With the exception of early Yeats, Djuna Barnes is probably the most overtly decadent of the high modernists. To be decadent, for Barnes, is to be haunted by the specter of biology. But while Barnes registers the symbolic power of decadent and degenerationist thinking, she is too much a parodist to take it quite seriously. If the female dandy has a privileged relationship to parody, *Nightwood* is a parody of decadence raised to a pitch of high modernist virtuosity. But Barnes doesn't just parody decadence: she also suggests that modernism cannot break from it. More: like the parodies of *Ulysses*, Barnes's decadent style both celebrates and undermines literary style as such.

Nightwood and Decadent Style

Barnes's career and its reception can therefore tell us something general about modernism's ambivalence toward decadence and aestheticism. The story begins with her 1915 volume of poetry, *The Book of Repulsive Women*. With its Beardsleyesque illustrations and its lovingly evoked figures of decay ("Though her lips are vague as fancy/In her youth/They bloom vivid and repulsive/As the truth"), Barnes's early volume of poems could seem a mere tissue of fin de siècle mannerisms, a last little gasp of the Yellow Nineties.[41] Barnes herself tried to suppress a 1949 reprint of *The Book of Repulsive Women* and left it out of the vita she sent to *Who's Who*.[42] This unsuccessful suppression—the reprint went forward without her blessing—might stand as an emblem for the suppression of modernism's debt to decadent style more generally.

In fact, all of Barnes's work and especially *Nightwood* would remain signally indebted to the textures and themes of decadence, as the critical consensus of the last few years has come to reflect. Erin G. Carlston sums it up well when she writes that "all of the varied genres and styles Barnes explores exemplify the definition Arthur Symons formulated of decadence in 1897: 'That learned corruption of language by which style ceases to be organic, and becomes, in the pursuit of some new expressiveness of beauty, deliberately abnormal' [Symons 149]."[43] David Weir's inclusion of Barnes at the end of his survey of decadent culture in the United States handily enumerates the characteristically decadent aspects of her career and art, from her association with Guido Bruno (1884–1942), publisher of decadent texts including *Repulsive Women*, to her exploitation in *Nightwood* of such decadent topoi as the "'fatal woman' theme"—the canonical treatment of which is Wilde's *Salome*—and degeneration theory.[44] Furthermore, and crucial for our purposes, there are "the varieties of sexuality that can be called 'decadent' because they are at some remove from heterosexual 'norms'";[45] as adumbrated above, *Nightwood*'s interest in transvestism taps into a decadent-dandiacal lineage whose ancestral locus classicus is Gautier's *Mademoiselle de Maupin* (1835), and which also includes Meredith's *The Ordeal of Richard Feverel* and Rachilde's *Monsieur Vénus* (1884).

Thematically, *Nightwood* partakes of decadence's focus on elaborate artificiality, non-normative sexuality, and extremes of psychological investigation. Formally, it inherits decadence's conflation of exceptional fineness with deliberate grotesquerie, a grotesquerie specifically, even obsessively, invested in discovering the bestial in the human. As early as *Repulsive Women*, Barnes had explored in "Twilight of the Illicit" an animalizing rhetoric soaked in decadent tropes; the accompanying illustration depicts a sort of hybrid lizard-woman, an icon of the degenerate paradoxically ascendant, triumphant. The poem itself describes a weariness entirely at odds with the erect posture of the figure in the illustration; between them, poem and illustration map out the dialectic of savage energy and world-weary exhaustion characteristic of decadence in general and of the discourse of degeneration theory in particular. An uncomplimentary verse portrait, "Twilight" begins, "You, with your long blank udders / And you calms / Your spotted linen and your / Slack'ning arms." Prefiguring Doctor O'Connor's sloppy bedroom in *Nightwood*, this interior tips over from decadent excess to mere messiness. Its aggressively unflattering portrait continues:

> You, the twilight powder of
> A fire-wet dawn;
> You, the massive mother of
> Illicit spawn:
> While the others shrink in virtue
> You have borne.[46]

Vincent Sherry has observed that *Nightwood*'s "aftermath imaginary" exploits images of "the puppet impersonating the human," which he sees as characteristic of the "poetics of decadence."[47] But this early poem weds its aftermath imaginary—its "fire-wet dawn" after the party's over ("shivering in the junk-sick morning," as Burroughs would have it)—not to images of automatons or puppets but, instead, to a figure of monstrous biology: "the massive mother of / Illicit spawn." Decadence, here, finds in biological maternity itself—in the very engine of the natural—its master image. Not only is human maternity translated into the language of (mere) animal reproduction ("dugs," "spawn"), but the figure of the "massive mother" seems poised to crowd out whatever we take "the others" (other mothers? other children? other people in general?) to refer to—they "shrink" while the "massive mother" expands alarmingly. The final two lines are punningly polysemous. "Shrink in virtue" might on first reading appear to mean "shrink by virtue of," though the direction of the sentence after the line break will not permit this reading to stand. Do we hear "born" (i.e., "birthed") in "borne," so that, with fine decadent irony, the addressee's "spawn" is itself the bearer of virtue? Or do the "others" shrink in the virtue that the poem's addressee has overcome or suffered ("borne") in order to produce her "illicit spawn"? Only the last reading is fully reconcilable with Barnes's syntax and spelling, but the lines are deliberately ambiguous nevertheless; they are struggling, it seems, to articulate some complex paradox about the relationship between "spawning" and virtue.

Whatever their exact sense, they leave us with that impression of disproportion that is one of decadence's hallmarks. As discussed at greater length in the previous chapter, when applied formally "decadence" usually denotes, as Regenia Gagnier has it, "a decomposition or deformation of the relationship between the part and the whole."[48] Such decadent themes find exemplary form in *Nightwood*'s long, strange sentences. Weir sees *Nightwood*'s style as enacting the passage from a decadent to a modernist aesthetic: "[*Nightwood*] is a kind of modernization of decadence in which decadent material is subjected to the narrative and stylistic procedures of modernist fiction. . . . As extended by Bourget, Nietzsche, and other writers, the theoretical paradigm of decadent style has come to describe a manner of writing that places the greatest degree of artistic emphasis on the smallest unit of a literary composition."[49] I want to build on Weir's argument with three goals in mind. First, I will attempt to define "decadent style" as it operates in Barnes with as much formal specificity as possible, taking up Weir's observation that *Nightwood* "can be used to illustrate the emergence of a modernist literary aesthetic out of the style of decadence" by articulating the means of this emergence at the level of the sentence. For Barnes, a nineteenth-century "decadent style" will be crucially rerouted through the conceptual and syntactical grid of the Renaissance conceit. Second, I will suggest that the decadent archaism of Barnesian style achieves its effects via what Carolyn Williams, writing of Pater, has called "aesthetic historicism." Barnes's own version of this aestheticist appropriation of historically marked forms—what I call her "decadent historicism"—will fully exploit degeneration theory's fascination with the bestial in the human, and *Nightwood's* animal motifs can illuminate the decadent formal texture of its prose. Third, I will briefly consider Barnesian decadent style in terms of the broader phenomenon of modernist engagement with parody.

Nightwood's Decadent Conceits

Nightwood brings to perfection the taste for stylistic pastiche which Barnes had begun with *Ryder* (1928). In the earlier novel, various phases of English literary history—Chaucer, the King James Bible, Renaissance prose generally, and a certain Irish-inflected rollicking demotic—are lovingly, and expertly, imitated. Though the pastiche is not as systematic as in *Ulysses*'s "Winds of Aeolus," it is usually not too hard to identify a source. Here, for instance, Barnes describes a father and newborn in prose recognizably derived from the King James Bible: "And he saw that it was small and red, and that its flesh was dry in the ear and the navel, and between the hands and between the feet; and between the nates it did perspire and give off a heat and a sourness."[50] The pastiches are distinct enough never to resolve into a default idiom—there is no solution to the heterogeneity of the prose's ingredients.

In *Nightwood*, decadence itself will provide the rhetorical solvent in which the diverse targets of Barnes's pastiche come to stylistic equilibrium. The resolution of diverse stylistic precedents within the common idiom of decadence makes sense, since the repeated staging of a curatorial fascination with the high aesthetic production of a distant cultural past is one of decadence's most recognizable tendencies. Like *Ryder*, *Nightwood*'s most obvious precedents are the styles of the Renaissance. T. S. Eliot recognized this debt when he famously declared that the novel attains "a quality of horror and doom very closely related to that of Elizabethan tragedy."[51] Certainly *Nightwood*'s effects—its "doom" but also its humor—depend on its deliberate plundering of archaic idioms, though its extended comparisons and hypertrophic similes have to my ear more in common with the conceits of the Metaphysicals than with Elizabethan tragedy.[52]

The peculiar effect of Barnes's prose depends on the mediation of markedly "old-fashioned" sentential rhythms by an (equally marked) decadent style.[53] Michael Riffaterre has analyzed the formal mechanisms by which decadent writing, in his view, re-scripts Romantic writing, subjecting it to the ironizing operations of "paradox":

> [Paradox] first proposes an object, and then offers an aberrant point of view that falsifies the representation of that object. The effect of surprise caused by an expression that seems inadequate, or even by a systematic mismatch between form and content, is a consequence of the combination of the two stages. The first, prior to the paradoxical transformation, is the *given*. The second, following the transformation, is the *derivation*, the form of the incongruity.[54]

Decadent writing, therefore, forces on the reader a kind of consciousness of the operations of style and form related to that of parody. With this in mind, we can see Dr. Matthew O'Connor's transvestism as an emblem of *Nightwood*'s far broader skepticism about the relationship between style on the one hand and essence or truth on the other.

This skepticism—a *loving* skepticism, a skepticism charged with affection for its object—results in a kind of stylistic pastiche that cannot but be a kind of literary-historical inside baseball; like so much modernist irony, you have to know a lot to get the joke. As Riffaterre concludes, "Everything lies in the internal games of writing, and this provides an extra point of interest in the decadent text . . . the power they have to make this truth visible through their formal eccentricity, and to require of us a reading that demands full awareness and complete participation."[55] What Riffaterre says of decadence is doubly true of Barnes's "neo-decadent performance,"[56] which famously demands such "full awareness." Barnes's parodic style imitates decadent imitation. Its "given" is both decadence proper (with its own internal parodied given, Romanticism) and the Renaissance rhythms Barnes loves. Barnes's derivations are double: faintly parodied decadence and faux seventeenth-century at once. And the particular aspects of Renaissance style to which Barnes is most drawn— the long, accretive sentences of Burton and the baroque surprises of the Metaphysicals' complex metaphors—resonate nicely with the familiar profligacy of nineteenth-century decadent prose, what Riffaterre calls its "acceleration towards superlative summits—an acceleration entirely pertinent to the deca-dent quest for excess and satiety."[57]

Burton's "loose free style" is usually thought of in contradistinction to the intricate conceits of the Metaphysicals, though in Barnes's hands, these two ostensibly opposed means become reconciled.[58] The most famous definition of the Metaphysical conceit comes, of course, from Samuel Johnson's essay on Abraham Cowley in *The Lives of the Poets.* Johnson identifies a characteristic

> combination of dissimilar images, or discovery of occult resemblances in things apparently unlike. . . . The most heterogeneous ideas are yoked by violence together; nature and art are ransacked for illustra-tions, comparisons, and allusions; their learning instructs, and their subtlety surprises; but the reader commonly thinks his improvement dearly bought, and, though he sometimes admires, is seldom pleased.[59]

Helen Gardner defines a "conceit" as "a comparison whose ingenuity is more striking than its justness." A *Metaphysical* conceit is distinguished by the pres-ence of a kind of argumentative intellection, "an appearance of logical rigour." The Metaphysical conceit is further distinguished by its conclusion, what Donne famously called "the impression of the stamp"; this epigrammatic thrust reflects its argumentative character.[60]

Nightwood's outlandish figures and comparisons not infrequently reflect Donne's call for an "impression."[61] Barnes is fond of yoking her elaborate im-agery to some point, often a generalizable claim about eros or human nature. Here is an example:

> Love becomes the deposit of the heart, analogous in all degrees to the "findings" in a tomb. As in one will be charted the taken place of the body, the raiment, and the utensils necessary to its other life, so in the heart of the lover will be traced, as an indelible shadow, that which he loves. In Nora's heart lay the fossil of Robin, intaglio of her identity, and about it for its maintenance ran Nora's blood.[62]

The epigrammatic thrust of the conceit—the deposit of the heart (love) is like the remnants in a tomb—precedes its fuller development, though the "impression" here can be thought of as the application of the lesson to the novel's dramatic situation enacted by the final sentence. It would also be possible to read the first, epigrammatic sentence—the most compact statement of this particular conceit, elaborated on in the sentence that follows—as the "impression," in which case the comment is not on Robin and Nora in particular but on love in general; Robin and Nora become mere instances of a broader phenomenon.

Nevertheless, there is a sense in which this conceit simply will not cohere satisfactorily. Where, for instance, is the "other life" of either the corpse in the tomb or the "deposit of the heart"? Heaven or the afterlife in the first instance, and the beloved's real existence in the second? Or, rather, is it the beloved's ideal existence as beloved that depends on the "deposit"? The narrator insists that the two sides of this comparison are "analogous in all degrees"—but in that case, what, in the tomb, corresponds to the heart's "blood," which "maintains" the "fossil" of Robin? The point is that the difficulty is not merely a matter of complex syntax but of cloudy logic: far from being "analogous in all degrees," this conceit is evocative but, on inspection, untenable: two things are placed side by side, but the machinery by which they are linked together is faulty, deliberately imperfect.

I am suggesting, then, that Barnes's metaphoric imagination courts solecism intentionally. In a line of dialogue that might be taken for a metacomment on Barnes's method, Nora at one point tells the doctor, "In the beginning, after Robin went away with Jenny to America, I searched for her in the ports. Not literally; in another way."[63] Nora, here, calls attention to the ontological instability effected by excessive figuration. Tenor and vehicle can become confused. Alan Singer observes that an "asymmetrical relation between tenor and vehicle [is] the foundation of Barnes's style." He finds this asymmetry "catachrestic" in the specific Renaissance sense of "a trope that stray[s] beyond the field of contextual determinations warranting its usage."[64] When confronted with a metaphor that has apparently left its context behind, the reader becomes confused, unsure how to focus her attention and concerned that she has lost the thread. In some cases—as in the "remnants" example above—confusion will remain, even with care and attention. This confusion accounts for a large part of the difficulty of reading *Nightwood:* it is cognitively taxing to keep track of the direction of a figure. The blurring of tenor and vehicle for the fatigued reader should be understood as a deliberate effect of Barnes's poetics; and, in some cases, even the most vigilant reader might find herself unable to resolve local difficulties.

Barnes's conceits often begin pithily but then refuse to stay that way, as if the compulsion to proliferate comparisons gets the better of them, or as if the satisfaction of a neat figure or an epigrammatic stamp must be denied or deferred. Here is Doctor O'Connor on his special topic, the night:

The darkness is the closet in which your lover roosts her heart, and that night-fowl that caws against her spirit and yours, dropping between you and her the awful estrangement of his bowels. The drip of your tears is his implacable pulse. Night people do not bury their dead, but on the neck of you, their beloved and waking, sling the creature, husked of its gestures.[65]

"The darkness is the closet in which your lover roosts her heart" is clear enough, but trouble begins in the second clause. Is "darkness" also the night-fowl's antecedent, so that "darkness" is a "closet" and a "night-fowl"? Grammatically it would seem so, though the sense is somewhat dubious. Alternatively, the night-fowl could be a second object of the verb "roosts": your lover roosts both her heart and the night-fowl in the darkness. (More normally, a night-fowl would roost itself, but "to roost" can function transitively.) In any event the night-fowl has, by the sentence's end, taken over the conceit; the two following sentences continue to be controlled by it: the drip of tears is the night-fowl's pulse, and night people sling the night-fowl on the necks of their beloved. In this most radical instance of the asymmetry between tenor and vehicle in Barnes's style, sense recedes almost to the vanishing point as the night-fowl—standing for what, exactly?—takes on an uncanny life of its own. "Husked of its gestures," the bird is also shorn of its function within a comparison. It risks standing for nothing but itself. It's as if Donne's "A Valediction: Forbidding Mourning" were actually about a compass.

The most prominent conceits in *Nightwood,* if not in fact the most frequent, entirely give in to the compulsion to reiterate and multiply comparisons and to grant the vehicle a startling independence, though they are rarely as difficult to parse as the figure of the night-fowl. As with the night-fowl above, in the conceit below "*corsage*" takes on a life of its own, an effect heightened by the introduction of the tenor only at the end of the paragraph:

As the altar of a church would present but a barren stylization but for the uncalculated offerings of the confused and humble; as the *corsage* of a woman is made suddenly martial and sorrowful by the rose thrust among the more decorous blooms by the hand of a lover suffering the violence of the overlapping of the permission to bestow a last embrace, and its withdrawal: making a vanishing and infinitesimal bull's eye of that which had a moment before been a buoyant and showy bosom, by dragging time out of his bowels (for a lover knows two times, that which he is given, and that which he must make)—so Felix was astonished to find that the most touching flowers laid on the altar he had raised to his imagination were placed there by the people of the underworld, and the reddest was to be the rose of the doctor.[66]

By the time one has finished this passage, it is easy to feel that the doctor has bestowed a literal red rose upon Felix.[67] Horticulture was a favorite topic of decadence—as Riffaterre observes, its paradoxical "artifice in nature" was irresistible to decadent writers—but the "decadent" character of Barnes's "*corsage*" conceit goes beyond its citation of the botanical topos.[68] It inheres instead in the formal imbalance between tenor and vehicle. Recall the formal definition of decadence offered by Paul Bourget and discussed in the previous chapter.[69] For Bourget, language and literary style develop and decline in a manner analogous to the life processes of animal organisms. Bourget's notions of organic deterioration and its literary corollaries rhymed with contemporary theories of hereditary degeneration as propounded by thinkers like Nordau and Lombroso. Just as a degenerate human specimen possesses some traits in preposterous disproportion to others, so too in literary decadence "the page decomposes to give way to the independence of the sentence, and . . . the sentence decomposes to give way to the independence of the word."[70]

Weir refers to this well-known definition of decadence in explicating T. S. Eliot's comment that "only sensibilities trained on poetry can actually appreciate" *Nightwood:* "The word or phrase is polished to a point that the reader's attention is attracted to such smaller units at the expense of the whole."[71] This is insightful but imprecise; a poetic prose is not, after all, necessarily a decadent one. As the foregoing analysis of Barnes's conceits suggests, a major aspect of the "decadence" of Barnes's style (as distinct from the "decadence" of her thematic preoccupations, which I will return to at length below) obtains in the perverse autonomy granted to a metaphoric vehicle. If "decomposition" is Bourget's master trope—a "decomposition" that organicizes the experimental disarticulation of the formal parts of a work of art—then we might think of Barnes's severing of vehicle from tenor as a signal instance of such decadent decomposition. Furthermore, and to stay with Bourget's insistent organicism, we might think of the uncanny *growth* of the vehicle, its eerie metastasization, as involving *Nightwood*'s decadent modernism in a genre often associated with decadence but not usually with Djuna Barnes: the fantastic tale of terror. I will return to this possibility below.

Degeneration, Cross-Gendering, and *Nightwood*'s Decadent Historicism

The lover who "knows two times" might apply as much to a lover of English sentences as to anything else, though does Barnes stop at two? I have already mentioned the self-reflexive temporal multiplications involved in Barnes's parodied decadence, the vertiginous sense that her sentences occupy (at least) three periods: her own, modernist one; the fin de siècle proper; and a more distant past, replete with the aura of the Renaissance and of the canon. Kannenstine has observed that Barnes's work draws on diverse threads both late Victorian and modern (he names "*fin de siècle* decadence, expressionism, imagism, surrealism, stream-of-consciousness, and possibly others") but that "the late books form a body of work which seems both innovative and traditional.... Various critics, working backward from contemporary references, have called them Gothic, Jacobean, and Elizabethan."[72] The vagueness Kannenstine perceives in the criticism is a deliberate effect of Barnes's method in *Nightwood*, a method marking something of a break with that of *Ryder*. Whereas in *Ryder* period pastiche can be identified with some degree of precision (there is no doubt about the faux Chaucerisms, say, of "The Occupations of Wendell"), in *Nightwood*, the effect is rather one of generalized archaism, as if textures of various literary pasts have been stitched together or overlaid such that any too specific referent is obscured. But these archaisms are always recognizably filtered through the idiom of decadence.

Nightwood's decadent texture is derived above all from the palimpsestic wistfulness of Pater, a debt rendered explicit in Felix's appreciative ruminations on Robin Vote's appearance:

> She was gracious and yet fading, like an old statue in a garden, that symbolizes the weather through which it has endured, and is not so much the work of man as the work of wind and rain and the herd of the seasons, and though formed in man's image is a figure of doom. Because of this, Felix found her presence painful, and yet a happiness. Thinking of her, visualizing her, was an extreme act of the will; to recall

her after she had gone, however, was as easy as the recollection of a sensation of beauty without its details. When she smiled the smile was only in the mouth and a little bitter: the face of an incurable yet to be stricken with its malady.[73]

Impossible not to hear, here, echoes of Pater's description of the Mona Lisa, whose "eyelids are a little weary," who "is older than the rocks among which she sits; like the vampire, she has been dead many times."[74] But Barnes's debt to this most decadent moment of Pater's oeuvre goes beyond the rhythmic echoes of his prose or the doomful tolling of an aestheticism half in love with death. Barnes shares with Pater a certain aesthetic approach to history, what Carolyn Williams has called Pater's "aesthetic historicism."[75] Williams suggests that Pater's authorial voice, so instantly recognizable, paradoxically depends on the masterfully managed echoes of past styles: "His prose feels haunted, as if the spirits of the dead come out when no one else is home." This feature of Paterian prose is the formal expression of his theory of "aesthetic poetry," which, as Williams has it, "strategically alludes" to "earlier poetry" even as it insists on its "historical difference." A certain tragic and, from our perspective, protomodernist shoring of fragments attends this aesthetic historicism, since "Pater's sense of time passing in the flux of present consciousness works both within and against his conservative desire to recontain fragments of time in some imaginary place." This "place of transhistorical unity is most often embodied as the personal figure of an infinitely capacious mind."[76]

For all his clownish excess, is not Dr. Matthew Dante O'Connor precisely such a "capacious mind," however parodied? His transvestism is therefore an emblem for an even larger kind of capaciousness; his is a total self that can resolve or contain opposites, binaries, contradictions—just as the Barnesian conceit both enacts and refuses identity between vehicle and tenor. O'Connor's transvestism therefore becomes, as it were, a metaphor for metaphor. For Garber, "the compelling force of transvestism in literature and culture comes . . . from its instatement of metaphor itself, not as that for which a literal meaning must be found, but precisely as that without which there would be no such thing as meaning in the first place."[77] O'Connor's cross-dressing is the condition of his endless yarning; both point toward a kind of infinite discursive prolixity, the ground and horizon of all verbal meaning. If Nora is *Nightwood*'s emotional heart, O'Connor is its condition of poetic possibility.[78]

This capaciousness is why, with respect to Dr. O'Connor's desired biological sex, size matters—he wants "a womb as big as the king's kettle," from which all of culture might issue.[79] The stylistic correlative of such capaciousness is *Nightwood*'s decadent style itself. "The reason I'm so remarkable," the doctor says, "is that I remember everyone. . . . It's the boys that look as innocent as the bottom of a plate that get you into trouble, not a man with a prehistoric memory."[80] Even down to his middle name, the doctor—like the two novels in which he appears—is a vast repository of past literary styles, the alchemical synthesis of which produces his own unmistakable "voice." But the element of parody is crucial, and helps distinguish Pater's "aesthetic historicism" from Barnes's "decadent" one. (Of course, historical allusiveness of the sort Pater finds in "aesthetic poetry" is always proximate to parody—just as aestheticism is always proximate to decadence.) Kannenstine writes that Barnes "seeks to erase the line drawn between past and present" and that "her final achievement is a manner and style of no particular era, and thus of any era."[81] This is finely observed, but requires a qualification: the very medium of Barnes's transhistorical prose is a historically marked decadent style for which the dissolution of historical boundaries is, as Williams shows of Pater, a constitutive theoretical and formal feature.

There is pleasure in the allusions to past styles, a pleasure exemplified by O'Connor once he gets going, but there are risks, too: that the past might engulf the present, drown it out, like a gothic curse or the appearance of a hereditary disease. As Daniela Caselli puts it, "The constant exhibition of linguistic corruption accounts for the obsessive, torrential, and self-destroying quality of the narrative in this novel that is never able to forget its own status as writing."[82] A literary harkening back becomes conflated with the threatening harkening back dwelt on by the late Victorian pseudoscience of degeneration theory, a dead end as far as the life sciences went but endlessly productive aesthetically, as the scores of naturalist novels dramatizing it attest. "Decadence" and "degeneration" were conceptually closely linked, with the latter drawing, through the language of science, on the broader cultural logic of the former. When, of aristocratic lineages, O'Connor says, "The last muscle of the aristocracy is madness . . . the last child born to aristocracy is sometimes an idiot," he is merely voicing a degenerationist cliché.[83] *Nightwood*'s slightly belated engagement with degeneration theory is part and parcel of its slightly belated engagement with aesthetic decadence.

Such decadent—or degenerate—historicism draws, rhetorically and conceptually, on the urtext of degeneration theory, Max Nordau's *Degeneration*. "Among the women," Nordau writes of fin de siècle degenerates, "one wears her hair combed smoothly back and down like Rafael's Maddalena Doni in the Uffizi at Florence"; another "has hers cut short in front on the brow and long in the nape, waved and lightly puffed, after the fashion of the fifteenth century, as may be seen in the pages and young knights of Gentile Bellini, Botticelli and Mantegna."[84] The inflection of characteristically modern decadent/degenerate human types (medicalized and pathologized in Nordau's scientist account) by recognizably Renaissance aesthetic styles is the most Barnesian note in *Degeneration*, and Nordau's description of fin de siècle aesthetic degeneracy might double as a description of Barnes's own style: "The unity of abiding by one definite historic style counts as old-fashioned, provincial, Philistine, and the time has not yet produced a style of its own."[85]

Degeneration at the level of plot can be seen most clearly in the description of the Volkbein line, with its sad culmination in Robin and Felix's abnormal son Guido, but all of *Nightwood*'s characters are haunted by atavistic returns—returns which seem to illustrate Nordau's insistence that degeneration involves "the unchaining of beast in man."[86] In her robust analysis of degeneration theory in *Nightwood*, Dana Seitler reads the novel alongside Frank Norris's *Vandover* (1914), a far cruder, and far less ironic, degenerationist allegory. Seitler finds in Norris a normative, bourgeois vision that "recast[s] the homosexual dandy as the atavistic brute"; Barnes, conversely, achieves something less repressive: "[I]f the bestial is the most clarifying index to what degenerationism seeks to police, the ironic reappropriation of this thematic . . . constitutes a very different kind of imaginary; it layers its representational economy with bodies that are not so much subversive as they are contradictory and hybrid . . . in a state of spiritual ascension and a position of human-to-animal collapse."[87]

Seitler recognizes that far from merely "subverting" degenerationist tropes, Barnes gets a great deal of creative mileage out of them. Indeed, much of *Nightwood*'s eerie intensity depends on its characters' uncanny flickering between their hypermodern (and modernist) poses and the grinning animal underneath—two poles that become, as in post-Stoker representations of the vampire (*Dracula* being a classic instance of degenerationist fantasy), thrillingly identical. "[Robin] yet carried the quality of the 'way back' as animals do," we are told early on; she is an "infected carrier of the past." Nora, likewise, contains the past within her, a past figured as beyond even the advent of the animal, as aligned with the mute materiality of plant life: "[T]here could be seen coming, early in her life, the design that was to be the weather-beaten grain of her face, that wood in the work; the tree coming forward in her, an undocumented record of time."[88]

Bestial Transvestism

What is the relationship between *Nightwood*'s obsessive imagination of the bestial in the human on the one hand and its interest in transvestism and cross-gendering on the other? Paul de Man's gloss on "catachresis" and "mixed modes" offers a clue: "They are capable of inventing the most fantastic entities by dint of the positional power inherent in language. They can dismember the texture of reality and reassemble it in the most capricious ways, pairing man with woman or human being with beast in the most unnatural shapes."[89] For Barnes, likewise, "man with woman" and "human being with beast" are potential conjunctions arising out of the deployment of the impossible possibilities offered by metaphor. Writing of Barnes's representation of Robin, Clare Taylor observes that *Nightwood*'s "conceptualiz[ation of the] masculine woman" depicts her as "an 'impossible,' or excessive, subject": "The text, pushing Robin to the limits of representation, subjects her to the bestial."[90] The "impossibility" Taylor perceives is a function of Robin's female masculinity, but the equation between cross-gendering and the bestial had already been proposed in the scene in which Nora mentally compares Dr. O'Connor in drag to the wolf from Little Red Riding Hood. Indeed, we might think of Dr. O'Connor's drag as a kind of transposition of the cross-gendering of Robin—the "impossibility" of representation that Taylor perceives of Robin finds its compensation in O'Connor, in whom transvestism and the bestial are posited as co-constitutive. Drawing energy from degeneration theory's peculiarly poetic phobias, Barnes yokes transvestism to the bestial in order to make a more comprehensive statement about the animal substrate of human sociality—a statement she shares with the Darwinian sci-fi of H. G. Wells before her and with William S. Burroughs after her.

Nightwood is not, of course, "Darwinian sci-fi." But its version of modernist interiority, of modernist psychology, is so extreme as to offer something like a generic revolution. As Emily Coleman said in a letter to Eliot, "Can you read [*Nightwood*] and not see that something new has been said about the very heart of sex?—going beyond sex, to that world where there is no marriage or giving in marriage—*where no modern writer ever goes?*" (emphasis Coleman's).[91] In her apparently retrograde reliance on the tropes and clichés both of decadence and of degeneration theory, Barnes in fact pushes the novel of modernist interiority toward its limit, a limit approached via the destabilizing, weirdly literalizing force of her metaphors, which insist so relentlessly and so eerily on the presence of the animal in the human. As Bonnie Kime Scott observes of *Nightwood's* "beasts turning human," for Barnes, "nature does not stay conveniently separate or 'other' from culture, and . . . evolution has not safely or permanently delivered human beings to civilization."[92] For Barnes, metaphor is the trope whereby beasts turn human, and humans bestial.

Nightwood's fascination with human-beast hybrids occasionally approaches not just sci-fi but horror fiction (Eliot's "quality of horror"?). Its famous concluding scene, in which Robin and a dog square off on all fours, gathers together the various threads from which *Nightwood* derives its uncanny effects: cross-gendering, degeneration theory (Nordau himself insists that one of the "stigmata of degeneracy" is "zoöphilia, or excessive love for animals"),[93] and the curious independence granted the metaphoric vehicle in Barnes's poetics. Robin's imitation of a dog—an imitation that results in a transformation—literalizes the human-animal motif threaded throughout the novel:

> Her pose, startled and broken, was caught at the point where her hand had reached almost to the shoulder, and at the moment Nora's body struck the wood, Robin began going down. Sliding down she went; down, her hair swinging, her arms held out, and the dog stood there, rearing back, his forelegs slanting; his paws trembling under the trembling of his rump, his hackle standing; his mouth open, his tongue slung sideways over his sharp bright teeth; whining and waiting.[94]

This is the most exhaustively interpreted passage in all of Barnes; it seems to hold the key to her entire poetics, though no one can agree on just what it means. As Tyrus Miller observes, there is a fundamental "undecidability" between two competing interpretive programs: on the one hand, Robin's performance looks pathetic, degrading, an instance of "abject breakdown." On the other hand, there is something hieratic in her transformation—think of

Zeus turned to a swan, or any number of comparable classical precedents—in which case perhaps this is an instance of "divine communication."[95] Such "undecidability" is a hallmark of decadence proper, with its visions of excremental transcendence. Though he doesn't invoke decadence, Kenneth Burke reads *Nightwood* as manifesting a "transcendence downward"; in Robin's canine mimicry "corruption and distinction become interchangeable terms."[96] Alan Singer grounds these interpretive ambivalences in a compelling formal analysis that finds in *Nightwood*'s final scene not the "climactic development of a latent image pattern" but instead something like the exposure at the level of theme of the novel's experimental imbalance between tenor and vehicle. For Singer, *Nightwood*'s final scene

> incurs self-consciousness about the relational hierarchy that conditions the significance of such patterns in the first place. In effect, the metaphoric dog (beast), which has been lurking within the doctor's monologue as a second-order meaning, leaps dramatically into the foreground of this narrative to rout those meanings constraining metaphor to a purely heuristic role. What was figurative in previous contexts becomes literal, thus inhibiting a reader's attempt to value one over the other.[97]

The movement of the "metaphoric dog" to the narrative "foreground" accomplishes the victory of vehicle over tenor always implicit in Barnes's extended conceits. Understood in terms of *Nightwood*'s debt to decadence, we might take the ascendance of second-order meanings to first-order meanings as indicating the potential for a decadent style of metaphor, in which the vehicle expands endlessly, to give rise to a decadent genre: the Darwinian horror novel, in which the continuity between man and beast is always more than merely figurative.[98] Robin Blyn finds Barnes's "neo-Decadence" "challeng[ing] the equation of Decadence with degeneracy,"[99] but this is not quite right. Barnes, in fact, doubles down on the equation of decadence with degeneracy, but not in order to use degeneration theory to impugn decadence. Rather, degeneration theory offers an index of decadence's truths. Barnes's felicity with parody permits her to harness the energy of degeneration theory without endorsing its phobic stigmatizations—she knows that it's potentially very silly stuff, but she takes it just seriously enough to get its images of atavism and the bestial to work in the service of her decadent vision. Indeed, degeneration theory's thematic preoccupations are productive of decadent style itself. Like such late Victorian fantastic tales as *The Island of Dr. Moreau* or *Dracula*, the conclusion of *Nightwood* shows the beast actually, not figuratively, turning human—or, more precisely, it takes a figurative metamorphosis and pushes it to its most extreme point: if it goes any further, it tips into sci-fi.

Contemporary readers, as well as later critics, have not infrequently read *Nightwood*'s final scene as describing a human-animal sexual encounter, an interpretation Barnes rejected: "The dog is *not* being romantic towards Robin! It is furious at the mystery of her drunkenness, a kind of exorcism of what it does not understand."[100] But the attractiveness of the bestiality reading reflects the sense that what the scene literally describes—a woman imitating a dog, and a dog growling back at her—is inadequate to its poetic radicality. There is a felt need to insist that the scene *goes further* than it does, because, although taken in isolation it merely describes a woman pretending to be a dog, in the larger fabric of Barnes's decadent conceits it performs a kind of magic trick: it dissolves the logic of metaphor. Or, to put it differently, the scene allows metaphor to come to a complete resolution—a resolution normally denied it—so that the vehicle finally takes over, supplants its tenor, and becomes real.

Nightwood's evocations of temporal return, of the biological hauntings of the past, can be illuminated by its most Paterian sentence: "When she smiled the smile was only in the mouth and a little bitter: the face of an incurable yet to be stricken with its malady." "Degeneration" wasn't part of Pater's imagination, but his discussion of the Mona Lisa certainly figures the aesthetic past as a kind of titillating illness, perverse, appealing, and dangerous—not unlike the evolutionary past whose return degeneration theory tracks with appalled fascination. For Barnes, the insistent rhythms of the past do indeed represent a kind of "degeneration narrative," as Seitler has it, in which thematic decadence "shift[s] its terms from a case of 'style' to a biological condition."[101] Or perhaps, as I've suggested above, the order of operations runs the other way: perhaps degeneration theory granted Barnes the permission she needed to let her metaphors run free, unconstrained by the normal logic of tenor and vehicle. By articulating an admittedly ironized degeneration narrative within the medium of Paterian aestheticism, the biological "malady" itself becomes *a kind of style*, one more sampled literary template with which, and within which, the modernist can play. The style of decadence is *Nightwood*'s master code, a gauzy medium through which Barnes effects her persistent filtration of the idioms of the past, "as if," as the Baron says of the Baronin, "the past were a web about her, as there is a web of time about a very old building."[102] Or, as Paul West has written, "There is a Chaucer inside her Baudelaire."[103]

Decadence and the Science-Fictional Metaphor

"Every science-fictional world," writes Seo-Young Chu in a brilliant analysis of science fiction's relationship to metaphor, "is a metaphysical conceit literalized as ontological fact within a narrative universe." For Chu, "science fiction" means "a mimetic discourse whose objects of representation are non-imaginary but cognitively estranging." Science-fictional genres and aesthetic tendencies can be taxonomized according to their referents, which are in every case difficult to imagine, at least in comparison to the world of familiar people and things treated by realism: "*Surrealism,* for example, is a type of science-fictional mimesis whose cognitively estranging referent is the phenomenon of dreaming . . . . *Detective fiction* is a type of science-fictional mimesis whose cognitively estranging referent is the mystery of ratiocination."[104] Following Chu's lead, I would suggest that the generic templates drawn on by Barnes involve the following cognitively estranging referents: *degeneration theory* is a type of science-fictional mimesis whose referent is the fact of evolution and descent by natural selection; *decadence* is a type of science-fictional mimesis whose cognitively estranging referent is the interpenetration of biological and social drives in the production of human culture, including the vexing question of the relationship between biological sex and gender roles. One way decadence points to its referent is by projecting metaphors of organic decomposition onto textuality, which is why decadence has a privileged relationship to the mode of parody. Like parody, decadence is *always about* the deterioration of linguistic, cultural, and textual scripts into their ingredients. Like William Burroughs after her, Barnes's "science fiction" is obsessed with demonstrating the interpenetration of parody as an experimental mode with science fiction (or magical realism, or the metaphysical conceit stretched to its breaking point, or whatever else one wants to call it) at the level of both theme and language.

Barnesian prose, then, is constructed out of a tissue of other styles, other voices. We might take "tissue," here, quite literally. Like Burroughs after her and H. G. Wells before her, Barnes takes from "decadence" in general a permission to stretch figuration to its limit, to replace metaphor with metamorphosis.

As Chu says, expatiating on *trope's* etymological link to the verb "to turn," literary tropes can seem uncannily similar to an "organism *turned* by mutation into something else."[105] "Madame Collects Herself" (1918), one of Barnes's early short plays, renders this logic very explicit. Madame Zolbo, visiting her hairdresser, Fifine, and a barber, Monsieur Goujon, makes a remark about what we might now call patriarchal gender constructs: "Shaw says—I'm perfectly sure it's Shaw—that a woman is only what a man, or men, make her."[106] In Madame Zolbo's case, this is literally true: she is, as we discover over the course of the play's few short pages, constructed out of the discarded body parts of various men from her past—a lock of hair from one, blood from another, a patch of skin from a third, a finger from a fourth. When, aghast, Fifine the hairdresser stabs Madame Zolbo through the heart, the wound proves nonfatal—Zolbo's heart, too, is imported. Fifine, in what might seem a general statement about the unlocatability of human essence, is also asking a very specific medical or anatomical question: "Where are you, Madam, in what spot are you yourself?"[107]

> MADAME ZOLBO: Ah, Monsieur, that is a very elusive thing. Can I call it my soul, a blithe atom, a canary at song in the wilderness of my body?
> MONSIEUR GOUJON: [*turning to his wife*] This is a woman's job. Strip her of her gifts, unravel the horrid spool until we reach the end—let us see what she is like.[108]

The hairdresser, aligned with surfaces, masks, and externality, is enemy to the forces of baroque interiority obsessed over by decadence. As the barber and the hairdresser finish removing all of Madame Zolbo's parts, she "disappears and a blond canary rises up toward the ceiling."[109] This transformation bears some obvious affinities with Robin's imitation of a dog in *Nightwood*, although it goes further and, for that reason, cannot attain to the same uncanny ambiguity. (With Madame Zolbo in mind, we might say that the power of Robin's "transformation" is that it *comes so close* to being a literal metamorphosis, but stops just short of it—it is like a fantastic tale, but it is not one.) Madame Zolbo appears to compare her soul to a canary, but as we discover, she is not, in fact, making a comparison at all. She is speaking a literal truth. Nor is this metamorphosis unidirectional: the play ends with Zolbo's canary-soul reacquiring the grisly materials of her prosthetic humanity, turning back into Madame Zolbo.

Unlike *Nightwood*, then, "Madame Collects Herself" is, generically, a fairy tale. But its representation of a literal transformation—from human to canary and back again—partakes not of the literature of magical enchantment but, rather, of the materialist fantastic tale. Degeneration theory is again in the background—Nordau describes fin de siècle degenerates as "dummies patched together at haphazard, in a mythical mortuary, from fragments of bodies, heads, trunks, limbs, just as they came to hand."[110] Like the creatures in *Dr. Moreau*, the construction of Madame Zolbo is medical and surgical; she is made of "a pint of blood," a "little square of skin," a transplanted heart, and so on. Like one of Dr. Moreau's vivisected beasts, Madame Zolbo is assembled piecemeal—but, if their essence is in the larynx, hers is even harder to pin down. Like Moreau's creatures, though, she too is just a creature inside: a lovely blond canary, aspiring to the higher air of metaphor.

The "mechanistic aesthetic" of Chanel's dandyism is meant to discipline nature, at least the "bad nature" that Barnes, in her interview with Chanel, finds the fashion designer condemning. But for the Barnesian female decadent, all nature is "bad" nature, and there's no point in condemning it or trying to bring it into line. The task of Barnes's decadent style is to render bad nature gloriously excessive, to transform the recesses of decadent interiority into a highly formalized, richly allusive rhetoric. If Chanel, to recur to Hulme's dichotomy, is "classical," Barnes's answering "romantic" interiority is positively animalistic: the soul is a beast, but that beast is a Renaissance poem.

PART III

EXTREMES AND END-TIMES

5

THE PSYCHOPATHIC DANDY

A Survey

His crimes seem to have had an important effect upon his art.
—OSCAR WILDE, "Pen, Pencil, and Poison"

Gary Gilmore, an intelligent psychopath and double murderer who, in 1977, became the first person executed in the United States since the 1972 suspension of capital punishment by the Supreme Court, was not a dandy. He was, however, a skillful artist and a capable writer. In a prison letter to his girlfriend, Nicole, he describes "a picture of Christ by a Russian artist that really haunted me for a long time":

> Christ didn't look anything like the popular beaming Western Christian version of the kindly shepherd we're used to. He looked like a man, with a gaunt, lean, sort of haunted face with deep set large dark eyes. You could tell he was pretty tall, angular, rangy, a man alone and I guess that was the most striking thing about the picture. No halo, no radiant beam from heaven above. Just this extraordinary man—this ordinary human being who made himself extra-ordinary and tried to tell us all that it was nothing more than any of us could do. Loneliness and a hint of doubt seemed to fill the picture. I would like to have known the man in that picture.[1]

It is perhaps not difficult to imagine why an imprisoned man, condemned to die, might identify with Christ, although the ranging of the psychopathic with the iconic disturbs. Gilmore's Christ is a figure of distilled opposition, "a man alone" who, absent his "halo" but driven to make "himself extra-ordinary," seems more *übermensch* than Savior.

This letter belongs to biography or to the literature of psychopathology or criminology, but it can nevertheless tell us something about fictional representations of the psychopath. Included in Norman Mailer's novelized journalistic account of Gilmore's trial and execution, *The Executioner's Song,* Gilmore's discussion of Christ gets to the heart of such diverse novelistic depictions of sociopathic violence as Patricia Highsmith's Ripley novels and Anthony Burgess's *A Clockwork Orange,* narratives that in different ways court an ambivalent identification with the distressingly fascinating figure of the murderer. (This is very familiar from the movies; films as different as Arthur Penn's *Bonnie and Clyde,* Terence Malick's *Badlands,* and Martin Scorsese's *Taxi Driver,* to name just three prominent instances of a probably endless series, all depend on, and often interrogate, the evocation of this queasy fascination. Mafia movies belong in a different but adjacent category.) Gilmore's interest in a desentimentalized Christ—or, more accurately, a Christ sentimentalized under a different sign than the more familiar one of forgiveness and endless love—reflects the most positive valuation of any audience's fascination toward and partial identification with the psychopath: antisociality is remade as a valorized apartness, and the violence of the killer converted to the (justified) violence against a social order. And society's retaliation becomes not legitimate punishment but the making of a martyr.

As a figure of literary and filmic interest, the psychopath often elicits representative strategies also proper to the dandy. Like the dandy, the psychopath exercises a powerful, if violently disruptive, form of masculine charisma appealing precisely because it is so dangerous.[2] Like the dandy, the psychopath's physical presence calls up a kind of excess of representational iconography: whether Marlon Brando or James Dean's slicked-back hair or the Taxi Driver's Mohawk, the pathological outsider is marked by magnetic stigmata. Like the dandy, the psychopath's sexuality is presented as suspect or compromised. He is either *excessively* heterosexual (Stanley Kowalski raping Blanche Dubois) or *insufficiently* heterosexual. Such pathologized sexuality has its roots in clinical portraits of psychopathy, for instance in Robert Linder's *Rebel without a Cause: The Hypnoanalysis of a Criminal Psychopath* (1944), which asserts that, for the psychopath, normal sexual instincts are largely absent or else "frequently homoerotic or perverse in some sense."[3] A classic instance of *insufficient* sexuality is Warren Beatty's impotence in *Bonnie and Clyde,* first indicated when he rebuffs Faye Dunaway's initial advances: "I ain't much of a lover boy. . . . [but] ain't nothing wrong with me—I don't like boys." A visibly disappointed Dunaway: "Boy. Your advertising's just dandy. Folks'd never guess you don't have a thing to sell."⁴ "Advertising" here captures the duplicitous force of this sort of masculine charisma: dangerous male sexual potency has been stream-lined into a set of conventionalized, and therefore commodifiable, signs, but in the process somehow emptied of its original charge. Paradoxically, though, this commoditization—this dandy advertising—enables the charming psycho-path's media citability and mass cultural fame, a historical circumstance of the real-life Bonnie and Clyde cleverly reenacted by Penn's casting of screen idol Beatty.[5]

Patricia Highsmith exploited the strange confluence of the dandy and the psychopath in the creation of Tom Ripley, the best-known psychopathic dandy in literary history, unless one counts the murderer Dorian Gray. In *Ripley Under Water* (1991), the Ripliad's ultimate volume, Ripley recovers from the pressures of serial murder with Richard Ellmann's *Oscar Wilde.* Like Gary Gil-more, Tom feels drawn to his version of Christ:

> Something about Oscar's life, reading it, was like a purge, man's fate encapsulated; a man of goodwill, of talent, whose gifts to human plea-sure remained considerable, had been attacked and brought low by the vindictiveness of *hoi polloi,* who had taken sadistic pleasure in watching Oscar brought low. His story reminded Tom of that of Christ, a man of generous goodwill, with a vision of expanding consciousness, of in-creasing the joy of life. . . . No wonder, Tom thought, that people of all types and ages kept reading about Oscar, not even realizing perhaps, why they were so fascinated.[6]

Ripley's identification with Wilde/Christ underscores the ease with which legitimate postures of martyrdom and oppositional energy can be hijacked by the psychopath. Or, more troublingly, it reveals the uneasy proximity of the just rebel and the unjust psychopath. Ripley, like Gilmore, finds in the rebellious figure of Christ a kind of narcissistic fantasy the apocalyptic hori-zon of which gives a theological-aesthetic turn to the destructive impulses of psychopathy, although, in true Ripley fashion and quite unlike Gilmore, his words are distinctly understated, free of any grandiose posturing. By routing this fantasy through the figure of Wilde, archetypal dandy, Ripley decks it out in a very specific cultural costume. Wilde himself would provide the template for the association of the (queer) dandy with the martyr; as discussed in my second chapter, he crystallized the force of his own heroism when, of the very nascent struggle for gay rights, he wrote, "The road is long, and red with monstrous martyrdoms." Ripley's own queasy identification with Wilde disturbs in part because it exemplifies the cultural logic by which a homophobic culture can make a queer cultural style seem the natural accouterment of villainy, as well as that by which the martyr can morph into the lunatic or terrorist, and vice versa.

In the period after World War II, an expansive history of romanticized outlawry would run headlong into the demystifications typical of the social-scientific interest in psychopathy and in antisocial personalities. Linder's *Rebel without a Cause* is the most prescient text here; it would set the stage for a range of later studies as varied as the group-authored *The Authoritarian Personality* (1950), Norman Mailer's "The White Negro" (1957), and Howard Becker's *Outsiders* (1965). For midcentury social theorists, rebellious oppositionality could even seem less an exceptional situation than an exemplary one, a model for all sociality. As Erving Goffman put it in *Asylums* (1961), generalizing from the case of the mental patient, "It is thus *against something* that the self can emerge" (emphasis in original).[7] In different ways and to different degrees, all of these studies orbited around the vexed quantity of the antisocial person's interiority. Mark Seltzer observes the "empty circularity" of the sociologically inflected self-understanding of a very extreme type—the psychopathic serial killer—for whom "social construction [itself] . . . becomes the point of attraction of the kind of person who traumatically experiences himself as nothing 'deeper' than a social construction."[8] Seltzer's sociologically self-reflexive serial killer offers a variation on the fundamental dialectic of decadent dandyism, in which the dandy's difference amounts *either* to a case of pathologized insides *or* to one of sheer, inhuman exteriority, pure performance. The "empty circularity" of Seltzer's serial killer is possible only because of postwar sociology's longstanding, even obsessive, interest in deviance and antisociality. As with the dandy proper, a homophobically pathologized queer sexuality was seen as central, even as causal, for psychopathy. As Theodor Adorno puts it in his chapter entitled "The Rebel and the Psychopath" in *The Authoritarian Personality*, "Symptomatically, [the rebel] is characterized, above all, by a penchant for 'tolerated excesses' of all kinds, from heavy drinking and overt homosexuality under the cloak of enthusiasm for 'youth' to proneness to acts of violence. . . . The extreme representative of this syndrome is the 'Tough Guy,' in psychiatric terminology the 'Psychopath.'"[9] Or, as Lindner puts it, "the universal sexual aims regarded as normal have little place in [the psychopath's] style of life."[10] The convergence of rebelliousness and a stigmatized nonnormative sexuality is the most prominent way in which the dandy makes his way into midcentury. In literature, he appears as *the homosexual villain*.

Tom Ripley is a particularly subtle instance of the homosexual villain, a cultural figment only very recently receding. As Michael Trask observes, "*The Talented Mr. Ripley* appears to revel in stereotypes of gay male villainy that a homophobic world has long presupposed."[11] In *No Future* (2004), Lee Edelman observes of the response to the gay serial killer Andrew Cunanan (Versaci's murderer) that a homophobic news media moved easily to the assumption that Cunanan's murderousness was an emanation of what one columnist called the gay "culture of death."[12] The cultural proximity of the queer and the psychopathic has a history, a history which, as far as I know, is earliest addressed by Norman Mailer in "The Homosexual Villain," a 1954 essay for the inaugural issue of the gay rights magazine *One*. Mailer begins by apologizing for his own homophobic reliance on the type. "I have been as guilty as any contemporary novelist in attributing unpleasant, ridiculous, or sinister connotations to the homosexual (or more accurately, bisexual) characters in my novels." He mentions *Barbary Shore's* Hollingsworth, "whose sadism and slyness were essentially combined with his sexual deviation." He even admits that this bias carried over into private life, since "I always saw [homosexual acquaintances] as at best ludicrous and at worst—the word again—sinister." His attitude changed, he writes, when a gay friend lent him Daniel Webster Cory's *The Homosexual in America*, after reading which he came to appreciate that the homosexual question was essentially political: "[F]or the first time I understood homosexual persecution as a political act and a reactionary act, and I was properly ashamed of myself."[13]

Interestingly, Mailer explains his personal prejudice, which his essay is largely concerned with repudiating, as basically an aesthetic problem: "What I have come to realize is that much of my homosexual prejudice was a servant to my aesthetic needs." As a contribution to literary history, this is the most important facet of Mailer's essay. He does not seek the origin of "the homosexual villain" where we might expect a psychoanalytically minded intellectual of Mailer's generation to look—in the presumptive heterosexual's infantile polymorphous perversity and its attendant mechanisms of neurotic disavowal and phobic compensation—but instead in terms of aesthetic appropriateness: "At the time I wrote those novels [*The Naked and the Dead* and *Barbary Shore*], I was consciously sincere. I did believe—as so many heterosexuals believe—that there was an intrinsic relationship between homosexuality and 'evil,' and it seemed perfectly natural to me, as well as *symbolically* just, to treat the subject in such a way." Further, "the difficulty of finding a character who can serve as one's protagonist is matched only by the difficulty of finding one's villain, and so long as I was able to preserve my prejudices, my literary villains were at hand."[14] In other words, homophobia is explained as a convenient position for the novelist because it facilitates plotting. Aesthetic exigencies are primary.

The homosexual villain—sadistic, sly, sinister—is in part an ambiguous hangover of such queer antiheroes as Dorian Gray. My second chapter glanced at the prosecutor's application of this logic of character to Oscar Wilde himself in the courtroom, while my third looked at William Burroughs's ambivalent inheritance of the evil decadent-dandy in such authorial stand-ins as Kim Carsons. Mailer's identification of the "homosexual villain" as an available novelistic template stops short of parsing the cultural logic—and the literary history—that produces him. The solution lies in the representative strategies deployed by any number of late-Victorian and modernist authors—including, for instance, Wilde and Proust—in depicting homosexuality and its necessary masks in an officially homophobic culture. From Dorian's "strange joys and stranger sins" to the elaborate codes by which the Baron de Charlus communicates his desire to Jupien in *Sodom and Gomorrah,* queerness obtains in the fascinating friction between various masks—some signifying homosexuality to those equipped to read them, others feigning "normalcy" for the larger culture—and the necessarily secret content of what Sedgwick calls "the homosexual topic."

Yukio Mishima's *Confessions of a Mask* is the most sustained treatment in modernism of the problem of the mask; it is the definitive articulation in fiction of the logic of masquerade as it relates both to queerness and to evil. An autobiographical coming-out novel set during the last years of World War II, *Confessions* is very much about Japanese culture in a period of convulsive transition, but its narrator, Kochan, understands his sexual difference in terms of an exclusively Western tradition: his touchstones include St. Sebastian, Stefan Zweig, Proust, the sexologist Hirschfeld, and Michelangelo. For my purposes, I will treat *Confessions* as a kind of theoretical text with relevance to American and English works of fiction in a similar vein; although a work of fiction, its analytic engagement with European sexological literature gives it the clarifying power of theory. Citing Hirschfeld as his authority, Kochan assumes that "the inverted and the sadistic impulses are inextricably entangled with each other";[15] his particular sadism involves elaborate fantasies of sacrificed young men in the postures of St. Sebastian. *Confessions of a Mask* develops what amounts to a full-scale account of the relationship between a sexual orientation (sadistically inflected homosexuality), a formal mode (the masquerade), and a moral category (evil). This theory provides the master key to a broad swath of modernist and postwar literary representation of gay male characters, from Gide's *L'immoraliste* to Proust's Charlus to Mailer's "homosexual villains."

Kochan's awareness of the potency of the mask begins when, as a child, he is caught making himself up with his mother's cosmetics and donning her apparel, in imitation of a well-known actress. "At about this time I was beginning to understand vaguely the mechanism of the fact that what people regarded as a pose on my part was actually an expression of my need to assert my true nature, and that it was precisely what people regarded as my true self which was a masquerade."[16] Kochan's sexuality renders intensely meaningful what for "normal" people is merely a cliché: "Everyone says that life is a stage. But most people do not seem to become obsessed with the idea, at any rate not as early as I did."[17] For Kochan, life's "masquerade" becomes more than a truism: it is the principle by which his world is structured. This has two effects. First, it suggests to Kochan that his own interior life, because it must remain censored, is somehow *more* interior than that of other people; and second, that interiority as such is a species of "evil." "My uneasiness," Kochan says, "was the same as that of which Stefan Zweig speaks when he says that 'what we call evil is the instability inherent in all mankind which drives man outside and beyond himself toward an unfathomable something.'" But "the other boys, having no need for self-awareness, could dispense with introspection."[18] Zweig's "unfathomable something" resonates both with Kochan's erotic desires and with a more generalized death drive ("I found myself deeply immersed in a desire for death. It was in death that I had discovered my real 'life's aim'").[19] For Kochan, erotic fantasies and the death drive are plainly intertwined, as the novel's many scenes of ritualized erotic violence—the material of Kochan's masturbation fantasies—attest. But the core of Kochan's erotic life consists not just of the imagination of violence per se but of the imagination of violent Christian martyrdom. Here is how he thinks about the expulsion from school of one Omi, a handsome roughneck loved by Kochan and admired by the other boys for his elegant toughness and his refusal to follow school rules:

> Upon further thought, however, his "evil" came to have a different meaning for me. I decided that a huge conspiracy into which the demon had driven him . . . was surely all for the sake of some forbidden god. Omi had served that god, had attempted to convert others to his faith, had been betrayed, and then had been executed in secret. One evening at dusk he had been stripped naked and taken to the grove on the hill. There he had been bound to a tree, both hands tied high over his head. The first arrow had pierced the side of his chest; the second, his armpit.[20]

St. Sebastian serves as the compressed, highly aestheticized symbol for all opposition, for every rebel—sinister or beautiful, depending on one's angle of vision—against society. He is the locus of a "conspiracy." He is an icon crucially inflected by sadomasochistic identification. He is "evil," but his evil might be another name for divinity. And he is also a gay villain, whose very spectacularized punishment constitutes a further degree of magnetic villainy. Kochan imagines Omi, and by extension himself, as St. Sebastian because he requires an image of revolt that is also an image of punishment, of mortification. And, paradoxically, the icon of an interiority perceived as richer or deeper than usual—since "other boys could dispense with introspection"—is drawn from the two-dimensional picture plane of an art history book. The complex dialectics of dandiacal decadence traced in my third chapter find neat expression here: psychical recesses are also, somehow, utterly flattened.

Around this image, the core of Kochan's interiority, he constructs what he calls a "machine of falsehood." "All these facts taken together made it difficult for me to know the psychology of any of my schoolmates. . . . my only recourse was to infer from theoretical rules what 'a boy my age' would feel when he was all alone." This formula for Kochan's personality is distinctly psychopathic. Obsessed with "visions reeking with blood," he can only extrapolate "normal" psychology through deduction from observation. Like the clinical psychopath, Kochan's understanding of the psychology of others depends not on empathy but on theory. Here is the kernel of the logic of the homosexual villain: the sexual minority's sense of his own difference within a culture that either reviles or does not recognize him slides into another, more absolute sense of difference, that between normal sociality and the psychopath, who can merely infer but cannot participate in or experience social community. And the exile from community gives rise to images of apocalypse, Kochan's "desire for death"—and not just his own: "I was convinced that I would soon be called into the army and would die in battle, and that my family also would mercifully be killed in the air raids, leaving not a single survivor."[21]

Kochan, in other words, represents the queer subject's embodiment of the death drive. Lee Edelman has identified the dominant culture's figural queering of the death drive at some length; he suggests that this phobic affiliation might be strategically embraced to produce "a queer oppositionality that would oppose itself to the structural determinants of politics as such, which is also to say, that would oppose itself to the logic of opposition."[22] I leave to others a discussion of the political efficacy, or lack thereof, of Edelman's position; for my part, I'm interested in tracing the relationship between the figural abjection of the queer and the psychopath, two varieties of antisocial opposition represented along different but occasionally overlapping lines. Like the gay villain as Mishima presents him, the psychopath, too, is a figure of the death drive; he represents the cancellation of the human and of the world. In Edelman's Lacanian scheme, the queer exerts "a pressure both alien and internal to the logic of the Symbolic": it presents a "negativity opposed to every form of social viability."[23] Edelman finds a compelling allegory for such pure negativity in Hitchcock's eponymous birds, "which could only sound to human ears like the permanent whine of white noise, like the random signals we monitor with radio telescopes trained on space, or perhaps like the electronically engineered sound with which Hitchcock ends *The Birds*."[24] Like Edelman's evocation of the inhuman whine of the birds, the figural burden of the "psychopath" often calls forth visions, chilling but also sublime, of phenomena beyond or without humanity. Such visions of negative sublimity are part of the aesthetic repertoire for the representation of psychopathy and extreme villainy. *The Executioner's Song*, for instance, makes of "the desert, that had no smell at all, but was dry in the nose and left you for dust" a symbol of whatever blankness is inside Gilmore; the desert is the death drive spatialized, just as *The Birds'* "electronically engineered sound" is the death drive auralized.[25]

Dandiacal psychopathy, then, linked to but not identical with gay villainy, involves the paradoxically pleasurable aestheticization of the death drive. "A jubilation can proceed from the consciousness of the desert," Jean-François Lyotard writes in "Sublime Aesthetic of the Contract Killer," which alongside

"Libidinal Economy of the Dandy" constitutes a little-known pair of essays on the French neorealist painter Jacques Monory. Taken together, these essays offer a suggestive theory of the dandy as psychopath—though Lyotard doesn't use that word. I will look at Lyotard's theory of dandiacal aesthetics and capital at greater length below; here I want only to note how his analysis of the dandy can illuminate the gay villain's most threatening association, his link to apocalypse and extinction: Edelman's "no future." "Dandyism," Lyotard writes, "would be [Romanticism's] remedy or its failure: the transformation of this suffering of nostalgia into deliberate destruction, active nihilism."[26] Monory, whose "painting is dandy," employs a monochromaticism "so strong that it destroys the personal identities of objects. . . . Here there is no longer a subject in the world to distinguish objects or traces or atmospheres by their shades. The violence of the charge is such that not only do objects fade away, but also a subject to distinguish them."[27] In such visions of a desubjectivized world, the formal principle of dandiacal flatness is raised to a kind of negative theology. The psychopath doesn't so much stalk this land as give rise to it: it is the fulfillment of his deepest wish. It is the apocalyptic threat he embodies and desires.[28]

Highsmith's Tom Ripley is the summa and autocritique of the homosexual villain. That the Ripley novels flirt with homophobic representations has long presented interpretive difficulties. As Trask puts it, "The pleasure Highsmith takes in stereotype is a feature of her work that readers have found hard to recuperate for a progressive agenda."[29] The problem is not only political but tonal. How should Highsmith's ironies be parsed? Can we find in them an "explor[ation of] cultures of homophobia in the 1950s," as David Greven asserts?[30] For his part, Trask suggests that neither those readings which treat Highsmith as "symptomatic of the Fifties repression of sexual nonconformity" nor those which discover her texts as "queer *avant la lettre*" will do. Instead, Tom's "discovery of the arts of secrecy" produces a "glamorization of the closet"; in the process, Highsmith "severs the association between the closet and queerness while universalizing the link between closeting and desire."[31]

In this regard, Ripley represents a kind of anachronism: he returns the "gay villainy" engendered by a post–Wilde trial but pre-Stonewall culture to the kind of generalized fin de siècle indeterminacy animating the literary 1880s and '90s. In his self-conscious aestheticism, Ripley allies the gay villain to the dandiacal connoisseurship established at the fin de siècle, even as his involvement in the art world—he eventually becomes the mastermind behind a group of forgers—combines criminality and artistic bohemianism. Tom's tendency to compensate for stigmatization with dandiacal elegance is established at the very beginning of the series. Tom remembers his Aunt Dottie's cruelly labeling him a "sissy" as a child: "Tom writhed in his deckchair as he thought of it, but he writhed elegantly, adjusting the crease of his trousers."[32]

To writhe elegantly represents one path for the dandiacal psychopath in an aestheticist key. *The Talented Mr. Ripley* offers an aestheticist *Bildung*. Tom's progress as a psychopathic killer rhymes with his progress as a dandiacal aesthete. When his friend Dickie, whom he will soon murder, shows him his amateurish paintings ("My surrealist effort"), "Tom winced with almost a personal shame. . . . Tom wanted to forget all about the paintings and forget that Dickie painted."[33] From one point of view, Dickie must die because of his embarrassing pretensions to being an artist. As the novel progresses, Tom's increasing confidence in his new identity is registered by his newly certain aesthetic sensibility: "He had given his undivided attention to decorating his house for more than a week. There was a sureness in his taste now that he had not felt in Rome, and that his Rome apartment had not hinted at. He felt surer of himself now in every way."[34] Highsmith establishes the congruence between Ripley's increasing aesthetic sensibilities and the materialism that motivates his various criminal schemes:

> He loved possessions, not masses of them, but a select few that he did not part with. They gave a man self-respect. Not ostentation but quality, and the love that cherished the quality. Possessions reminded him that he existed, and made him enjoy his existence. . . . The money gave him the leisure to see Greece, to collect Etruscan pottery if he wanted to . . . to join art societies if he cared to and to donate to their work. . . . He had just bought a two-volume edition of Malraux's *Psychologie de l'Art* which he was now reading, with great pleasure, in French with the aid of a dictionary.[35]

Toward the beginning of *Ripley Under Ground*, Ripley must pretend to be an artist named Derwatt, who is dead. He puts on a fake beard and does his best *artiste* for a roomful of eager journalists: " 'I have no periods,' Tom said. 'Picasso has periods. . . . That's all right. But by doing this he destroys what might be a genuine—a genuine and integrated personality. What *is* Picasso's personality?"[36] The joke is that Derwatt's allegedly integrated artistic personality is a fraud, since Ripley's art-forging collective has been successfully selling forged Derwatts alongside originals. Ripley's career begins, after all, when he murders Dickie and then briefly assumes his identity—in other words, Ripley himself is less an integrated personality than a man who integrates others into his personality. Extolling the integrated personality while impersonating a dead man might stand as an emblem for the unnerving force of Ripley's character, which consists of an endless succession of masks and assumed roles. Back when Dickie was still alive, Ripley has a premonition of what might be called the metaphysical underpinnings of his psychopathic potentiality. "He stared at Dickie's blue eyes. . . . You were supposed to see the soul through the eyes, to see love through the eyes, the one place you could look at another human being and see what really went on inside, and in Dickie's eyes Tom saw nothing more now than he would have seen if he had looked at the hard, bloodless surface of a mirror."[37] For Tom, the psychopathic cancellation of depths is both affliction and opportunity.

But Tom's reduction to a "hard, bloodless surface" doesn't stop us from liking him. The oddly perverse effect of the Ripliad inheres in how comfortable we become with Ripley in spite of his essential falseness, his lack of not just a moral center but a metaphysical one. Ripley is a screen, yet we learn to find him familiar—until we remember, or are reminded, that he is very foreign indeed. Highsmith's genius was to infect psychopathy with an almost maudlin vulnerability. As Leonard Cassuto observes, "Tom fears being branded a pervert from the first, but he is one. Not the sexual kind, though. Tom is a pervert of sentimentality."[38]

In the Ripliad's penultimate novel, *The Boy Who Followed Ripley* (1980), the queerness Highsmith had carefully suggested from the beginning receives its most explicit treatment—a necessary development in a post-Stonewall culture. This is also, not coincidentally, the novel in which Ripley comes closest to being a hero rather than a villain. Tom has gone to Berlin with a wealthy American teenager, Frank, who over the course of the novel is kidnapped by a gang of ransomers and eventually rescued by Tom. Even before their trip to Berlin, Tom seems to recognize that the city will serve as a site of liberated sexuality. He and Frank visit Berlin's gay bars, in one of which a disco ball entices him: "The rotating grey object, no bigger than a beachball and quite ugly *per se,* looked like a relic of the Thirties, evocative of pre-Hitler Berlin, and strangely fascinating to the eye."[39] Tom wishes he might better fit in:

> "*Hoppla!*" roared another figure in drag into Tom's ears, and Tom realized, almost with a twinge of shame, that it was perhaps because he

looked straight. A miracle they didn't throw him out, and maybe he had Frank to thank for being in. This led to a happier thought: Tom himself was an object of envy for having a nice looking boy of sixteen in his company.[40]

Tom's fascination with appearances continues after Frank is abducted. After hatching a plan to identify the kidnappers by requesting that they appear at a gay bar in order to receive payment—a plan hinging on Tom's reverse gaydar, which will supposedly allow him to identify the heterosexual kidnappers by their distinctly nongay appearance at the bar—he soaks up the atmosphere: "'I love this crazy fantasy here!' Tom said to Eric. He meant the occasional figure in drag, the makeup, the mock flirtations, and the laughter and good humour everywhere. It gave Tom a lift, as *A Midsummer Night's Dream* overture always gave him a lift before he went into battle."[41] The fluid sense of identity accomplished by drag seems magical to Tom—the bar becomes a place of wondrous transformations and appealingly misleading appearances not unlike *Midsummer*'s Fairyland. If Tom has always been a wearer of masks, the gay bar rinses his propensity for duplicity of its sinister aspect, converting it instead to a charming and rather innocent game. Tom decides to have his friends dress him in drag in preparation for their evening of spying at the bar; his *toilette* is accompanied by Lou Reed's "Make Up," about Andy Warhol drag superstar Candy Darling.[42] It is as if the masks, the assumed identities, which have always been the source of Tom's sinister power and strange charisma have here been emptied of their immorality by being brought into the realm of drag and thus overtly queered. Further, Tom in drag—that is, Tom assuming a mask in its specific queerness—is Tom no longer as villain but as hero, since *this* Tom is engaged in the noble work of rescuing a minor from a group of criminals. One can imagine a parallel Ripliad in which, instead of being a serial murderer, Tom is a sort of flamboyant detective, navigating the codes of a queer subculture to do good. Highsmith means to critique the underlying logic of the gay villain from which she admittedly gets so much mileage. Tom's brief career as a gay good guy in *The Boy Who Followed Ripley* exposes this characterology even as it subverts it. Furthermore, the *apartness* effected by psychopathy is canceled in this version of Tom—no longer a loner, he is briefly a member of a queer community.

Tom's involvement with Frank marks his temporary departure from psychopathy, and it culminates in the trauma of Frank's suicide (Frank, it turns out, had been burdened by guilt for patricide), which affects Tom more strongly than anything else in his saga. "Tom thought of ringing [his wife] Heloise, since it would be around nine in the morning there, and didn't. He realized that he was shattered. *Shattered.*"[43] Highsmith's flattened, oddly uninflected prose has a knack for communicating sincerity or straightforwardness alongside a kind of winking, ironic distance; here, the emphasized second "shattered" intensifies our sense of Tom's distress even as it reminds us that there's something a bit rich about a serial killer's grief. Tom soon gets over it, in a sentence typifying the very dry humor that is the Ripliad's default manner: "Only by 9 p.m. the next evening did Tom regain some kind of composure, a sense of returning to himself."[44]

By the next, and final, volume in the series, *Ripley Under Water,* Tom will be happily returned to his old murderous self. When Tom and Heloise, who live in the French countryside, acquire new neighbors in the American Pritchards, we know something is wrong even before we discover that Mr. Pritchard has been tracking Tom's nefarious activities for some time and would like to expose him. How do we know? Because of the Pritchard's poor taste in interior decorating: "Tom's impression of horrid made-yesterday antique was confirmed by the heavy dining-table and the high-backed chairs around it, with seats that looked as uncomfortable as church-pews."[45] The Pritchards' bad taste is not just an indication of their potential danger for Tom, but also—and this is the dandiacal core of the Ripliad, which is above all else a satiric fantasy about the difficult cultivation of taste—a justification for Tom's eventual murder of Mr. Pritchard. "Pritchard wore white shoes with a basket-weave structure that let the air in, the kind of shoes Tom couldn't abide. Funny how everything about Pritchard irked him, even the wristwatch, the stretchable gold-bracelet variety, expensive and flashy. . . . Tom preferred infinitely his conservative Patek Philippe on a brown leather strap, which looked like an antique."[46] Tom identifies himself with "good taste" so intensively that he assumes (correctly, as it turns out) that an ugly raincoat constitutes a passable international disguise: "It was in bad taste, and Tom thought it would help him on entering London—just in case one of the immigration inspectors actually remembered what Thomas Ripley looked like."[47]

What Thomas Ripley "looked like" is a dandy, but behind this pose he looks *like nothing at all*—he is a master of disguises, capable of assuming identities (Dickie Greenleaf's, Derwatt's) with the magical efficacy of the shapeshifter. The default costume for this kind of characterological negativity is the dandy's. In the Ripley novels, the nothingness behind the dandy's mask has its grotesque corollary in the disappearing acts Ripley must impose on his victims—he spends a great deal of time eliminating bodies, an act that often involves literal effacement. There is, for instance, the cremation of Bernard in *Ripley Under Ground*, or the slow disintegration of Murchison's body, immersed in water for years, in *Ripley Under Water*: "Tom thought of the word maceration, the flaking off in layers of the outer skin. Then what? The nibbling of fish? Or wouldn't the current have removed pieces of flesh until nothing but bones were left?"[48]

"Maceration," which means "to soften or break up by soaking in a liquid" but also contains an archaic sense of "to cause to grow thinner or waste away," might be thought of as Tom Ripley's secret truth, the animating principle of the Ripliad. In *Ripley Under Water*, water's cleansing properties are repeatedly invoked, as when Tom, in a hotel on vacation, says, "A bucket of clean water! Not that I'd want to drink it, but to wash with."[49] Or, later, cleaning bloodstains: "A second wash now with warm water and some soap of the kind that made no suds, but was still effective."[50] Water erases crime, removing its stains and, more radically, disintegrating its objects. But it also threatens to erase the whole world. Tom, whose parents drowned, has always feared water, a phobia announced toward the beginning of *The Talented Mr. Ripley*: "It gave Tom a sick, empty feeling at the pit of his stomach to think that in less than a week he would have water below him, miles deep, and that undoubtedly he would have to look at it most of the time, because people on ocean liners spent most of their time on deck. And it was particularly un-chic to be sea-sick, he felt."[51] To be *chic* is to succeed in one's dandyism, but Tom's dandyism is predicated on the elimination of others via bodies of water: Dickie Greenleaf, after all, was murdered in a boat and disposed of in a lake. Water is Tom's element in the same way the desert is Gilmore's—it is the elemental symbol of his hatred of being. Perhaps Tom even drowned his own parents, in an act of primal parricide whose meaning expresses the psychopath's ultimate wish: the desire never to have been born.

Hipsters and Capitalists
"The White Negro" and *The Wild One*

Ripley represents the psychopathic dandy at a crossroads, caught between competing models: the dandy as bohemian, and the dandy as capitalist (his crime, after all, is highly remunerative, permitting him to enjoy a high standard of living and the pleasures of conspicuous consumption). Dandiacal psychopathy takes two forms. First, the Victorian dandy's opposition to bourgeois norms is hyperbolized such that he becomes truly antisocial. This type is often butch, and includes the rebel without a cause, unassimilable but charismatic and compelling, and even, from a certain angle, the locus of just critique. The oppositional bohemian's canon includes macho screen roles like Brando in *The Wild One* or James Dean in *Rebel without a Cause*: putatively straight loners whose sexual energy is powerfully homoerotic, a productive contradiction captured by such queer explorations of the type as Kenneth Anger's *Scorpio Rising*. Such rebels might seem on their surface to have little to do with dandyism classically conceived, but their dependence on a charismatic iconography is profoundly related to the dandy's. As the sociologist Rupert Wilkinson asks, "What, for instance, are we to make of the tough-guy rooster in American history? His showiness brought him close to the tough-guy's antithesis, the dandy."[52]

On the other hand, the commodity cathexis associated with the dandy can render him, in his psychopathic mode, an evil figure of pure capitalism, of unchecked ruthlessness figuring the cruelties of an order that puts profit over people. The first is exemplified by such "hipsters" and rebels as Mailer's "White Negro," Johnny Strabler in Lázsló Benedek's film *The Wild One*, and Randle McMurphy in *One Flew Over the Cuckoo's Nest*; the second is epitomized by Patrick Bateman in *American Psycho*, novel and film. For both the rebel and the capitalist, dynamics of audience investment and identification constitute a primary source of aesthetic force.

Norman Mailer's seminal essay "The White Negro" triangulates the "hipster," the psychopath, and the "Negro" as variously self-conscious representatives of rebellion against an increasingly totalitarian modern order. For Mailer, the "hipster" is a peculiar variation of the psychopath emerging against the background of an unprecedented conformity whose immediate cause is the imaginative havoc wrought by World War II. "The hipster is a psychopath, and yet not a psychopath but the negation of the psychopath for he possesses the narcissistic detachment of the philosopher, that absorption in the recessive nuances of one's own motive which is so alien to the unreasoning drive of the psychopath." Possessed of "hip," or "the sophistication of the wise primitive in a giant jungle,"[53] the hipster is a figure of self-conscious impulsivity, a paradoxical quantity which suggests that hipness (unlike psychopathy proper) can be *cultivated*: it is not a pathology but a social practice.

The hipster is white, but his social style depends on an idea of blackness: "The bohemian and the juvenile delinquent came face-to-face with the Negro, and the hipster was a fact of American life."[54] The "Negro" provides a useful template for the hipster because the fact of his oppression has forced him to develop the kind of self-conscious psychopathy the hipster assumes by choice. (It is worth noting that, pace critics of the ostensive racism of "The White Negro," black psychopathy and physicality are not assumed and naturalized so much as posited and historicized as reaction formations against oppression— and Mailer's quarry is the fantasy of blackness *for whites*, not "blackness" it-self.)[55] Mailer is attentive to the sociology of libidinized racial borrowings in a manner prefiguring Eric Lott's *Love and Theft*, though his essay is less explicit about the class content of the hipster. We can infer that he issues from within a spectrum between working and middle class, the poles of which correspond to the "juvenile delinquent" and the "bohemian," rebels against working- and middle-class culture respectively. An upper-class Mailerian hipster is impossi-ble to imagine, and there is a sense in which the cultural attainments associated with the upper class, like Mailer's own Harvard education, disqualify one from partaking of hip beyond the roles of interpreter or chronicler.[56] This is because a certain inarticulateness always attends hipness. Mailer quotes Caroline Bird to that effect: "The hipster may be a jazz musician; he is rarely an artist, almost never a writer."[57] If the hipster, as I suggest, shares a genealogy with the dandy, the dandy's verbal brilliance survives only very faintly in the hipster as a rather impoverished variation on the "tough talk" discussed in my second chapter.

Lázsló Benedek's biker film *The Wild One* (1953) gives us "The White Negro" *avant la lettre,* right down to the white flirtation with symbolic blackness: the (all-white) biker gang of which Johnny (Marlon Brando) is leader (although throughout he seems curiously outside them, apart) calls itself the BRMC, or Black Rebels' Motorcycle Club, and in one scene members of the club mystify an aging small-town bartender with a rendition of jive talk and newfangled hand gestures. Johnny's tough talk is at once painfully inadequate—the very act of enunciation seems difficult for him—and pragmatically efficacious. The most canonical instance of this efficacy is Johnny's reply to a question asked by one of the local girls, Mildred, "What are you rebelling against?" Johnny, famously: "Whaddaya got?"[58] Like Wilde's epigrams, like Philip Marlowe's best lines, this rejoinder has transcended its dramatic context and entered the culture; in Amanda Anderson's terms, it is successful. Unlike Wilde's and Marlowe's epigrams, though, it is hardly some jewel-like unit of language, some well-wrought barb bespeaking its enunciator's forbidding competence. Indeed, it probably seems wittier in citation than on screen, where Brando's nasal muttering suggests none of the satisfaction of the clever riposte: it is a sullen admission offered more in sadness and resignation than anything else.

Interestingly, though, it is immediately *taken* as wit by Mildred, who, in tones of hilarity, repeats the conversation to Kathie, Johnny's love interest. "I said what are you rebelling against, Johnny? Johnny said, 'What have you got?' What have you got! Isn't that cute?" Kathie only nods, because—we take it—she *understands* Johnny, which in this case means understanding that he's not being witty. This is to say that she understands his psychopathy, although (Mailer's essay not yet having been published) she probably wouldn't have put it that way. She understands that this isn't an act, that Johnny simply can't help it, that far from being fraudulent his posture of rebellion is inadvertent, hapless, probably hopeless. *The Wild One* revels in the conversion of the antisocial personality into the material of romantic fantasy, even as it refuses to fully countenance that conversion. The potential for the romantic elevation of the psychopathological is present even in Lindner's clinical *Rebel without a Cause: The Story of a Criminal Psychopath,* if only in the first half of the title. The "rebel" who emerges in Lindner's case study is a pretty sad character, in and out of jail for petty crimes and impossibly far from heroics or romance. But who can miss the loftier promise of that title? Nicholas Ray couldn't, and his *Rebel without a Cause* (1955) completed the metamorphosis, begun by *The Wild One,* of the psychopath into romantic icon.

This metamorphosis is prefigured in the shift of angles between reading "Whaddaya got?" as the ironically eloquent repartee of the romantic outsider and as the involuntary and rather pathetic expression of isolated antisociality. Mildred and Kathie's incommensurate interpretations point toward a constitutive paradox of the hipster himself, his status as both "psychopath" and "the negation of the psychopath," as Mailer has it. (Even here the distinction is not so cut-and-dried, as Kathie's proper recognition of Johnny's damaged psyche becomes the basis for her erotic interest in him, which she recodes as an investment in his social redemption.) The hipster is a figure of dandyism insofar as his self-conscious summoning of psychopathy involves him in a kind of acting, complete with its own epigrammatic zingers and sartorial iconography.

Bird suggests that though the hipster "may affect a broad-brimmed hat or zoot-suit," he "usually prefers to skulk unremarked." However true this may have been for "actual" hipsters, the hipster could become iconic only because remaining unremarked was the *last* of his goals, as Bird herself seems to recognize when she observes that "James Dean, for one, was a hipster hero."[59] The appearance of Brando's Johnny—with his cocked cap, leather jacket bearing his name, sunglasses—encapsulates the iconography of the hipster, near the historical inception of the phenomenon, with a panache bordering on self-parody.[60]

One Flew Over the Cuckoo's Nest

Ken Kesey's *One Flew Over the Cuckoo's Nest* (1962) is the most explicit literary treatment of the rebel-without-a-cause. Its half-Indian narrator, "Chief" Bromden, cannot finds words sufficient to describe the fascination evoked by Randle McMurphy, a charming clinical psychopath institutionalized for a pattern of offense including statutory rape:

> He's got on work-farm pants and shirt, sunned out till they're the color of watered milk. His face and neck and arms are the color of oxblood leather from working long in the fields. He's got a primer-black motorcycle cap stuck in his hair and a leather jacket over one arm, and he's got on boots gray and dusty and heavy enough to kick a man in two. . . . The way he talks, his wink, his loud talk, his swagger all remind me of a car salesman or a stock auctioneer—or one of those pitchmen you see on a side-show stage, out in front of his flapping banners, standing there in a striped shirt with yellow buttons, drawing the faces off the sawdust like a magnet.[61]

Embarrassing in the worshipful quality of its attention, Bromden's description of McMurphy's masculine charisma checks all the boxes. Like hard-boiled tough guys, McMurphy is a figure of labor, an association which, far from barring him from the pleasures of fashionable costume, instead invests that costume with legitimacy and force. The tokens of this macho fashion—motorcycle cap, leather jacket, boots—were by 1962 already well established by films like *The Wild One*. If the private eye was, as Leslie Fiedler had it, "the cowboy adapted to life on the city streets," the biker-as-outsider would achieve this adaptation without sacrificing a mount.[62]

Despite his infatuation, Bromden may be cannier about the nature of McMurphy's appeal than he at first seems. His likening McMurphy to a car salesman and pitchman underlines the affiliation between popularly conceived personal charisma and advertising. After all, the tough-guy act, with all its obvious oppositional purpose, is nevertheless supremely susceptible to commodification, made up as it is of a collection of fetishized products. (It's no coincidence that the Triumph brand of motorcycles now uses images from *The Wild One*, which featured a Triumph bike, to sell their brand.) Bromden's comparison of McMurphy to a guy with a sales pitch "drawing the faces off the sawdust like a magnet" suggests that personal magnetism as such is figured as the lure of the commodity.

Like Hemingway code heroes and tough-guy private eyes before him, McMurphy's brand of machismo must be set up in opposition to "dandyism" precisely because it shares so much with it. A sartorial iconography, a certain way of talk, a constituted threat to the bourgeois order—all of these suggest the proximity of the spectacularized tough guy ("You're making a spectacle of yourself," Nurse Ratched at one point says to McMurphy, and never spoke truer) to the dandy.[63] The difference is labor. As Bromden says, "[N]ever before now, before he came in, [did we know] the man smell of dust and dirt from the open fields, and sweat, and work."[64] Or, as Nurse Ratched, the figure of matriarchal control, says of a patient with marital difficulties, "He has been heard to say, 'My dear sweet but illiterate wife thinks any word or gesture that does not smack of brickyard brawn and brutality is a word or gesture of weak dandyism.'"[65] In McMurphy's case, and in the case of all such causeless rebels, "brickyard brawn and brutality" constitute not the repudiation of "dandyism" but the conditions of its strategic reclamation.

Kesey presents McMurphy's psychopathy as a kind of harmless, even enviable, constitutional nonconformity, complete with an appealing virility: "[The doctor] told me that 'psychopath' means I fight and fuh—pardon me, ladies—means I am he put it *over*zealous in my sexual relations. Doctor, is that real serious?"[66] If both the clinical and the popular psychopath are, in this period, either excessively or insufficiently heterosexual, there's no doubt about where McMurphy falls, though Kesey is careful to suggest that McMurphy's sexual offenses are, in spite of initial appearances, relatively benign. Nevertheless, he is punished with the asylum's notorious electroshock therapy—"You are strapped to a table, shaped, ironically, like a cross, with a crown of electric sparks in place of thorns"—and, eventually, lobotomy. Like both Christ and the dandy, McMurphy is an emblem of male-male erotic energy, a figure of cathected masculinity whose homoerotic appeal is acknowledged by Bromden in order to repudiate it: "If I was one of these queers I'd want to do other things with him. I just want to touch him because he's who he is."[67] Kesey anticipates a broadly psychoanalytic or erotic interpretation, only to offer in its place the theological register he has been pushing all along. The libidinal and the Christological resonances are enmeshed: Bromden wants to touch, as it were, the hem of McMurphy's garment. That tautological "he's who he is" is a formula for the divine, but it also suggests the admirable self-sufficiency that is the hallmark of the rebel and the dandy.

The novel's denouement, in which Nurse Ratched turns the rest of the men against McMurphy by convincing them that he's only out for money, foregrounds this posture of affective investment and identification by challenging it. Ratched rejects Bromden's and the other inmates' interpretation of McMurphy's character; she observes that, though "he seems to do things without thinking of himself at all, as if he were a martyr or a saint," he nevertheless always makes money. "Would anyone venture that Mr. McMurphy was a saint?" Put this way, the proposition sounds too absurd; the men demur, though Bromden, in his role as narrator, offers the most literal version of faith in McMurphy: "I still had my own notions—how McMurphy was a giant come out of the sky to save us."[68] But the nurse's insinuations are largely successful, as evidenced by the response of Harding, the most intellectual of the inmates: "Let's be honest and give this man his due instead of secretly criticizing his capitalistic talent. What's wrong with him making a little profit?"[69]

McMurphy, as psychopathic rebel, is the consummate outsider: in the archetypal history I am tracing, he synthesizes the traditions of the valorized outlaw with those of the spectacularized dandy. As such, his oppositionality is figured as a force for justice. But another possibility has been lurking all along, a possibility dramatized by the new interpretation with which Nurse Ratched stamps McMurphy toward the novel's close. The psychopath might just be a capitalist, boiled down to his essence.

American Psycho, or *Snooty Baronet* Redux

Bret Easton Ellis's *American Psycho* presents the dandy as the serial-killing apotheosis of all that is ugliest in capitalism. Patrick Bateman is not a force of antisocial opposition but rather of antisocial celebration, and his amoral cathexis of commodity consumption—Lord Wotton's appreciation of objets d'art raised to a hellish power—is the sign not of the outsider status of even the most aristocratic of his dandiacal predecessors but rather of his absolute *insiderness*: he is late capitalism's animating demon.

And like Pound's Mauberley, he is a creature of masks. A latter-day dandy-aesthete and Wall Street executive who, like the aristocratic dandy proper, seems never to have to actually work, Bateman puts it this way: "Surface, surface, surface was all that anyone found meaning in."[70] *American Psycho* works out the problem of masquerade under the aesthetic sign of a postmodern emphasis on surfaces. Ellis explores flatness—for the postmodern dandy, both an aesthetic and a metaphysical category—as a question of both style and theme. Mary Harron's film version (2000) is particularly keen on translating this flatness into a visual language, a transposition that feels especially appropriate, as if film were the book's ur-medium, and Harron's movie less an adaptation than the excavation of an original. And perhaps, in a sense, it is. In a *New York Times* review of Joan Didion's novel *Democracy* (1984), Mary McCarthy ambivalently suggests that "one way of looking at [that novel] is to decide that it has been influenced by movies; hypnotized by movies would be more appropriate."[71] Ellis, who has called Didion his greatest influence, announces his own novel's movie-hypnotized status early on, with such film-saturated sentences as "Pan down to the *Post*," "Like in a movie another bus appears," "A slow dissolve and Price is bounding up the steps."[72] In other words, the management of novel time is effected in the technical language of the movies. Some current European editions of the book (though not, as far as I can discover, American ones) feature Christian Bale, the star of the movie, on the cover; rarely has this kind of tie-in felt so right.

American Psycho demonstrates the passage from a modernist aesthetic of externality to a postmodern aesthetic of surfaces in which, as Fredric Jameson puts it, "depth is replaced by surface, or by multiple surfaces."[73] In *American Psycho* the aestheticist cult of surfaces becomes terrifyingly all-encompassing. Ellis returns the aestheticist interest in objects to the realm of commodity consumption—his is a doubly fin de siècle text, its critique of capitalism at the end of the twentieth century echoing the preoccupation with fine commodities and objets d'art marking one strain of aestheticism at the end of the nineteenth.[74] Here is a representative passage, in which Bateman immerses himself in the offerings of Bloomingdale's:

. . . vases and felt fedoras with feather headbands and alligator toiletry cases with gilt-silver bottles and brushes and shoe-horns that cost two hundred dollars and candlesticks and pillow covers and gloves and slippers and powder puffs and hand-knitted cotton snowflake sweaters and leather skates and Porsche-design ski goggles and antique apothecary bottles and diamond earrings and silk ties and boots and perfume bottles and diamond earrings and boots and vodka glasses and card cases and cameras and mahogany servers and scarves and aftershaves and photo albums and salt and pepper shakers and ceramic-toaster cookie jars and two-hundred-dollar shoehorns and backpacks and aluminum lunch pails and pillow covers . . .[75]

As Ellis's ellipses on either side of this litany indicate, such lists of consumer goods are potentially infinite and can, when enumerated at length, shed their local significance in favor of a kind of massive, mute meaninglessness. In *American Psycho,* Ellis takes one prominent topos of the nineteenth-century aestheticist novel—"reminiscent," as Rita Felski observes, "of nothing other than the lavish prose of a consumer catalog"[76]—to its formal limit. Like actual advertisements, you can't miss the point of *American Psycho*: it repeats its central motifs so exhaustively as to abandon the conventions of the novel in favor of those (accretion, repetition, enumeration) of the catalog, a tendency Ellis crystallizes with section headings like "Shopping": "I move like a zombie toward Bloomingdales . . ."[77]

American Psycho is notorious not for its catalog prose but for its scenes of serial murder, in which Bateman rapes, tortures, and dismembers innumerable victims, largely but not exclusively women. The alternation of these nearly unreadable scenes of violence with scenes of high-end consumption—fine dining, expensive drug taking, shopping at Bloomingdale's—suggests, all too readily, that Ellis intends a satirical critique of New York City's Wall Street overclass for its ruthlessness and exploitation, its misogyny and contempt for the poor. But what if, rather than shoehorn *American Psycho* into a glaringly obvious critique of consumerism and ruling-class privilege, we read it for its aesthetic stakes? Freed of the need either to endorse Ellis's bloody satire as a necessarily extreme reaction to increasingly intolerable conditions of capitalism or to dismiss it as banal, half-baked, and boring, we will discover *American Psycho* pushing to the point of crisis an aesthetic and formal tendency occupying one strain of serious fiction from modernism through the *nouveau roman* and beyond: the purgation (or the fantasy of the purgation) of human subjectivity and its attendant representational modes from the novel. This tendency has its emblems and its thematic preoccupations, of which aestheticized commodity fetishism is the best recognized. Psychopathy, less familiar, is another. Both meet up in the figure of the dandy, for is not Dorian Gray himself, murderer, the aestheticist psychopath at something like the beginning of the tradition?[78]

There are, moreover, suggestive connections between the postmodern flatness associated with the seventies, eighties, and nineties and the macho modernism of Lewis and Pound, itself strongly predicated on the aestheticism it often purported to repudiate. *American Psycho* has been interpreted under the sign of "hyperreality," Jean Baudrillard's characterization of a postmodernity marked by the autonomy of images and the signifier from any "reality" they were once thought to represent.[79] Such a flattening of the world to images recalls Wyndham Lewis's Snooty Baronet, whose emphasis on "looking" is an exemplary instance of the belief in the "superiority of the eye" that, according to Vincent Sherry, distinguishes the "radical modernism" of Lewis, Pound, and Hulme from other developments of the period.[80] This hypervisuality, which Lewis associated with a hard-minded seriousness opposed to the popular and the commoditizable, finds one paradoxical culmination in a leveling postmodern aesthetics associated not just with the commodity but with visual pornography, a genre in which, as Snooty Baronet has it, "that word *looked*, that was for me *everything*."

Like *Snooty Baronet* before it, *American Psycho* understands the tendency to objectification as a property of the psychopathic protagonist. In these novels, commodity fetishism and psychopathy join forces, working together to produce a universe of objects without subjects. As Baudrillard has it, "dandyism" is "nihilism" in its nineteenth-century guise—we might think of Dorian Gray, but also of Snooty's advertising puppet, "a little dandyish"—while, by the end of the twentieth century, we are left with only "desertlike, aleatory, and indifferent form."[81] As Bateman puts it late in *American Psycho*, "[W]here there was nature and earth, life and water, I saw a desert landscape that was unending ... so devoid of reason and light and spirit that the mind could not grasp it on any sort of conscious level."[82] This figurative desertification is psychopathy's master trope; it is no coincidence that Snooty murders Humph in an actual desert.[83] Like Snooty Baronet, Patrick Bateman is a psychopathic object—capable of action but with no "insides." Like Wyndham Lewis, Bret Easton Ellis uses the character of the psychopath to interrogate an aesthetic he had previously exploited (in *Less Than Zero* [1985] and *The Rules of Attraction* [1987]) and to which he remains attracted—a disillusioned minimalism best described by the vernacular label "cool," a postmodern American variant on Burstein's "cold modernism," opposite and challenge to that "hot modernism" for which "subjectivity" is "bedrock."[84] Like Snooty, Bateman is a characterological experiment by which Ellis tests and critiques his own aesthetic habits.

In *American Psycho*, then, an aestheticist tradition in which objects are cathected according to the logic of the catalog runs headlong into what Francis Ferguson has called its "account of the pornographic as part of a representational strategy."[85] Bateman converts women into objects via the medium of the camera: "As usual, in an attempt to understand these girls I'm filming their deaths. With Torri and Tiffany I use a Minox LX ultra-miniature camera that takes 9.5mm film, has a 15mm f/3.5 lens, an exposure meter and a built-in neutral density filter and sits on a tripod."[86] Bateman's dwelling on these detailed technical specs ushers his victims into the representational sphere of the devices filming them: they are less corpses in a private snuff catalog than objects on the level of the camera itself. We might as well be reading *Popular Photography* or *Gear: Camera Magazine*. This is the core of hyperrealism's pornographic deflation, in which reality is reduced to its media of representation.

Snooty Baronet, too, converts women into objects, but according to the pattern of Lewis's mechanized aestheticism, a mode of objectification that would have to wait until later in the century to find its genuinely pornographic corollary (although we might think here of the sexy female robot in Fritz Lang's 1927 *Metropolis* as a precocious instance of the meeting of the mechanical and the pornographic). In what has to be the oddest sex scene in modern literature, Snooty here seduces his sometime girlfriend, Val:

> She grappled with me at once, before the words were well out of my mouth, with the self-conscious gusto of a Chatterley-taught expert. But as I spoke I went to meet her—as I started my mechanical leg giving out an ominous creak (I had omitted to oil it, like watches and clocks these things require lubrication). I seized her stiffly round her body. All of her still passably lissom person—on the slight side—gave . . . It fled into the hard argument of my muscular pressures. Her waist broke off and vanished into me as I took her over in waspish segments, an upper and a nether.[87]

Here, Snooty Baronet, psychopathic object—more machine than man—counters Val's earthy Lawrentian eros, her "Chatterley-taught" "gusto," with his own creaking, inhuman mechanism. The passage describes an erotic conversion: an object himself, Snooty turns Val into an entity similarly objective: her "lissom," that is to say still *human*, "person" is "taken over" by Snooty, turned into a "waspish" carapace. As Burstein observes, Snooty's prosthetic leg "has the effect of rendering mechanic even those fleshier bits" of both his own and Val's bodies.[88] If Tarr prefers the outside of things, the "armoured hide . . . turtle's shell, feathers or machinery" to messy interiors, Snooty actively converts his lover *into* a shell. This is, as yet, far less sinister than *American Psycho*— Snooty never kills Val—but in having Snooty turn murderer at the novel's end, Lewis prefigures Ellis in tethering an objectifying aesthetic mode to the actions of the psychopath.

Indeed, *American Psycho* can help us to recognize retrospectively *Snooty Baronet*'s own interest in aestheticism as proper to the commodity, and the proximity of the consumer catalog to the aestheticist novel discussed by Felski can tell us something about Lewis's modernist avant-garde. Sianne Ngai has suggested that a modernist tradition including Gertrude Stein is invested in an aesthetic of "cuteness," grounded in a certain relation to the commodity, in which "things can be personified" (for instance, Stein's "tender buttons").[89] This tradition stands in ostensible opposition to that Hulmean and Lewisian "antisentimental avant-garde . . . conventionally imagined as hard and cutting edge"; it is instead an aesthetic of "familiar 'small things.'"[90] But the emphasis on "smallness" can make the "antisentimental avant-garde"—which, after all, is marked by the beauty Hulme finds in "small, dry things"—look rather closer to the "cute" than it might at first appear. Snooty's encounter with the puppet, who, pushing his wares in a shopwindow, is a literal agent of the commodity, confirms Ngai's insight regarding cuteness—"if things can be personified, persons can be made things"[91]—while expanding its range of applicability. For Ngai, the cute object, by projecting powerlessness, invites fantasies of its own annihilation, an effect not without consequence in novels of psychopathy, in which the conversion of subjects to objects entails their destruction.

As a late inheritor of Snooty's psychopathic objectification of himself and others, Bateman's willingness to murder is the result of an aesthetic commitment to externality. Just as Snooty comes to doubt his subjectivity after encountering a "hatter's automaton," so Bateman wonders, "If I were an actual automaton what difference would there really be?"[92] As Ferguson puts it, "The interesting feature of *American Psycho* is that Bateman doesn't just objectify his sexual victims; he also objectifies himself"; furthermore, "his victims are those who are described as having interiors."[93] It is as if Bateman's crimes put into practice Tarr's opposition to "the naked pulsing inside of life." And as in macho modernism proper, the phallus provides an aesthetic principle. As Namwali Serpell writes, *American Psycho* "is hard, shiny, brittle. Instead of softness and flaccidity, we are in a world of hardbodies, sharp knives, and Patrick Bateman's erect phallus."[94] Ellis and Lewis alike felt that the requirements of the psychological novel were illegitimate or irrelevant, but the cost of this renunciation is registered in the appearance—one might, in a psychoanalytic mood, call it symptomatic—of the psychopath as the sort of character uniquely appropriate to the novel of antihumanist objectivity. This is not an influence claim—I doubt Ellis has read much Lewis—but rather a demonstration of Lewis's prescience. Lewis, as Edwards puts it, "discovers (sometimes in desperation) the conditions that are a presupposition of Post-modernism."[95]

What Bateman, in both book and film, later calls a "mask of sanity" hiding "nightly bloodlust" exhibits more than a passing resemblance to the situation of Mishima's Kochan, though any specifically queer content has been evacuated or reduced to a trace, namely Bateman's homophobia, which we are welcome to read either psychoanalytically (i.e., Bateman's phobic compensation for his own homoerotic impulses) or as an arrow in the narrative's socio-critical quiver (i.e., Bateman is just a murderous intensification of the evil impulses of the patriarchal overclass, already replete with misogyny, homophobia, contempt for the poor, and so on). In other words, *American Psycho*, as Norman Mailer observed in his ambivalent and perceptive *Vanity Fair* review, is a novel with a "thesis"—"the eighties were spiritually disgusting"[96]—and it develops this thesis not by the progress of argument but by blunt accretion and by the grisly shock tactics of its scenes of violence, scenes comically juxtaposed with the shiniest markers of late-capitalist refinement. Standing in front of a Paul Smith store and spooked by a passing gay pride parade, Bateman "sprinted over to Sixth Avenue, decided to be late for the office and took a cab back to my apartment where I put on a new suit (by Cerruti 1881), gave myself a pedicure and tortured to death a small dog I had bought earlier this week in a pet store on Lexington."[97] Frozen with "a certain traumatized fascination," Bateman is sandwiched between the markers of high-end consumption *American Psycho* enumerates at such tedious length—here, the Paul Smith store—and the politically powerful spectacle of the Pride Parade, to which he responds with a distaste he knows quite well to be phobically excessive. Ellis is satirizing the hypermasculine yuppie's fear that the patterns of refined consumption marking his class dominance will indeed render him, as Bateman's friend calls him, a "decadent faggot."[98]

But readings of *American Psycho* as satire are too anxious to suppress the injunction to identification that is a hallmark of the novel of dandyism. As Serpell puts it, "To make violence aesthetically potent . . . is to make it flat but it is also to make it seductive."[99] The representation of the "spiritually disgusting" has its own aesthetic seductions, toxic lures to identification recognized, however unsubtly, by the outraged feminist response (from the National Organization for Women and others) that met the book's publication.[100] The standard rejoinder to such outrage is to assert that since *American Psycho* is obviously satire, its representations of pornographic violence are in the service of its critique. However true that may be, it will not do to erase Ellis's invitation to identify with Bateman from an account of how *American Psycho* works. In this respect, the novel's early feminist critics were on to something important. Like all dandy heroes, Bateman is a figure of *taste,* and taste is something everyone wants to have. In *American Psycho,* the dandy's curation of objets d'art has taken the sinister turn latent in aestheticism from as early as De Quincey's "On Murder as One of the Fine Arts." As Seltzer puts it, "The question of serial killing cannot be separated from the general forms of seriality, collection, and counting conspicuous in consumer society . . . and the forms of fetishism—the collecting of representations, persons, and person-like bodies—that traverse it."[101] *American Psycho*'s dandyism underscores the continuity between this macabre seriality and the exercise of connoisscurship, of taste.

We should not, in other words, underestimate Patrick Bateman's coercive appeal. Blakey Vermeule has discussed the centrality of "Machiavellian" figures to novel history—she understands the term in its cognitive-science acceptation (which is also its popular one) to refer to characters with a high capacity for "cunning," requiring that they be especially good at reading other people. Examples include Satan, Robert Lovelace, Gilbert Osmond, and Humbert Humbert.[102] In the case of *American Psycho,* Vermeule finds Bateman "obliterating the thin line dividing high Machiavellianism from sociopathy."[103] Machiavellian characters are always villains, but they are villains who—like Satan, Lovelace, and Humbert Humbert—seduce one into complicity by the force of their language. But unlike Satan, Lovelace, or Humbert Humbert, Bateman is not a high rhetorician. How, then, does Ellis's seductiveness work? What *American Psycho* achieves is a kind of canniness, an unsettling precision of discernment, about some of the imaginative effects of consumer culture, including the coercive force by which the possessions of the materially successful elicit a fantasy identification with the possessor—or, more radically and as is perhaps the case in *American Psycho,* with the objects themselves. In his *Why We Love Sociopaths* (2012), his study of the sociopathic hero who has dominated television for the last decade (from *The Sopranos* to *Breaking Bad*), Adam Kotsko suggests that rich sociopathic characters effect, in their audience, an uneasy movement from "'I hate that guy' to 'I wish I were that guy.'"[104] *American Psycho* coerces a similar response from its readers—the enforced, or involuntary, identification with power and its trappings—but it does so at a much more intimate level precisely because it is always hectoring us *not* to identify; its scenarios of violence are like formalized prohibitions on identification. The queasiness inspired by *American Psycho* results from the failure of its glaringly obvious critical stance to prevent the reader from forming a fantasy attachment to Patrick Bateman and his opulent lifestyle. As Ngai puts it, "It is difficult to critique the fetishism of commodities . . . without somehow entering into its logic."[105]

Put a different way, the persistence of this identificatory spur is the most nuanced thing about Ellis's critique—it is the privilege of his enormous cynicism to understand that no intensity of satire can rinse the magical luxury he describes of its allure. Ellis doesn't even need to describe a "real" highlife, as when he parodies high-end foodie culture in a way that ought to cancel its appeal: "For dinner I order the shad-roe ravioli with apple compote as an appetizer and the meat loaf with chèvre and quail-stock sauce for an entrée. She orders the red snapper with violets and pine nuts and for an appetizer peanut butter soup with smoked duck and mashed squash which sounds strange but is actually quite good."[106] The deep perversity of *American Psycho* is that the excessiveness of its critique makes identification obviously inappropriate, so that, when it surfaces anyway, it does so with redoubled fury and a very bad odor. This is true, perhaps, of many satires against materialism and consumerism—it is partially true of Martin Amis's *Money* (1984), for instance—but *American Psycho*'s achievement is to bring both the revulsion against materialism and the guilty seduction by it to a peculiarly extreme pitch. We are in the realm of what Lyotard calls "magazine time," a frozen expanse of libidinally saturated commodity fetishism whose function "is that of suspending the enjoyment, containing the expiring—not of taking, but of contact.["107] This is a version of what Lyotard calls the "consciousness of the desert"[108] of nihilistic psychopathic fantasy, and at its center is the commodity.

Lyotard's theory of hyperrealist painting—painting that imitates photography—as a dandiacal aesthetic mode can elucidate the formal nature of *American Psycho*'s queasy seductiveness, and clarify those of its effects remaining unaccounted for by the label "satire." For Bateman, sex as such is pornographic ("Sex happens: a hardcore montage"). Martin Weinreich has coordinated Bateman's equation of sex and pornography with Baudrillard's characterization of pornography as "the hypersexuality contemporaneous with the hyperreal," which Weinreich understands as "the effect of a total visualization of everyday life under the sign of the commodity."[109] Lyotard, likewise, understands "hyperrealism" in the visual arts as "an art of *catalogues*: objects exhibited to arouse and suspend the desire to take them, the drive to acquisition"; he sees in this tendency a "*dandyism*, the bringing to light, a century after Baudelaire and Constantin Guys, of that style of 'modernity' presaged in [Baudelaire's 1868] *L'Art romantique*."[110] Lyotard calls this temporal suspension "magazine time" and "blue time," the libidinal structure of which is frozen, permanently dilating, or precipitately arrested orgasm: "Blue time begins as it ends, discontinuous, abrupt; to open it you would have to imagine an erection as sudden as the ejaculation which closes it. . . . Immobilisation leads to nothing, except death."[111] Transposing this account to *American Psycho*, we can read Bateman as a "*dandy monster*" (as Lyotard calls Baudelaire)[112] in a hyperrealist key—he is an aestheticist psychopath, a serial murderer whose world is structured like a catalog offering up objects for sexual delectation and sacrifice.

The aesthetic effect of "hyperrealism"—a category that can productively be transposed from painting to the novel in the case of *American Psycho*—is a twinned and contradictory impression of reality and "de-reality": "Reality because reiteration. But de-reality because loss of anchoring . . . dissolution of exteriority inside a *process of exteriorization*." At its root this paradoxical aesthetic, which "represents representation" and in the process withholds the pleasures and convictions of "illusionist realism," is a question of "[f]etishisation, which is what representation becomes in capitalism."[113] But this is a radical fetishization that, instead of grounding the subject (as it does, however tenuously, in Freudian and post-Freudian traditions) undoes it altogether:

This fissured art makes us see what is called consumption, etc., and what is probably as yet only a nostalgic way of situating the problem of the object today. Consuming is just this constraint, this set-up imposed on the flows of libidinal energy, of having to be discharged exclusively according to the channels of law and value. I say that it is still romantic to speak of consumption because it is speaking of a place where this discharge might happen in a way that was *authentic, originary, "specific"* (in the sense in which Freud speaks of the specific action), a place of innate or natural complicity between desire and its object. Obviously, there is no such place, it is there as counterpoint and exteriority *within the system*, which instead brings about the emergence of the anti-romantic ("modern," postmodern) theme of the (absolutely compelling) modalities of discharge.[114]

The replacement of a "natural complicity between desire and its object" with mere "modalities of discharge" suggests that a certain libidinal circuit (desire, acquisition, satisfaction) has been shorted, supplanted instead by a kind of libidinal economy whose basic unit is not subject-object but, as in the world of Snooty Baronet, object-object, although—and here is a crucial difference between modernist "hardness" and postmodern "flatness"—the objects themselves become unreal, existing only on the plane of representation. Lyotard writes of one of Monory's works, "The 'objectivity' of this painting is disobjectification and desubjectification, the two of them going together as effects of capitalist production."[115] In *American Psycho* this is the dandiacal cult of surfaces, which was always also a cult of the consumer good, raised to a terrifying metaphysical principle.

Patrick Bateman translates the monstrous dandyism Lyotard finds in Baudelaire into the idiom of hyperrealism. The entire history of decadent dandyism has involved the negotiation of a dialectic between pathologized depths on the one hand and polished surfaces on the other, but hyperrealism reduces the "depths" term to a ghostly trace; "surface, surface, surface" is all that remains. Just as Burroughs, in what I referred to as his "pop" Westerns, pastiches genre to write a kind of melancholy cartoon the canceled history of which is the psychological novel, the pornographic logic of *American Psycho* cannot but eschew the potentialities of the traditional novel. *American Psycho*'s "account of the pornographic" involves not just the systematic transformation of subjects into objects and of insides into outsides but the recognition that a world thus flattened can be pleasurable.[116]

American Psycho demonstrates the long reach of dandyism's aesthetic effects. Even at his worst, the dandy is a figure of ambivalent identification—there are insistent continuities between the ideas of Snooty and Bateman on the one hand and the ideas of their authors on the other, and in both cases the characters themselves exert a pull on the reader that is at odds with the repellence of their behavior and ideas. In these novels, the seductions of the dandy and the seductions of aesthetic abstraction merge completely. The pleasure of identification with the cathected materialism of the psychopathic object can shed light on what, beyond or besides its eventual affiliation with fascism, has always made the macho modernism of the *BLAST* crew disturbing. Inheriting the mantle of Lewisian externality, Williams's "No ideas but in things" was a productive mantra, but as Snooty Baronet demonstrates, it had its risks. Patrick Bateman, too, has "no ideas but in things," the commodities and corpses of which his world consists, tokens of total desubjectification. One of the pleasures of abstraction—particularly the still part-figural abstraction at which Lewis excelled in painting—has always been its promise that the body might become an object or a machine, like Bateman's victims, or indeed Bateman himself, reduced to—or glorified by—their conversion into not inert flesh but gadgetry, on display in a high-end shop window, talked up by a puppet.[117]

The End: *A Clockwork Orange* and the Psychopathic Christ Dandy

In his film adaptation of Anthony Burgess's *A Clockwork Orange*, Stanley Kubrick capitalizes brilliantly on the implicit dandyism of the story's antihero, the murderous young Alex. Malcolm McDowell's futuristic dandy styling—fake eyelashes, all-white suit, suspenders and cane—became as iconic as Brando's outfit in *The Wild One*. As Berthold Schoene-Harwood observes, "Alex and his droogs are typical representatives of the in-vogue fantasy of young male rebellion against conformity . . . inscribed in mainstream culture by Hollywood movies celebrating the impetuous individualism of iconic vanguard figures like, for example, James Dean and Marlon Brando."[118] Kubrick's emphasis on Alex's appearance takes its cue from the novel, in which Alex regularly reiterates that he and his "droogs" "were dressed in the heighth of fashion."[119] For Alex, dandyism and physical viciousness go hand in hand, as his contempt for his sloppy comrade Dim attests: "I didn't like the look of Dim; he looked dirty and untidy, like a veck who'd been in a fight, which he had been, of course, but you should never *look* as though you had been."[120] Alex's ideal of dandiacal continence rhymes with the self-assurance of the private eye and with the aristocratic reserve of the Hemingway code hero.

During his imprisonment for murder, Alex is given a copy of the New Testament by a kindly prison chaplain; he happily imagines himself joining in with the Roman police: "So I read all about the scourging and the crowning with thorns and then the cross veshch and all that cal, and I viddied better that there was something in it. . . . I closed my glazzies [eyes] and viddied myself helping in and even taking charge of the tolchocking [beating] and the nailing in, being dressed in like a toga that was the heighth of Roman fashion." But Alex's identification with Christ's tormentors shouldn't mask his identification with Christ's torments, an underlying masochism typical, as we have seen, of psychopaths in both clinical and imaginative literature. Like Christ, Alex was "never . . . much of one for following the law," as his father says.[121] And like Christ, Alex will be singularly sacrificed to preserve the system he threatens.

Unlike other fictional psychopaths of the period, though, like *Cuckoo's* McMurphy, Alex's refusal to play by the rules of society seems genuinely evil; it is far less susceptible to being rescued by a countercultural interpretive frame that reads it as the expression of justified resistance to an oppressive society. An unrepentant murderer and rapist, Alex's crimes are gratuitous and brutal. Burgess does have Alex allude to the possibility that his criminal violence has a redemptive aspect, though chiefly in order to repudiate this line of thought. Like *1984*, *A Clockwork Orange* is set in a Sovietized near future in which totalitarian modernity has usurped the prerogatives of the liberal subject. "And is not our modern history, my brothers," Alex asks, "the story of brave malenky selves fighting those big machines? I am serious with you, brothers, over this. But what I do I do because I like to do."[122] Even as he raises the possibility that his behavior contains the seeds of justified revolt, he insists that, for him, evil is its own gratification.

While this brief gesture underscores Alex's continuity with the psychopathic Christ figure as exemplified in *Cuckoo*, Burgess's vision is darker. If Christ is a figure of oppositional goodness at utter odds with the evils of this world, Alex is Christ's counterimage. Like Christ's, Alex's opposition entails the apocalyptic cancellation of the world. During his time in prison, one of the effects of Alex's psychological reprogramming is that he can no longer listen happily to the classical music he loves; he finds it physically painful. He is eventually able to reverse this effect, regaining access to his sustaining kernel—a nihilistic scene of apocalypse in which he is the gleeful agent of the world's destruction: "Oh, it was gorgeosity and yumyumyum. When it came to the Scherzo I could viddy myself running and running on like very light and mysterious nagas [feet], carving the whole litso [face] of the creeching world with my cut-throat briva [knife]."[123] This is the *echt* psychopath's hatred of the world as it exists, a hatred here cast as an aesthetic modality, a way of responding to art.

In extremely condensed form, Burgess's characterization of Alex and his droogs summons up the dandy's history as viewed in its broadest frame: as the final transmutation of a series of types beginning with the early modern libertine, progressing to the eighteenth-century rake, and eventuating in the dandy of modernism and beyond. Pejorative conceptions of "libertinism" in the seventeenth century transformed Hobbesian materialism and freethinking into a "libertine disorder" threatening "obscenity, drunkenness, swearing, promiscuity, and irreligion."[124] Burgess attaches libertinism's "recommend[ation] . . . that life give way to death as quickly as it can" to dandyism's valorization of aesthetic experience.[125]

The perverse twist by which high aesthetic experience might constitute the soundtrack of destruction is one of *A Clockwork Orange*'s central gimmicks, its impact no doubt conditioned by the (still-current) clichés about the Nazis listening to Mozart while committing mass murder. But Burgess intended a far deeper perversity, namely, that psychopathy itself should be aligned with Christian moral choice. The book's "moral lesson," Burgess writes, "is the weary traditional one of the fundamental importance of moral choice."[126] Famously, the novel opposes techniques of behavioral conditioning that would eliminate free will. It insists on this lesson, though, by making Alex at his most psychopathically nihilistic—"carving the whole litso of the screeching world"— identical with the free subject. The formula is familiar enough, but its extreme expression somehow unbalances its logic. Only Christ, and perhaps Milton's Satan (an avatar of libertinism), are free to oppose the world as radically as the psychopath in the throes of his hatred.

Is Alex a figure on the scale of Christ or Satan? Or is he a humbler kind of novelistic personage? This is finally an impasse for *Clockwork*, which Burgess resolves by disaffiliating Alex from Christ/Antichrist and placing him, as he says, in the realm of "genuine fiction," in which change is possible: "When a fictional work fails to show change, when it merely indicates that human character is set, stony, unregenerable, then you are out of the field of the novel and into that of the fable or the allegory."[127] (This "change" appeared originally only in the twenty-one-chapter English version of the novel, in which Alex begins to reform; in the twenty-chapter American version, Alex remains un-regenerate.) No matter that *A Clockwork Orange* hardly presents a convincing instance of the kind of interior transformation marking the English psycho-logical novel from Richardson through, say, Elizabeth Bowen—its twenty-one-chapter version is as much a "fable or allegory" as the version shorn of the final chapter, and the change it tracks has little in common with the "realist" novel typically conceived. The point is that Burgess's didactic moral purpose required that the novel end by emphasizing those aspects of Alex's character that are less sublimely, or terrifying, absolute. Alex must become a mere juve-nile delinquent, thereby susceptible to moral change, rather than a principle of destruction and opposition.

Alex begins to undergo his moral revolution when, back on the streets, he experiences less zest for the old ultraviolence than before. He begins, unac-countably, to carry around a photograph of a baby: "It was of a baby gurgling goo goo goo . . . its flesh was like in all folds with being a very fat baby." When his friends nearly discover his secret, "I had to snarl at them and I grabbed the photo and tore it up into tiny teeny pieces and let it fall like a bit of snow on to the floor."[128] Alex must not betray to his old droogs that he no longer stands on the side of destruction—that he is ready to enlist in what Edelman calls "the cult of the Child."[129]

In other words, Alex's redemption is marked and catalyzed by the ideo-logically pregnant signifiers of heterosexual reproduction, what Edelman calls "pronatalism," and as such he is, before his reformation, proximate to the gay villain. "There was something happening inside me," Alex says; when he runs into a newly married friend, it's clear what that "something" is: "Wife wife wife? Ah no, that cannot be. Too young art thou to be married, old droog. Impossible impossible." Marriage and reproduction represent the magic road away from psychopathic oppositionality: "I kept viddying like visions. . . . For in that other room in a cot was laying gurgling goo goo goo my son. Yes yes yes, brothers, my son. And now I felt this bolshy big hollow inside my plot, feeling very surprised too at myself. I knew what was happening, O my brothers. I was like growing up."[130] This sentimentalized instance of pronatal ideology is the agent of maturation and whatever psychological "transformation" *A Clockwork Orange* tracks.

Burgess, it seems, is aware that this sentimental journey might ring false, and it's possible to read it as parody ("I knew what was happening, O my brothers. I was like growing up"). The novel's final passages execute a dizzying blend of parody and didactic sincerity, in which the optimistic message of redemption-by-reproduction is presented alongside or within a comically grim meditation on the cyclical violence of successive generations:

> My son, my son. When I had my son I would explain all [my past misdeeds] to him when he was starry enough to like understand. But then I knew he would not understand or would not want to understand at all and would do all the veshches I had done, yes perhaps even killing some poor starry forella [lady] surrounded with mewing kots and koshkas [cats and kittens], and I would not be able to really stop him. And nor would he be able to stop his own son, brothers. And so it would itty on to like the end of the world, round and round and round, like some bolshy gigantic like chelloveck, like old Bog Himself [God] . . . turning and turning a vonny grazhany orange in his gigantic rookers.
>
> But first of all, brothers, there was this veshch of finding some devotchka [girl] or other who would be a mother to this son. I would have to start on that tomorrow, I kept thinking. That was something like new to do. That was something I would have to get started on, a new like chapter beginning.[131]

This is hardly a redemptive vision; even if Alex is reformed—even if, via the magical moral agency of ideologically sanctioned sexual reproduction, he has "chosen" good—each new generation's violence will "itty on to like the end of the world." And this vision, in its pointless repetition not unlike the activity of "Bog Himself," represents *Clockwork's* rueful return to the register of the nihilistic sublime of the "old ultraviolence": the scarring of the very face of the world to the strains of Beethoven. This is what Lisa O'Connell calls libertinism's "paradoxically lively sense of an existential void."[132] This is the territory of Antichrist, or Satan, or "Bog"—not of the human-scaled moral transformations of didactic realism. A "new like chapter beginning" can only sound parodic or bathetic, here. So what if Alex is no longer a psychopathic dandy, but just another pram-pushing aspirant to the bourgeoisie? Aestheticized psychopathy isn't some deviation suffered by a few wayward "droogs," but the structuring principle of the cosmos: it is the "nothingness" Wyndham Lewis worried lay just beyond the flatness and abstraction he was nevertheless at-tracted to. As Tom Ripley says, "If I could take a giant eraser and rub out everything, starting with myself."[133]

As a figure of what Baudelaire called "opposition and revolt," the dandy had been opposed to what *is* since (at least) the middle of the nineteenth century. But only at the end of the twentieth could this opposition eventuate in what Lyotard calls the "consciousness of the desert," a consciousness that is also a desire. Every dandyism has its form, and the psychopathic dandy is no differ-ent: Marlon Brando's tough talk, the stylistically flattened menace of Ripley, the catalog prose of *American Psycho*'s brutalizing minimalism. I have offered a range of reasons for dandyism's availability as a cultural idiom for these scenar-ios of violence, emptiness, desertification. There is the history of the gay villain and the masks, fascinating and repellant, from which he cannot be divorced. There is aestheticism's proximity to a culture of consumption that could seem, in the Reagan years, sublimely massive and murderous. There is decadence's hundred-year-old fixation on violence and transgression, a canonical reper-toire lying in wait for repurposing by a later fin de siècle. Perhaps above all, there is aestheticism's desire to correct an ugly world. If the world cannot be made beautiful, it can at least be destroyed.

CODA

THE DANDY AND THE HIPSTER
AFTER THE APOCALYPSE

I wonder whether, underlying all of these powerful causes, lies an ultimate one: a new anxiety about the worthiness of aesthetic experience as such. In closing, I want briefly to consider the twenty-first-century hipster as the dandy's pale afterlife, perhaps as the dandy's terminus. By "hipster," I am not speaking primarily of the hard-partying nightlife creature celebrated by the early run of *Vice* magazine, but of his more erudite older brother, the Brooklyn-centered intellectual hipster whose image and persona have become a dubious icon of the intellectual life of the early twenty-first century. The intellectual hipster shares a certain look with the *Vice* hipster (skinny jeans, etc.), though he is less hedonistic and more obviously a part of the professional-managerial class, bohemian wing. I speak of "him" advisedly. As Jennifer Baumgarden puts it, hipsters "*are* feminized (skinny, fashion-y, coiffed) but they are also . . . mostly men." She goes on to wonder "whether there is homophobia in . . . hipster-hating."[1] Analogously to the dandy, from whom he is descended, the hipster is an originally male figure who is, in his essential constitution, suspected of both androgyny and queerness. And like the dandy from Pelham through the Hemingway hero to Patrick Bateman, the hipster is associated not just with a sartorial style but with culinary aestheticism. As one commentator put it, "Portland is a really great place as a sort of metaphor [of hipsterism]—It has a really great restaurant scene."[2] In its cruder orientation as represented by *Vice*, hipsterism's emphasis on consumption can sound decadent, in the specific nineteenth-century sense, as Mark Greif points out: "The big publication of the early hipster moment was called *Vice* precisely because that was the hipster schtick, to lump consumer and Gothic into the same category of transgression:

We will show you how to buy pleasures which some liberal prude of our fantasies considers immoral."[3] But just as, for dandyism proper, the prerogatives of consumption can provide, paradoxically, the tools for an oppositional subjectivity, so too can hipsterism provide a refuge for people disconnected, for reasons sexual or intellectual, from the dominant requirements of the culture.[4]

In a scene that has become an instant classic in the contemporary literature of consumption, the hero of Ben Lerner's 2014 novel *10:04*, having recently signed an exciting book contract, enjoys a celebratory meal with his agent in a hip Chelsea restaurant. (Lerner's narrator is unnamed and shares many features with Lerner himself—as ever in the history of the dandiacal novel, the collapse between author and character is aggressively courted.) The meal "included baby octopuses that the chef had literally massaged to death. We had ingested the impossibly tender things entire, the first intact head I had ever consumed."[5] Like the meals in *American Psycho*, it's hard to tell whether this luxury item exists in the real world; unlike in *American Psycho*, the satire is rueful and self-skeptical rather than savage and self-loathing. In Lerner's delicate (not to say precious) autobiographical metafiction, a critique of the privileges and habits of New York's gentrifying classes is elaborately buffered by ironic involutions. "I'll project myself," the narrator imagines himself saying of his own authorial strategy, "into several futures simultaneously . . . I'll work my way from irony to sincerity in the sinking city, a would-be Whitman of the vulnerable grid."[6]

Like Hemingway before him, Lerner's aestheticist sensibilities play out around culinary connoisseurship, which might at first seem like a mere digression but in fact offers something like the heart of *10:04*'s sensibility. Unlike Hemingway, Lerner offers an overt interpretive agenda right alongside the evocation of rarified consumption. "It was quiet enough to hear the bartender shaking an artisanal cocktail," the narrator says, and the joke is that the language of advertising has infected the narrator's perception. "Sharon ordered what I thought was a simple drip coffee that turned out to be an exorbitantly priced single-origin Chemex affair."[7] This, like many other lines isolated from their context in *10:04*, could be Bret Easton Ellis. As could this: "Dessert was a yuzu frozen soufflé with poached plums. Money was a kind of poetry."[8] But this, on the miracle of the commodity during the run-up to a hurricane, is pure Lerner:

> . . . the seeds inside the purple fruits of coffee plants had been harvested on Andean slopes and roasted and ground and soaked and then

dehydrated at a factory in Medellin and vacuum-sealed and flown to JFK and then driven upstate. . . . It was as if the social relations that produced the object in my hand began to glow within it as they were threatened, stirred inside their packaging, lending it a certain aura.[9]

Lerner contributes to the literature of hip consumption a somewhat maudlin but nevertheless highly precise analytic self-reflexivity. For all his intellectual sophistication, Lerner's protagonist is a transparent variation on that debased and apparently ubiquitous type, the twenty-first-century hipster. As Greif puts it, "The 'hipster' is the name for what we might call 'the hip consumer,' or what Tom Frank used to call 'the rebel consumer.'"[10] At bottom, the rebelliousness of this hip consumer is what separates him from the yuppie, and also what connects him to the longer history of the dandy.

Greif's astute characterization of the hipster as a member of "a *subculture* of people who are already *dominant*" resonates particularly well with the history of the dandy, who is, in his most recognizable form—at Oxford or Cambridge at the fin de siècle or in the first decade of the twentieth century—precisely a subcultural member of the ruling class.[11] More broadly, this position links the dandy to the *intellectual*, who is, as Bourdieu has it, "the dominated fraction of the dominant class."[12] Indeed, like his cousin the *flâneur*—"the *flâneur* is, in fact, the critic"[13]—so too the "dandy's immaculate self-consciousness and disdain for sentimental effusions is perfectly attuned to the scholarly zeitgeist, allowing the critic to carve out a skeptical distance from the mainstream."[14] Lerner's variety of hipster inherits all of these tendencies: he is urbane, hypercritical, and acutely aware of both his membership in the dominant class and his lack of power within it. The lurch from semiparodic aestheticist delectation to Marxist-analytic dissection of the "aura" of the commodity performs (or exposes) the formation that links the intellectual to the aestheticist connoisseur in a way that Patrick Bateman never could. We might even say that Bateman, in his hyperbolic revoltingness and his finance-class affiliations, represents something like an attempted disavowal on the part of the intellectuals of styles of connoisseurship and consumption with which intellectualism itself is intimately connected.

10:04 aims to expose this mystification by frankly avowing an aestheticism of intense momentary experience drawn from Pater but politicized and desolipsized, made a feature of communal experience. One must, as the narrator puts it in lyrical jargon, embrace "the possibility of a transpersonal revolutionary subject in the present and co-construct a world in which moments can be something other than the elements of profit."[15] Lerner's narrator offers a dandiacal-utopian vision in which intense experience is decoupled from the prerogatives of capitalism.

Is this a parody of the overheated jargon perpetrated by some left academics? Or is Lerner sincere? I am genuinely unsure, and one of the things that can make Lerner's work seem irritatingly self-regarding is that even its parodies of critical affectation seem to flatter their objects. This is potentially a feature of all parody, but it is particularly salient in the history of dandyism, in which the parody and the "real thing" exist in a kind of symbiosis, with the parodic imitation often giving cues to the original: like Oscar Wilde and his images in Gilbert and Sullivan's *Patience*, original and parody together "co-construct a world," as Lerner's narrator might put it.

Hurricane Irma and Occupy Wall Street offer two instances of apocalypse and utopia respectively in *10:04*, a novel whose imagination of aftermath—to recur to Vincent Sherry's useful label—is characteristically decadent. Lerner's narrator's most important meditation on such aftermath occurs in a consideration of the potential for the work of art to be released from its bondage to the "monetizable signature" and its status as a "commodity": "[I]t was incredibly rare—I remembered the jar of instant coffee the night of the storm—to encounter an object liberated from that logic. What was the word for that liberation? *Apocalypse? Utopia?*"[16] The intellectualized hipster's quest for this transcendent aesthetic encounter is a descendant, refined and delibidinized, of the midcentury hipster's for "kicks." In both cases—remember that Mailer opens "The White Negro" with an evocation of the atom bomb—apocalypse is the backdrop and even the condition for the quest for high experience.

10:04's narrator does not, as it happens, realize the utopian "transpersonal revolutionary subject"; nor does the hurricane inaugurate an apocalypse in which he is caught and destroyed, or raptured. Instead, he decides to procreate. The last movement of the novel offers an ambivalent response to Edelman's polemic in *No Future* (a text which the theory-savvy Lerner, who has published essays in academic journals like *boundary2*, is much more likely than most novelists to be familiar with). The narrator agrees to impregnate his friend Alex; tentatively and without the usual commitments or ceremonies, they are planning to constitute a heterosexual family unit. Pronatalist sentiment will replace the utopian "transpersonal subjectivity" earlier gestured to as a redemptive mode: "Neither Alex nor I speak, have any questions for the doctor, or take each other's hand, but there is that intimacy of parallel gazes I feel when we stand before a canvas or walk across a bridge."[17] Reproduction gives rise to the same emotional ties normally generated (when it is generated at all) in the narrator's life by experiences of works of art. Walking with Alex in the area of an Occupy Wall Street protest toward the very end of the novel, the narrator has a vision of fertility that is also a vision of Hades:

> A steady current of people attired in the usual costumes was entering the walkway onto the bridge and there was a strange energy crackling among us; part parade, part flight, part protest. Each woman I imagined as pregnant; then I imagined all of us were dead, flowing over London Bridge. What I mean is that our faceless presences were flickering, every one disintegrated, yet part of the scheme. I'm quoting now, like John Gillespie Magee.[18]

As in the concluding paragraph of Burroughs's *The Western Lands*, Lerner's narrator synthesizes moments of the most intense experience via a tissue of literary quotations. Unlike in *The Western Lands*, he is not an old man but a young one; the quotational strategy, by which life is converted to literature, serves not so much to evoke the pathos of aging and memory as to buffer experience itself by literary allusiveness, or to suggest that, in a novel at least, experience itself is *nothing other than* belletristic allusion. Louis Menand has written of T. S. Eliot that "the literary quotation marks of imitation and allusion" allow for the "neutralizing" of the poet's own suspicions about his emotional authenticity."[19] Lerner inherits an amplified version of this dilemma, an extreme self-doubt and anxiety about affectation that is characteristic of the intellectualized hipster. This self-doubt extends to the sentimentalized pronatalism offered in *10:04*'s lyrical final passages, in which "Alex is pregnant and the seas are poisoned and the superstorm has shut down all the ports."[20] While the apocalyptic scenarios of *A Clockwork Orange* are overcome, however parodically or unsatisfactorily, by Alex's sudden, sentimental commitment to fatherhood, in *10:04* parenthood involves a melancholy rapprochement with the climate apocalypse that is already upon us. This is one possible response to a millennial attitude recently described by Gabriel Winant in *n+1*, in which "nobody . . . wants to have kids because of climate change." Lerner's narrator's answer: have kids anyway, but work them into an elegiac, fragmentary prose-poem drawn from *The Waste Land* and leavened with Whitman. The hipster's preoccupations—aestheticized culinary consumption, the construction

of aesthetic "moments" drawn from Pater, the ambling *flâneurie* of the priv-
ileged urban male—are here sublimated or transcended in favor of a sort of
love-among-the-ruins rumination, a resigned spawning in the decadent aftermath of the apocalypse. But that very response comes swaddled in quotation,
its sincerity and authenticity buffered, held in suspension.

Self-doubt is not a dandiacal quality. The intellectualized hipster's tenta-
tiveness involves a stark discontinuity between the hipster and the dandy—
a discontinuity that, in terms of the history of archetypes I have been tracing, is most strongly to be noted between the midcentury hipster and the
twenty-first-century hipster. As Greif asks, "Why would 'hipster,' this archaic
term of the '50s, be on everyone's lips at the turn of the 21st century?"[21] Greif
offers three connective planks. First, both hipsters are primordially white—the
earlier dialectically constituted by his fascination with a fantasized black other,
the later by a nostalgic preoccupation with the white suburbia of the 1970s.[22]
Second, just as the twenty-first-century hipster negotiates "the very old dyad of
knowingness and naïveté, adulthood and a child-centered world,"[23] the '50s
hipster is constituted above all by his "claim to knowledge."[24] Third, and
perhaps most important, the hipster in both historical periods *knows how to
consume:* "The hipster is the cultural figure of the person, very possibly, who
now understands consumer purchases within the familiar categories of mass
consumption . . . like the right vintage T-shirt, the right jeans, the right foods
for that matter—to be *a form of art.*"[25]

This generalized lifestyle aestheticism connects the semicriminal hipster of,
for instance, *The Wild One* to the intellectualized hipster of *10:04.* But while
the '50s hipster is all blustery self-assertion, a self-assertion whose extreme
is actually psychopathic, the intellectualized hipster is hampered by layers of
self-reflexivity and doubt, a doubt that extends to his aestheticism itself. Is it
really possible for Lerner's narrator to "work [his] way from irony to sincerity,"
as he announces he intends? Such a path is a signal instance of what Lee Konstantinou calls "post-irony," an ethos captured by writers like Dave Eggers and
David Foster Wallace.[26] Lerner represents a further stage in this post-ironic
trajectory. One can imagine some version of post-irony that would permit a
full-throated return to a confident aestheticism, an unabashed neo art for art's
sake. Although there is a sense in which the dandy has always been linked
to criticality, the peculiar species of self-doubt suffered by the intellectualized
hipster blunts his critical arsenal, a dilemma having everything to do with that
originary "supermaleness" shared by the hipster and the dandy. As Schwenger

puts it, "the masculine mode" is marked by a "despair that shadows the reflexive life." For the hipster, as Schwenger says of the practitioner of the masculine mode more generally, "Self-consciousness is a crack in the wholeness of his nature."[27] Such despairing self-consciousness is, arguably, Lerner's major novelistic theme.

The aestheticist dandy is an ironist, sure, and all irony is marked by reflexivity, but he is not ironical about the importance of art. Such a path does not seem possible for Lerner's hero, though, who instead embraces—though in quotation marks, as it were—that least dandiacal of options, fatherhood. On the terms established by *10:04*, fatherhood is a solution to the failure of the aesthetic object to transcend its context or to redeem its world. (To be sure, this, too, is ironized: but post-irony is not non-irony.) By reproducing, the intellectualized hipster will attempt to corner the apocalypse into a draw, not art for art's sake but art for the sake of the child. Earlier I called Lerner "precious." I didn't mean it pejoratively. "Preciousness," in this context, is what happens to the aesthete who has become unsure about aestheticism. I am tempted to suggest that this uncertainty is the dandy's terminus. I am not sure, though, that a comeback is not somewhere in the offing.

.

NOTES

INTRODUCTION

1. Lewis, *Malign Fiesta*, 160.
2. Carlyle, *Sartor Resartus*, 207.
3. A detailed history of the dandy's multiform nineteenth-century guises lies outside my scope, though I rely throughout on scholars of nineteenth-century dandyism. The major English-language histories of nineteenth-century dandyism are Moers, *The Dandy*; Adams, *Dandies and Desert Saints*; and Garelick, *Rising Star*. Other accounts of dandyism I have especially relied on are Feldman, *Gender on the Divide*; Meisel, *The Cowboy and the Dandy*; and Glick, *Materializing Queer Desire*. See also Lavar, *Dandies*; Susan Fillin-Yeh, ed., *Dandies*; M. Miller, *Slaves to Fashion*, and Mann, *The Dandy at Dusk*.
4. Barbey d'Aurevilly, *On Dandyism*, 44–45, 65.
5. Ibid., 57.
6. Ibid.
7. Ibid., 116.
8. Ibid., 77.
9. Ibid., 117.
10. Ibid., 121, 141.
11. See Ellmann, *Oscar Wilde*, 47.
12. Ibid., 231.
13. Ibid., 252.
14. Chai, *Aestheticism*, 27. Chai is speaking here of the commonality of vision uniting Leconte de Lisle with Walter Pater.
15. Gagnier, *Individualism*, 92.
16. For studies of decadence, see Praz, *The Romantic Agony*; Dowling, *Language and Decadence*; Spackman, *Decadent Genealogies*; Felski, *The Gender of Modernity*; Pittock, *Spectrum of Decadence*; Weir, *Decadence and the Making of Modernism*; Constable, Denisoff, and Potolsky, eds., *Perennial Decay*; Bernheimer, *Decadent Subjects*; Weir, *Decadent Culture*; and Gagnier, *Individualism*. For studies of aestheticism, see esp., in addition to Chai, *Aestheticism*: Gagnier,

Idylls of the Marketplace; Williams, *Transfigured World*; Freedman, *Professions of Taste*; Mao, *Solid Objects*; and Mendelssohn, *Henry James, Oscar Wilde*.

17. I take "the decadent dandy" from Garelick, *Rising Star*, 4.
18. Ellmann, *Oscar Wilde*, 253.
19. For instance, while aestheticism is concerned with surfaces, it is also concerned with flux and evanescence, associated with interiority; while decadence, in its focus on peculiar forms of sexual fetishism, is often interested in cathected objets d'art.
20. On what I am calling Wilde's "sarcasm," see Kane, who reads the "all too moral narrative" of *Dorian Gray* as a "*parody* of the Gothic mode of Stevenson's *The Strange Case of Dr Jeckyll and Mr Hyde*, which is therefore not to be taken too seriously" (47).
21. Wilde, *The Picture of Dorian Gray*, 113–14.
22. See O'Connell, "The Libertine."
23. For a reading of Thurman's *Infants of the Spring* in terms of black dandyism, see Miller, *Slaves to Fashion*, 176–218.
24. See Nicholls, *Modernisms*. For Nicholls, the Baudelairean dandy's aloofness "allows him to remain uncompromised either by the ideological imperatives of academic culture or by what had become known . . . as 'industrial literature'— journalism, that is, and popular episodic fiction." For Baudelaire, "The figure of the leisured dandy thus aligned 'style' with the refusal to compromise" (12).
25. Fitzgerald, *This Side of Paradise and The Last Tycoon*, 95–96.
26. Glass, *Authors Inc.*, 140.
27. Nordau, *Degeneration*, 317.
28. Jaffe, *Modernism and the Culture of Celebrity*, 90. Although he doesn't put it this way, Jaffe's "imprimatur" is a version of Wayne Booth's "implied author," but its effects are both textual *and* social. At the textual level, the "imprimatur" authorizes and enables interpretation—for instance, when readers must decide how seriously to take Joyce's Stephen Dedalus, their readings are "propped up . . . by a particular recourse to Joyce the authorial coinage, the imprimatur." The implied author is a narratologically necessary feature of any fictional text, but the "imprimatur" is individualized, given a name and a personality. In this, the "imprimatur" merely identifies the phase of all novel reading in which we name the implied author, and there is no reason, as far as I can tell, why it should be restricted to modernism. One reads *Tristram Shandy* by the biographical personage Laurence Sterne; one imagines "Laurence Sterne," implied author, as controlling and ordering the narrative. But the imprimatur, unlike the more narrowly narratological implied author, names a wider social power.

29. Ibid., 20.
30. "Modernist work offers itself as a functional replacement for the biographical self" (ibid., 31). For more on modernism and celebrity, see Jaffe and Goldman, eds., *Modernist Star Maps;* and Goldman, *Modernism Is the Literature of Celebrity.*
31. Quoted in Arvidson, "Personality," 809. Arvidson relies on Saunders, *Self Impression,* 269. I will turn to Arvidson on Lewis at greater length below.
32. Feldman, *Gender on the Divide,* 53.
33. Ford Madox Ford (then Hueffer) quoted in Moody's *Ezra Pound,* 113. Moody warns that the notoriously unreliable Hueffer was probably exaggerating or inventing.
34. Meyers traces Eliot's green cosmetics to his interest in the fin de siècle and in Baudelaire ("T. S. Eliot's Green Face Powder").
35. Braudy, *The Frenzy of Renown,* 477. And as Philip Mann writes, "Given the dandy's nature as work of art, the passing of time poses particular problems for him. . . . The most radical solution to this problem is suicide" (35–36).
36. O'Keeffe, *Some Sort of Genius,* 4.
37. Hiney, *Raymond Chandler,* 221.
38. Quoted in Herring, *Djuna,* 136, 131.
39. Dearborn, *Ernest Hemingway,* 68. In Hemingway's case, such nattiness was not long-lived—in his middle and especially later years he was downright slovenly. See ibid., 418, and elsewhere.
40. Dandiacal texts' verbal stylishness reflects the more strictly sartorial focus on the "detail" ("the buttons on a waistcoat, the buckle on a shoe") that Roland Barthes names as the essence of dandyism: only by such minutiae can the dandy distinguish himself from the normally well-attired man in an era of broadly available off-the-rack fashion. "The job of the 'detail' . . . is to allow the dandy to escape the masses and never to be engulfed by them; his singularity is absolute in essence, but limited in substance, as he must never fall into eccentricity, for that is an eminently copyable form" (*The Language of Fashion,* 61, 62).
41. Garelick, *Rising Star,* 11.
42. Ibid., 3.
43. R. Williams, *Dream Worlds,* 114.
44. Widiss has identified in a range of twentieth-century American novels something like this spur to authorial identification at work, what he calls an "obscure invitation . . . to a self-conscious apprehension of, and perhaps by extension a form of communion with, [a text's] author. At its most basic this is no more than a simple structural homology between reader and author,

at its most extreme a full-on annexation of Eucharistic ritual." See *Obscure Invitations*, 2.

45. Quoted in Dearborn, *Ernest Hemingway*, 7.

46. This is especially true of both Hemingway and Chandler. Alcoholic and despairing in his final years, Chandler's self-descriptions are indistinguishable from a characterization of his wisecracking fictional hero Philip Marlowe. Here is Chandler bragging about talking his way out of an insane asylum, where he'd been committed following a drunken suicide attempt: "I out-talked them and out-thought them, so that in the end they sent me home in a limousine, merely because they were dazzled by the display of wit and courage I put on" (quoted in Hiney, *Raymond Chandler*, 256).

47. Braudy, *The Frenzy of Renown*, 28.

48. Schwenger, *Phallic Critiques*, 3. Schwenger borrows "supermale" from the title of Alfred Jarry's dandiacal fantasy novel *The Supermale* (1902).

49. Buchbinder, *Masculinities and Identities*, 52.

50. Schwenger, "The Masculine Mode," 108.

51. Cleland, *Fanny Hill*.

52. For a look at *Lolita* as about "the situation of the corrupt aesthete," see Green, *Children of the Sun*, 452.

53. Easthope, *What a Man's Gotta Do*, 41.

54. Buchbinder, *Masculinities and Identities*, 43, summarizing Easthope, *What a Man's*, 35–44.

55. Simpson, *Male Impersonators*, 4.

56. As Mann puts it, "The dandy knows to hide the pathological side of his character through masks, which are second nature to him" (*The Dandy at Dusk*, 30).

57. Modernist dandies are a signal instance of what Feldman has called "Victorian modernism" in her study of that title, which, like *Dandyism*, examines the relationship between nineteenth-century aestheticism and modernism. For Feldman, though, the quintessential "Victorian moderns" inherit and rework Victorian sentimental domesticity; Proust, for instance, "rewrites in high-Modernist fashion a literary form from the past: the sentimental tableau" (13). The "Victorian moderns" under discussion here, on the contrary, are antisentimental and antidomestic.

58. Christ refers to modernism's "anti-Victorianism," observing in particular that "Pound rarely mentions [Pater], and Eliot aggressively belittles him, claiming that Pater had not influenced 'a single first-rate mind of a later generation'" (*Victorian and Modern Poetics*, 149; quoting from Eliot, *Selected Essays*, 392). But Pound's inclusion of Pater in *BLAST* (see below) is foundational, and

Eliot claims not that Pater failed to influence any first-rate minds of a later generation but that *Marius the Epicurean* failed to do so, an entirely different proposition (Christ provides the fuller quotation on 154). Modernism's anti-Victorianism was real, but partial; just as often, modernists advertised their continuity with selected Victorian predecessors.

59. Lewis, ed., *BLAST*, 11.

60. Ibid., 15, 27, 41, 45.

61. Ibid., 154.

62. The continuities and differences between the symbol of the Romantics and the "image" of the modernists continue to prove contentious for critics. For a strong statement of the similarities between the Romantic symbol and the modernist "image," see Hay, "On the Shore of Interpretation." For a response to Hay that emphasizes differences between symbol and image, and an economic overview of the history of these debates, see Halmi, "Symbolism, Imagism, and Hermeneutic Anxiety." For Halmi, "the Romantic symbol and the Poundian image differ profoundly from each other inasmuch as the one is conceived as the objective manifestation of a harmoniously organized totality encompassing the individual subject, and the other as the subjective appropriation of a mentally represented external object" (136). I am less interested in adjudicating this complex chapter in the history of the philosophy of aesthetics than in drawing attention to the social and gender content that, for Hulme especially, would come to be associated with different aesthetic positions. Such content most often emerges—in such terms as "hard," "dry," or "damp"—at the level of figuration, not theory.

63. My reading complicates Lesley Higgins's account of the gender politics of the *BLAST* circle. Higgins sees modernism's "cult of ugliness" as predicated on the overt rejection, occasioned by homosexual panic, of Paterian aestheticism; for evidence, she compiles Lewis's and Eliot's hostile assessments of Pater, often marked by thinly veiled (or, in Lewis's case, entirely unveiled) homophobia. But she ignores Pater's central position in *BLAST* itself. See Higgins, *The Modernist Cult of Ugliness*, 79–119.

64. Quoted in Kemp, *The Desire of My Eyes*, 412.

65. Hulme, *Speculations*, 128, 130.

66. Ibid., 131, 126.

67. Moers, *The Dandy*, 287.

68. For a reading of Pater's metaphors and how they inflect his "surface/depth paradigm," see Mendelssohn, who reminds us that Pater's famous "gem-like flame" is complemented by images of water, through which "Pater encourages us to turn our gaze inward, to the very depths of our consciousness instead

of remaining on the surface of the self" (*Henry James, Oscar Wilde*, 113). The shuttling back and forth between surface and interior is the keynote of Pater's theory of aesthetics—a constitutive ambivalence that makes him a productive thinker for a huge range of modernists.

69. Pater, *Studies in the History of the Renaissance*, 120 (hereafter referred to as *Renaissance*).

70. Ryan, *The Vanishing Subject*, 4.

71. For a reading of Paterian subjectivity as a kind of domestic interiority purged of femininity, see Tamar Katz, for whom "the task Pater encountered in fashioning an authoritative aesthetic subject was to incorporate domesticity's promise—to remove the subject from the vicissitudes of the public world—while avoiding the domestic sphere's definition as specific and as female" (*Impressionist Subjects*, 25). For a sophisticated theoretical and historical overview of impressionism, see Matz, *Literary Impressionism*.

72. Quoted in Kenner, *The Pound Era*, 256.

73. Ibid.

74. Lewis, *Tarr: The 1918 Version*, 199. In *The Romantic Image*, Kermode similarly draws a line between nineteenth-century aestheticism and Wyndham Lewis, observing that the "cult of the dead face" observed in Pater's "The Child in the House" "later, separated from all obvious pathological interest, turns up in Yeats, and in Vorticism" (64).

75. Lewis, *Tarr* (1968 ed.), 280.

76. As Witemeyer points out, "The Image likewise has affinities with James Joyce's concept of the secular epiphany; both are pattern-disclosing revelations which manifest themselves in the course of everyday life" ("Early Poetry," 48). See also Bidney, *Patterns of Epiphany*; and Nichols, *The Poetics of Epiphany*. Nichols describes "the new form of the epiphany inaugurated by Wordsworth" as one in which "the perceiving self flows into the world. It then sees in the world its own powers, reflected in the processes of nature, manifested in particularly intense imaginative perceptions, and preserved by memory" (21). Hulme's interest in primitivist abstraction—which he sees as primitive man's ordering response to a hostile and nonhuman environment—is a rebuke precisely to this Romantic humanism.

77. Baudelaire, *La Fanfarlo*, 18.

78. I cannot attend to all of the nuances of the history of the modernist image here, but besides Levenson, see Schwartz, *The Matrix of Modernism*; and Kermode, *The Romantic Image*.

79. Levenson, *A Genealogy of Modernism*, 21.

80. Ibid., 133.

81. Levenson suggests that Hulme's final antihumanism is *not* a "classicism": Hulme "came to a position more extreme than the classical, and which is identified with classicism only on pain of confusion" (ibid., 94). "The romantic/classical opposition is simply not identical with the humanist/ anti-humanist opposition—not in ordinary use, not in Hulme's use. Once Hulme saw *humanism* as the root of the problem, he ceased to regard the romantic/classical division as fundamental" (98). This point seems important to me, and continues to be frequently overlooked.

82. Burstein dubs the literary aesthetic of which Vorticism is an exemplar "cold modernism": "Insofar as cold modernism engages a world without selves or psychology, it is not antihumanism, but ahumanism" (*Cold Modernism*, 2). Hot modernism, by contrast, concentrates on the inner lives of characters—Burstein names Joyce, Woolf, and Proust (24). Burstein's insistence that "one of cold modernism's central mainstays is that there is no difference between style and substance" (12) might be taken to reflect its affinity with dandyism. Though dandyism is not one of Burstein's focuses, sartorial fashion is.

83. In fact, H. Peter Stowell does indeed refer to impressionism as "subjective objectivism" (*Literary Impressionism*, 9, quoted in Matz, *Literary Impressionism*, 26).

84. Quoted in Levenson, *A Genealogy of Modernism*, 120. For more on the modernist negotiation of subjectivity and objectivity, including a useful discussion of the Eliotic "half-object," see Schwartz, *The Matrix of Modernism*, 203. And Mao observes that "it would be a mistake . . . to assume that an interest in the subject somehow precluded an interest in the object, since for fiction writers the fascination of 'internal' life clearly embraced the mystery of its interchanges with the radically other or external" (*Solid Objects*, 16).

85. Levenson, *A Genealogy of Modernism*, 134.

86. Lewis, *The Demon of Progress*, 3.

87. Matz, *Literary Impressionism*, 53. Matz brilliantly shows the "necessary connection . . . between sexual and epistemological orientations" in Pater. Pater's scandalous subjectivism was scandalous because, in short, it was so flagrantly libidinal (and therefore suggestively proto-Freudian): Pater "ensures the impression's juncture of intellect and sense by making [the impression] a function of desire felt by intellect for sense—by a connoisseurial mind for an idealized object of masculine vitality" (54).

88. Green, *Children of the Sun*, 34. From Baudelaire's "The Painter of Modern Life" (1863), in which the dandy is a figure of "opposition and revolt," to Camus's inclusion of the dandy in his *L'homme révolté* (1951), the French tradition is clearer than the English on the equation of dandy and rebel.

89. Ibid., 252.

90. Rosenfeld, "The Case of Ezra Pound."

91. Although Schwartz finds that T. S. Eliot sets up an opposition between "the conventional 'personality' (and the pose of the aesthete) versus the 'impersonality' of the serious poet" (*Matrix of Modernism*, 70), the imbrication of dandyism and modernism suggests rather that the "pose" of the aesthete is a path toward impersonality. For a modernist dandy like Pound, an apparent excess of personality in fact involves the cancellation of personality by its submission to, and occlusion by, a series of masks.

92. Pound, *New and Selected Poems*, 39, 129.

93. Mao notes that "critics have . . . strikingly ignored the continuity of *Hugh Selwyn Mauberley* with the polemics on hardness that both precede and follow it" (*Solid Objects*, 165). This absence in the criticism is all the more striking given that John J. Espey's important 1955 reading of Gautier's influence on Pound and *Mauberley* takes its cue from Pound's 1918 essay "The Hard and the Soft in French Poetry," "in which [Pound] spoke of Gautier as a 'hard' poet as opposed to a 'soft' poet like Samain" (*Ezra Pound's* Mauberley, 30). Espey also speculates on the influence of *Mademoiselle de Maupin* on *Mauberley* (37).

94. Pound, *New and Selected Poems*, 113.

95. Carolyn Williams's characterization of Pater's prose as "haunted, as if the spirits of the dead come out when no one else is home" is appropriate (*Transfigured World*, 45), but *Mauberley*'s focus on the war lends such ghostliness a different valence from Pater's wistfulness.

96. Quéma, *The Agon of Modernism*, 17.

97. Mao, *Solid Objects*, 104. Mao goes on to suggest that Lewis was aware of a possible contradiction between his avowed antiaestheticism and the implications of his own aesthetic, with its emphasis on externality, objectivity, and hardness, since aestheticism "also set so much store by the beautiful solid object . . . the gems of Dorian Gray or des Esseintes" (106).

98. Love, "Forced Exile," 26.

99. Higgins, *Modernist Cult*, 80.

100. Quéma is the exception to the rule when she observes that "Tarr's philosophy . . . stems directly from the dandy's discourse" and that Lewis's early work shares with Ezra Pound's *Hugh Selwyn Mauberley* a common source in "Oscar Wilde's theoretical texts that combine dandyism and mask" (*The Agon of Modernism*, 134, 135).

101. Lewis, *Blasting and Bombardiering*, 9.

102. Pater, *Renaissance*, 70.

103. Adams, *Dandies*, 180. Kermode, similarly, draws a line between nineteenth-century aestheticism and Wyndham Lewis, observing that the "cult of the dead face" in Pater's "The Child in the House" "later, separated from all obvious pathological interest, turns up in Yeats, and in Vorticism" (*Romantic Image*, 64). And for a treatment of Pater's influence on the doctrines of Imagism, see Menand, *Discovering Modernism*, esp. chap. 2, "Problems about Objects" (29–53). For a compelling art historical account of "flatness" in modernism, see Joselit, "Notes on Surface." Joselit draws a distinction between the modernist flatness championed by Clement Greenberg and the abstract expressionists on the one hand and "postmodern" flatness on the other: "The depth [the former] exhibits . . . is psychological. In art designated as *post*modern on the other hand, a different articulation of flatness and depth arises. In such works not only optical but *psychological* depth undergoes deflation, resulting in a visuality in which identity manifests itself as a culturally conditioned play of stereotype" (20, emphasis in original). Insofar as aesthetic ideologies of modernist flatness entail anxious suppressions, the anxiety is about the depth *not being deep enough:* "Greenberg's cocky advocacy of flatness veils a profound anxiety over the 'legitimacy' of abstraction. For, in this art, optical flatness is validated by psychological depth" (22). However true this is generally, in the case of Wyndham Lewis visual flatness is indeed intended, at least in part and some of the time, to "deflate" or even defeat psychological depth—it is therefore more continuous with postmodern flatness than Joselit's dichotomy would suggest.

104. Agamben, *Stanzas*, 50.

105. Edwards, *Wyndham Lewis*, 435.

106. Trotter, *Paranoid Modernism*, 351.

107. Jameson, "Wyndham Lewis as Futurist," 309.

108. Lewis, *Snooty Baronet*, 133.

109. Ibid., 136.

110. Ibid.

111. Agamben, *Stanzas*, 46.

112. Brown, *The Sense of Things*, 18.

113. Ibid., 12, 7–8.

114. Lewis, *The Demon of Progress*, 32.

115. As Mendelssohn observes, aestheticist writers like Pater, Wilde, or James found their "stock-in-trade" in "the emblematic use of art and the deployment of tropes from the visual arts" (*Henry James, Oscar Wilde*, 115). Lewis deserves to be numbered among this group.

116. Lewis, *Snooty Baronet*, 132.

117. Ibid., 136.
118. Brown, *The Sense of Things*, 162.
119. Ibid., 161.
120. H. James, *The Golden Bowl*, 301.
121. Jameson, *Fables of Aggression*, 55. And elsewhere: "the body now fragments into hosts of objects which can be foregrounded in their turn" (44). One might add: so does the *mind*.
122. Burstein, *Cold Modernism*, 2.
123. Mao suggests that Lewis was not after a world "in which the subject . . . would congeal into the object" but "rather, one in which the two would remain side by side, each in its proper repose" (*Solid Objects*, 139). This may be true of Lewis in some of his phases—and is consonant with his own claims in his critical writings—but it seems to me that, just as often, he exhibits an antipathy to the subject as such characterized by Burstein's "ahumanism."
124. Arvidson, "Personality," 797. For Arvidson, Lewis—"impersonality's reverse engineer" (794)—considered modernist ideals of impersonality fatally infected by larger depersonalizing forces, including behavioristic psychology and technocratic scientism (803, 804). "As Lewis argues, 'this delusion of impersonality could be best defined as that mistake by virtue of which persons are enabled to masquerade as *things*'; in like fashion, the delusion of personality might be extrapolated as that mistake that allows things to masquerade as persons" (804–5, quoting Lewis, *The Art of Being Ruled*, 28). On this account, Lewis's puppet fictions exalt what Arvidson calls "personified detachment"—"the registration of puppet antics on the mind of a detached but visible observer-narrator." The "irony of Snooty's claims to . . . autonomy is that, as arch-behaviorist, he denies such an existence to all others in his aesthetic frame," just as does Lewis himself, who "habitually casts his own relationship to his characters as puppet mastery" (811).
125. Kenner finds Lewis's novels "incarnat[ing] the ideas the polemics are directed against"—depicting the behavioristic automatism Lewis attacked in his political and philosophical writing (*Wyndham Lewis*, 97). Mao, likewise, writes of Lewis's "cautionary rhetoric of robots and automatons" (*Solid Objects*, 132). It seems clear, though, that for Lewis the reduction of the human to a puppet or robot is in fact a very attractive option. *Snooty Baronet* critiques this attraction but also revels in it. For a reading of *Snooty Baronet* that, while noting that "the surface aesthetic Lewis employs is, in the end, uncomfortably similar to that achieved by the mind-killing science of behaviorism" (649), nevertheless finds the novel's surface aesthetic advocating "a love for the visible world" (641) ostensibly opposed to behaviorism, see Stephen E.

Lewis, "Love and Politics." To my mind *Snooty Baronet*, like Lewis's fiction before it, takes a degree of gleeful satisfaction in the nihilistic implications of his aesthetic of surfaces that is perforce deemphasized in a reading focusing, as Stephen Lewis's does, on "love and friendship" (618).

126. Lewis, *Snooty Baronet*, 240.

127. Perhaps Lewis is mocking his own earlier inclination, so typical of the prewar avant-gardists, to hope to find in the coming violence the supreme aesthetic satisfaction, an attitude he recollects in *Blasting and Bombardiering*: "for me [war] was only a part of Art: my sort of life—the life of the 'intellect'—come to life" (63).

128. Edwards, *Wyndham Lewis*, 436. And as Trotter points out, Snooty's psychopathy is linked not just to an aesthetic but to a politics, since *Snooty Baronet* "exposes, in Kell-Imrie's insouciance, the complicity of his own method with traumatizing violence which is fascism's signature" (*Paranoid Modernism*, 353). On Lewis's fascism, see Sherry, *Ezra Pound*; and Jameson, *Fables of Aggression*. For Jameson, Lewis's oeuvre is "great art" because it "distances ideology by the way in which, endowing the latter with figuration and with narrative articulation, the text frees its ideological content to demonstrate its own contradictions; by the sheer formal immanence with which an ideological system exhausts its permutations and ends up projecting its own ultimate structural closure" (23). This criterion for aesthetic value helps explain how Lewis, despite the recurrence of homophobia and misogyny in his work, can nevertheless anticipate the insights of queer theory.

129. This is the reverse or complement to the process, discussed by Cheng, by which Josephine Baker's skillful manipulation of the tenets of modernist primitivism serves to subjectivize objects: "the very process of objectification—even as it takes subjectivity from [Baker]—*also* invests the objects around her with subjectivity, which in turn provides a kind of cloak for her nakedness" (*Second Skin*, 116).

130. Lewis, *Snooty Baronet*, 155.

131. Ibid.

132. Lewis, *The Art of Being Ruled*, 247–51. See Carlston, "'Acting the Man,'" for an overview of Lewis's essentially constructivist theory of the sex/gender system in general and his "tireless denaturalization of masculinity" specifically (774).

133. Moers, *The Dandy*, 76.

134. Lewis, *Snooty Baronet*, 134.

135. Joselit, "Notes on Surface," 20.

1. FINE AND DANDY

1. Connolly, *The Rock Pool*, 64, 65.
2. Hemingway, *Death in the Afternoon*, 73.
3. See esp. Comley and Scholes, *Hemingway's Genders*; Spilka, *Hemingway's Quarrel with Androgyny*; Moddelmog, *Reading Desire*; Strychacz, *Hemingway's Theaters of Masculinity*; Burwell, *Hemingway*; and Kennedy, *Imagining Paris*.
4. Hemingway, *The Garden of Eden*, 134.
5. Feldman, *Gender on the Divide*, 2.
6. In fact, as Moers points out, "Yankee Doodle Dandy" was originally sung by British soldiers in the 1760s; it was an ironic jab meant to mock the tattered and ill-matching uniforms of colonial American militiamen (*The Dandy*, 2).
7. Early in Theodore Dreiser's *Sister Carrie*, for instance, Drouet can say of the countrified and unsophisticated young Carrie that "she was a little dandy," by which he would seem merely to mean "pretty" or "appealing" (54).
8. Hemingway, *Garden of Eden*, 192.
9. Comley and Scholes, *Hemingway's Genders*, 54–55. Rodin, who frequently gave his works multiple titles, also called this sculpture, intriguingly, *Volupté*, *The Gates of Hell*, and *Les fleurs du mal*.
10. Feldman, *Gender on the Divide*, 11
11. Comley and Scholes, *Hemingway's Genders*, 57.
12. Hemingway, *A Moveable Feast*, 5, 6, 11.
13. As Gaggin notes, "Lines judging experiences to be 'good' demonstrate the aesthetic dimension of objective analysis" (*Hemingway*, 1).
14. North, *Reading 1922*, 202.
15. "But if Alice Toklas is an appropriate member of the class 'all nice wives,' then perhaps the phrase 'like that' means something very different indeed. This alternative meaning would still be perfectly colloquial, but the inflection would simply be changed from '*like* that' to 'like *that*.' With this slight change of emphasis, the line 'All nice wives are like that' is changed from a smug assertion of uniform heterosexual conformity to a suggestion of ubiquitous secret homosexuality—'All nice wives are like *that*'" (ibid.).
16. Ibid. Walter Benn Michaels also examines the use of "nice" in *The Sun Also Rises*, but not in order to suggest any queer resonances. Rather, for Michaels, "'nice'—along with words like 'good' and 'true'—[are] at the heart of a prose style that no longer needs the explicit vocabulary of race (e.g., 'Nordic') to distinguish those who have breeding from those who don't. . . . 'Nice' has its pedigree; indeed, pedigree is its pedigree." According to this reading, "nice" is a key part of the armature of Hemingway's alleged sublimated nativism; as an

aesthetic descriptor, it enforces a regime of taste designed to separate the Jake Barneses and the Brett Ashleys from the (Jewish) Robert Cohns. Michaels's thesis is, at one level, compatible with North's, since according to Michaels, Hemingway stigmatizes *actual* breeding—sexual reproduction—as the province of racialized others (hence, Cohn has three children, while Barnes is impotent). Thus, queerness, if nonprogenitive, might be aligned with nativism as Michaels constructs it. See Michaels, *Our America*, 13–29.

17. See Bak, *Homo americanus*, 53–100. In the penultimate draft, Jake's famous line ran, "Isn't it nice to think so?" (see Dearborn, *Ernest Hemingway*, 282).
18. North, *Reading 1922*, 202.
19. Love, "Forced Exile," 23–24. Love's source is the OED.
20. "Fine" appears a lot in Hemingway, but as digitized searches reveal, less than a third as frequently as "good."
21. Kenner, *A Homemade World*, 140, quoted in Gaggin, *Hemingway*, 24.
22. Pater, *Appreciations*, 4–6.
23. Hemingway, *Green Hills of Africa*, unnumbered page.
24. Hemingway, *A Moveable Feast*, 12.
25. See http://www.time.com/time/printout/0,8816,935439,00.html.
26. Hemingway, *Green Hills of Africa*, 70.
27. North, *Reading 1922*, 198–99.
28. Pater, *Renaissance*, 119.
29. Ibid.
30. As Jonathan Freedman notes, Adorno theorizes the commodity structure of aestheticism: "In Adorno's *Aesthetic Theory*, it is precisely in aestheticism, and specifically in aestheticism's art-for-art phase, that the commodification of art in a market economy becomes clearest" (*Professions of Taste*, xx). Freedman usefully tracks "the eager adoption of [aestheticism's] central tenets by the commercial press, by the advertising industry, and by the manufacturers and vendors of new 'aesthetic' commodities" (13). For a related account of the importance of commodity structure to the dandiacal aesthete, see Glick, *Materializing Queer Desire*.
31. Hemingway, *Green Hills of Africa*, 134.
32. Hemingway, *Across the River and into the Trees*, 192.
33. R. Williams, *Dream Worlds*, 119.
34. Hemingway, *Garden of Eden*, 76.
35. Lytton, *Pelham*, 317.
36. Hazlitt, *Essayist and Critic*, 332.
37. Gigante, *Taste*, 9, 160, 161.
38. Baudelaire, *La Fanfarlo*, 47.

39. Freedman, *Professions of Taste*, 36.
40. Huysmans, *À Rebours*, 82–83.
41. Gigante, *Taste*, 3.
42. R. Williams, *Dream Worlds*, 109.
43. Felski, *The Gender of Modernity*, 92–93.
44. Ibid., 100.
45. Nordau, *Degeneration*, 305.
46. Ibid., 96. Indeed, the suspect gender and sexual identity of the connoisseur stretches back at least to the first third of the eighteenth century, as a 1735 satirical poem called "The Connoisseur; or a Satire on Men of Taste" attests:

    > And what the girls were deem'd in Ages past,
    > Are our top *Beaux*, and modern Men of Taste.
    > But now so lessen'd is the Progeny,
    > That the next Race will only Women be;
    > And tir'd Nature, having lost its Force,
    > Stop Propagation, and so end its Course. (quoted in Gigante, *Taste*, 14)

47. Wilde, *The Picture of Dorian Gray*, 47.
48. For more on vivisection as aestheticist metaphor, see Mendelssohn, *Henry James, Oscar Wilde*, 144–46 and 155–57.
49. See Comley and Scholes, *Hemingway's Genders*, for a good analysis of the role of homosexuality in *Death in the Afternoon*. Among other things, they note Hemingway's addition and multiple revisions in manuscript of a long glossary entry on the word *maricòn*.
50. Hemingway, *Death in the Afternoon*, 68.
51. Ibid., 10.
52. Hemingway frequently used "queer" to mean "homosexual"—it appears unambiguously in that sense a number of times throughout *Death in the Afternoon*.
53. Hemingway, *Islands in the Stream*, 24.
54. Hemingway, *For Whom the Bell Tolls*, 169.
55. Hemingway, *Islands in the Stream*, 28. For a discussion of the modern association of the interior decorator with homosexuality, see Elliot, "Art Deco Hybridity."
56. Hemingway, *The Nick Adams Stories*, 185.
57. Gaggin, *Hemingway*, 66. See also Stubbs, "Watch Out." For a reading of Nick's simple meal (alongside many other scenes of culinary consumption in Hemingway) in terms of the conceptual opposites "civilization" and "wilderness," see Justice, "The Consolation of Critique."
58. Hemingway, *A Moveable Feast*, 72–73.
59. Quoted in Armstrong, *Modernism, Technology, and the Body*, 42.

60. Hemingway carried a copy of James's *Little Tour* while on a honeymoon in France. Reported in Stoneback, "Memorable Eggs," 23. Stoneback also notes the James passage, and suggest that a passage on eggs in *Garden of Eden* is a conscious allusion to it. He goes on to read egg imagery in *Garden* in terms of patterns of change, renewal, fertility, and infertility.

61. Connolly, *The Rock Pool,* 67.

62. Quoted in Haralson, *Henry James,* 173.

63. Indeed, Evelyn Waugh thought Hemingway's style had been influenced by Firbank. See Canning's introduction to Firbank's *Vainglory.*

64. In discussing Hemingway's debt to James, I draw largely on Haralson's account, particularly his final chapter, "'The Other Half Is the Man': The Queer Modern Triangle of Gertrude Stein, Ernest Hemingway, and Henry James." Haralson reads Hemingway's masculinist code heroics as explicitly reacting to Jamesian precedent, and, indeed, James as implicitly anticipating Hemingwayesque machismo: "[J]ust as Hemingway (although certainly not he alone) shaped his masculinity in reaction against Jamesian interiority, so does the Jamesian critique of overdetermined manhood ('active,' externalized, commercial, hetero) anticipate an Ernest Hemingway, with his dire performance pressure and his violent energies" (*Henry James,* 174).

65. Ibid., 173.

66. Quoted in ibid., 200.

67. Vonnegut, *A Man Without a Country,* 23.

68. Adams, *Dandies,* 18. See also White, *The Uses of Obscurity,* for a fine examination of Jamesian concealment.

69. Quoted in Adams, *Dandies,* 207.

70. Critics of Hemingway have, of course, noticed that machismo and something called "reserve" are linked, though they have not, as far as I am aware, connected Hemingwayesque "reserve" to its Victorian antecedent. Schwenger, though, does note that macho "reserve" logically implies a "feminine" reverse that cannot but undo or trouble the masculinism of Hemingway's style: "Masculine reserve thus modulates imperceptibly into feminine unknowableness. And Hemingway becomes the ostentatiously masculine creator of 'feminine' absences" (*Phallic Critiques,* 50).

71. Quoted in Newman, *Apologia,* 22.

72. Adams, *Dandies,* 189.

73. Ibid.

74. Sedgwick, *Epistemology of the Closet,* 74. Boone remarks, relatedly, that "that the crises of narrative authority that have come to be seen as endemic to modern fiction must also be evaluated in light of the specifically sexual anxieties

to which the fictional exploration of interior consciousness and subconscious desires gives voice" (*Libidinal Currents*, 10).

75. My sense of the connection between professionalism and dandyism relies largely on Adams, who discusses at length the links between dandy, professional, and priest. See *Dandies*, 183–228.

76. Dickens, *Great Expectations*, 291.

77. Dickens, *Bleak House*, 148, 171, 512.

78. Ibid., 602.

79. Newman himself invokes the lawyer as a pejorative exemplar of reserved speech and acknowledges, in order to deny it, the popular association of Roman Catholic adherence with lawyerly reticence: "[I]t is not that a Catholic, layman or priest . . . will accept any thing that is placed before him, or is willing, like a lawyer, to speak according to his brief" (*Apologia*, 334).

80. Young, *Ernest Hemingway*, 11.

81. Ibid., 202.

82. Adams, *Dandies*, 195.

83. See Eby, *Hemingway's Fetishism*, 252; and Comley and Scholes, *Hemingway's Genders*, 57–59. Overt references to *Mademoiselle de Maupin* appear twice in Hemingway's corpus. In *Islands in the Stream*, one of Hudson's young sons is reading it, though "I don't understand [it] well enough to explain it" (68–69). And in the manuscript version of *Garden of Eden*, David and Marita discuss the book together and concur that it gave them an "erection" (quoted in Comley and Scholes, *Hemingway's Genders*, 57).

84. Gautier, *Mademoiselle de Maupin*, xiv–xv.

85. Hemingway, *Selected Letters*, 162.

86. Quoted in Haralson, *Henry James*, 194.

87. Gautier, *Mademoiselle de Maupin*, 45.

88. Edel, "The Art of Evasion," 170.

89. Spilka notes the "androgynous direction" of the gender-bending haircut scenes in *A Farewell to Arms*: "even their latent threat of manning and unmanning . . . now seems clear" (282). For a reading of patterns of "transvestic hallucination" across Hemingway, see Eby, "'He Felt the Change.'" And Altman has discussed the impression that *The Garden of Eden* can seem like "the key, or the magic decoder ring" to Hemingway's oeuvre. Altman, however, warns against this impulse: "The danger is that retrospective blurring can lead to over-reading, and misreading, the earlier text." Though I think this admonition is well taken, I agree with Spilka and others that *The Garden of Eden* does in fact retroactively transform the legitimate interpretive possibilities available to Hemingway's readers. As Altman herself puts it, posthumous

publication renders "the innocence of those first readers . . . irrecoverable, for better or for worse" ("Posthumous Queer," 130, 132, 136).

90. Knowles, "The Microcosm as Interior," 12.
91. Hemingway, *Garden of Eden*, 5.
92. Ibid., 150.
93. Feldman, *Dandy on the Divide*, 32, 38.
94. Gautier, *Mademoiselle de Maupin*, 62, 159.
95. Ibid., 45.
96. Ibid., 189.
97. Hemingway, *Garden of Eden* manuscript, 422.1/2, 4, quoted in Eby, *Hemingway's Fetishism*, 158.
98. Hemingway, *Garden of Eden*, 15.
99. Ibid., 184.
100. Ibid., 37.
101. Ibid., 84.
102. Ibid., 193, 67.
103. Szalay, *New Deal Modernism*, 95.
104. Ibid., 95, quoting Hemingway, "An Interview with George Plimpton."
105. Hemingway, *Garden of Eden*, 71. The English "fault" meant originally "deficiency, lack, scarcity, want of (something specified)." The manuscript returns repeatedly to David's suspected impotence (see, e.g., 422.1 11, 16–17).
106. As Comley and Scholes note of "Mr. and Mrs. Elliot," "the object of the satire is not the Elliots as individuals but the culture that has made procreation the sole legitimate object of sexual activity, transforming erotic play into alienated labor" (*Hemingway's Genders*, 82).
107. *Garden of Eden* manuscript, 422 1/17, 9, quoted in Spilka, *Hemingway's Quarrels*, 294. Comley and Scholes: "The published novel allows only part of this story to appear, conveying the impression by its omissions that Marita has restored David to a more 'normal' erotic life, whereas the manuscript indicates that it is precisely the 'abnormality' of their relationship that has refreshed and renewed his creative energies" (*Hemingway's Genders*, 102).
108. See Dellamora, *Masculine Desire*. Pater, for instance, recycles Gautier's 1857 discussion of Leonardo: "Just as Swinburne a few years earlier had turned to French models in order to renew English poetry, so too Pater turns to the French, especially Gautier. Because French writers show an open interest in the sexual ambiguity of Leonardo's life and work, they provide Pater materials for a more thorough analysis of sexual difference" (*Masculine Desire*, 134). On Pater's interest in androgyny, see also Herbert Sussman, *Victorian Masculinities*.

109. Pater, *Renaissance*, 60.
110. *Garden of Eden* manuscript, 422/1, 1, and 422.1/7, 13.
111. Hemingway, *Garden of Eden*, 4.
112. Ibid., 53.
113. Pater, *Renaissance*, 70.
114. Ibid., 163.
115. Mendelson, "Who Was Ernest Hemingway?"
116. *Garden of Eden* manuscript, 422/16, 3.
117. *Garden of Eden* manuscript, 422.1/10, 2.

2. RAYMOND CHANDLER'S DANDIFIED DICK

1. Raymond Chandler to Dale Warren, July 9, 1949, in Chandler, *Papers*, 120–21.
2. Quoted in Ellmann, *Oscar Wilde*, 447.
3. Quoted in Foldy, *The Trials of Oscar Wilde*, 1.
4. Besides Foldy, see Ed Cohen, *Talk on the Wilde Side.* The indispensable foundation for both of these accounts is H. Montgomery Hyde, *The Trials of Oscar Wilde.*
5. Cohen, *Talk on the Wilde Side*, 2.
6. While a discussion of theories of charisma lies outside the scope of this chapter, the model I have most in mind is what Joseph Roach calls "it": "An air of perceived indifference counts heavily in the production of this special allure, which must appear to be exercised effortlessly or not at all. . . . 'It' is the power of apparently effortless embodiment of contradictory qualities simultaneously: strength *and* vulnerability, innocence *and* experience, and singularity *and* typicality among them" (*It*, 5, 8).
7. Sinfield, *The Wilde Century*, 1–2.
8. On Chandler's pastiche of Hemingway, see Hiney, *Raymond Chandler*, 74. Hiney is quoting from Chandler's notebooks, kept at the Bodleian.
9. Corber observes of postwar film noir what is also surely true of the interwar novels of Dashiell Hammett and Chandler: "The men who were most likely to become objects of suspicion in the intensely homophobic climate of the postwar period were not those who participated actively in the domestic sphere or who submitted passively to corporate structures—modes of behavior that in another context might have marked them as insufficiently masculine—but those who refused to settle down and raise a family. Thus one possible function of the clearly marked gay male characters in film noir was to reassure spectators that the independent, self-reliant hero was straight" (*Homosexuality*, 12). Horsley notes that the Chandler hero's "tortured self perceives women as threatening his identity and fears losing control. Such anxieties

are projected, for example, in the fascinated disgust Marlowe expresses for effeminate men like Marriott in *Farewell, My Lovely*, Lavery in *The Lady in the Lake*, and Geiger in *The Big Sleep*" (*Twentieth-Century Crime Fiction*, 82). And Erin A. Smith observes that the ads in *Black Mask* "repeatedly urged readers to get the training they needed to obtain skilled work that retained a measure of autonomy," and that "autonomous work, plain speaking, and manliness meshed in the world of *Black Mask*" (*Hard-Boiled*, 58–59).

10. Chandler, *The Raymond Chandler Omnibus*, 216. Hereafter cited parenthetically by page number and abbreviated C.

11. "Theatrical Trailer," *The Maltese Falcon*, DVD.

12. Important and related late seventeenth- and eighteenth-century precursors to epigrammatic speech in the nineteenth and twentieth centuries might include the bawdy wit of Restoration comedy as well as the verbal one-upsmanship structuring such plays as Richard Brinsley Sheridan's *School for Scandal*. Also relevant: Samuel Johnson's famed verbal aggressivity and the many bon mots attributed to him. In the *Life of Johnson*, James Boswell repeatedly emphasizes the agonistic nature of conversation in Johnson's circle: "Boswell. 'But, Sir, may there not be very good conversation without a contest for superiority?' Johnson. 'No animated conversation, Sir, for it cannot be but one or other will come off superiour'" (589). This is but one instance among dozens in the *Life*.

13. B. H. Smith, *Poetic Closure*, 198n2.

14. Goffman, *Interaction Ritual*, 224–25.

15. Ibid., 227.

16. The hard-boiled private eye should be seen as an episode in the long diminution of normative emotional temperature which Stearns traces from the Victorian period to the postmodern one: "[T]he positive usage of 'cool,' along with its increasing usage, symbolizes our culture's increased striving for restraint" (*American Cool*, 1). Although Stearns does not discuss detective fiction, he does observe the importance of "coolness" in the children's adventure fiction of the 1920s and after: "Rather than grappling with fear, or even considering fear in retrospect, the new breed of Tarzans and, later, Supermen, had no emotions to deal with one way or another. Their coolness was as remarkable as their ability to fly or withstand bullets or communicate with apes" (109).

17. Porter has also noted the similarity between aristocratic speech and the American wisecrack: "As with the maxim of the European aristocratic tradition, the wisecrack combines at its level the quintessence of style with the body of wisdom. Like the maxim it is pointed and elliptical, but unlike

the maxim, since its point of view is from the bottom up, it relies for its power on a cynical irreverence often made memorable by the shock of the vernacular" (*The Pursuit of Crime*, 144).

18. Anderson, *The Powers of Distance*, 148.

19. Relatedly, Eve Kosofsky Sedgwick observes, "The prevailing grammatical mode of [*The Importance of Being Earnest*] is, of course, pointed wit—its almost ascetic paring down to the bare surface of the inversions, epigrams, double entendres that Camille Paglia rightly describes as 'smooth with Mannerist spareness,' 'spasms of delimitation,' 'attempts to defy the temporal character of speech.' Wilde's 'greatest departure from the Restoration dramatists,' Paglia points out, is to 'detach the witticisms from repartee, that is, from social relationship.' It isn't so much that nothing is spared as that nothing is to spare—nothing doesn't pay off; almost literally, not a word of the play fails to contribute its full quantum to the clockwork mechanisms of syntactic and semantic parsimony and hyper-salience" (*Tendencies*, 68–69, quoting Paglia, *Sexual Personae*, 549). What Paglia calls the epigram's "detach[ment] from repartee" and what Sedgwick calls its "hyper-salience" both contribute to the epigram's easy portability.

20. Wilde, *The Complete Works*, 1205. Gwendolen revises the phrase slightly: "In matters of grave importance, style, not sincerity, is the vital thing" (371).

21. See, e.g., "Chandlerisms: A collection of similes, one-liners, and turns of phrase that could be written only by Raymond Chandler," accessed April 23, 2013, http://home.comcast.net/~mossrobert/html/chandlerisms/chandlerisms.htm.

22. Freedman, *Professions of Taste*, 72.

23. Wilde, *Poems and Essays*, 266.

24. Beekman, "Raymond Chandler," 160.

25. Quoted in Joyce Carol Oates, "The Simple Art of Murder."

26. Guetti, "Aggressive Reading," 141.

27. Horsley observes that "Hammett's protagonists are also capable of speaking with a satirist's mocking insight, but Marlowe's perceptions are expressed in ways very unlike the savage ironies of the Continental Op. *Farewell, My Lovely* amply illustrates this habitual form of self-defence, teasing, elegantly phrased, and ironically guarded" (*Twentieth-Century Crime Fiction*, 83–84).

28. Irwin, *Unless the Threat*, 48. In Irwin's reading, Marlowe's enforcement of good manners with Mrs. Regan "make[s] clear that theirs is a professional relationship" rather than a romantic or a sexual one, while also reminding her that "she is still a married woman, and any dalliance would be adulterous" (48).

29. Christianson has, similarly, drawn a distinction in hard-boiled novels between "wisecracks"—tough-talking dialogue—and the "hard-boiled conceit," of which Chandler's famed similes are paradigmatic. The hard-boiled conceit may sometimes occur in dialogue, but, notes Christianson, "lend[s] itself to description within the first-person narrative better than within dialogue" ("Tough Talk," 157).

30. A scene in Henry James's *The Tragic Muse* (1890) can illustrate the way in which limited pragmatic efficacy is attached to the definition of "epigram." Nick Dormer is here discussing his engagement to Julia with Mr. Carteret, a wealthy potential benefactor whose largesse is dependent on Nick and Julia's marriage. Nick explains that Julia wants to wait a certain period before appointing a wedding day, and declares himself resultantly "exceedingly unhappy." "Mr. Carteret looked at his young friend as if he didn't strike him as very unhappy; but he demanded: 'Then what more does she want?' Nick laughed out at this, but he perceived his host had not meant it as an epigram; while the latter went on: 'I don't understand. You're engaged or you're not engaged'" (*Novels, 1886–1890*, 913). As a conversational turn, the deployment of an epigram is not taken to require a response, other than some sort of appreciative acknowledgment of the epigram itself (Nick's laugh). In fact, though, Mr. Carteret "had not meant it as an epigram," which is to say that laughing was the wrong thing to do; Nick should have attempted a serious response ("She wants a prenup").

31. Anderson, *The Powers of Distance*, 164.

32. Ibid., 170.

33. Hammett, *Complete Novels*, 38.

34. Quoted in Stephen L. Tanner, *The Function of Simile*, 174.

35. Mrs. Mounstuart raises the question generally of the female epigrammatist, a type which, in the period of the hard-boiled novel, most famously includes Mae West's screen avatars and Dorothy Parker. A discussion of female epigrammatizing lies outside the scope of this chapter, but see Lauren Berlant's rich reading of Parker and form, genre, and gender (though Berlant does not use the term "epigram"), "'It's Not the Tragedies That Kill Us, It's the Messes': Femininity, Formalism, and Dorothy Parker," in *The Female Complaint*. Berlant recovers the "sentimentality" behind "the pithy, skewering quip[s]" for which Parker is famous (215).

36. Meredith, *The Egoist*, 64.

37. Ibid., 96–97.

38. Ibid., 98.

39. Ibid.

40. Ibid., 309. And Herrnstein Smith likewise observes that "allusions to the punch, sting, bite, or sense of almost (and perhaps, for the nervous system, actual) physical assault [are] frequently associated with epigrammatic endings" (203).

41. Meredith, *The Egoist*, 64, 64, 97, 98. In fact, the etymology of "tattoo" is dual—it entered English both from Dutch, meaning to drum or tap rhythmically, and from Polynesian, meaning to mark with ink. Both resonances are present here. *Oxford English Dictionary*, 2nd ed., s.v. "Tattoo."

42. Guetti, "Aggressive Reading," 143.

43. Hyde, *The Trials of Oscar Wilde*, 22. Hereafter cited parenthetically by page number and abbreviated *T*.

44. Anderson, *The Powers of Distance*, 160. It is an irony of Wilde's courtroom strategy that in spite of the emphasis on his wit that characterized the trial as media event, in fact his most successful moment in court involved a markedly different rhetorical mode: the powerful (apparent) sincerity of the "love that dare not speak its name" speech (quoted in Hyde, *Trials*, 236), generally considered to have caused the second trial to end in a hung jury. This speech, which spoke movingly of platonic love between men, signaled a retreat from the epigrammatic style with which Wilde had hitherto conducted himself. Part of the defensive character of Wilde's epigrams during the trials inheres in the way they generate a certain ironic distance between Wilde and the degrading fact of having to lie in self-defense, but in the "love that dare not speak its name" speech Wilde abandons this distance and forfeits the protection it grants. The abdication of epigram in favor of a style meant to convey profound sincerity and ethical seriousness continues in the prison letter *De Profundis* (1897). Indeed, a good deal of what might be called the "sincerity effect" in both the trial speech and *De Profundis* depends on an audience or reader's registration of the contrast between this new style and an earlier abandoned epigrammatism. Recognizing that epigrammatic aggressivity has definitively failed him in the trial that, he knows, will define his life, Wilde committed himself to a revolution in his own style, a revolution designed to mark his martyrdom with appropriate pathos. For a somewhat different reading, see Foldy, who reads the apparently sincere speech as a supreme instance of Wildean irony, in which "Wilde's disingenuous but skillful appeal to the authority of Plato and the Bible proved successful because it was interpreted literally by those in the courtroom. Wilde's ironic redeployment of the Platonic ideal was doubly devious—a fact that must have greatly amused him—since he was actually appealing less to the authority of the established literary, artistic, and religious canons than to the authority of one of his own

works in which he had attempted to revaluate and subvert those same canons [his essay on Shakespeare's sonnets, 'The Portrait of Mr. W.H.']" (*Trials*, 118).

45. Bakhtin, *The Dialogic Imagination*, 389–90, quoted in Cohen, *Talk*, 251n4.

46. Anderson, *The Powers of Distance*, 70.

47. Wilde, *Complete Works*, 1044.

48. Fiedler, *Love and Death*, 498.

49. Meisel, *The Cowboy and the Dandy*, 4.

50. There is a structural analogy here to the patterns underlying blackface minstrelsy as famously described by Eric Lott. For Lott, blackface "arose from a white obsession with black (male) bodies which underlies white racial dread to our own day"; the affective burden of this performance involved "panic, anxiety, terror, and pleasure" (*Love and Theft*, 3, 6). The racism of blackface minstrelsy has its analogue in the homophobia of the tough guy's encounters with queer dandies; in both cases, "unexpected returns of identificatory desire" provide the libidinal scaffolding for the performance (29). The similarity between minstrelsy and dandiacal tough talk is not arbitrary, for "masculinity" is the common term between the two structures. As Lott puts it, "What appears to have been appropriated were certain kinds of masculinity. To put on the cultural forms of 'blackness' was to engage in a complex affair of manly mimicry" (52).

51. For an extended look at Chandler's engagement with literary decadence, see Norman, "The Big Empty."

52. Chandler, *Later Novels and Other Writings*, 259.

53. Ibid., 711.

54. For an examination of Chandler as "transatlantic" rather than "American," see Norman, "The Big Empty."

55. For a reading that finds both English country house and American hardboiled detective fiction primarily satirical, see Eden, "Detective Fiction as Satire." Eden sees English detective fiction as Horatian and American noir as Juvenalian.

56. Wilstach, *A Dictionary of Similes*, 371.

57. Marlowe's attachment to Norgaard has become the locus classicus of almost all critical readings seeking to complicate Marlowe's presumed heterosexuality, from Gershun Legman's homophobic 1949 critique of "the homosexualist element" in Chandler's fiction to Gill Plain's queer-theory inflected reading of the same scene in 2001, with many stops in between. For an overview of these readings (exclusive of Plain), see Abbott, *The Street Was Mine*, 73–89. Plain reads Marlowe as attracted to Red because he finds in Red an idealized version of himself: "Marlowe has finally encountered the masculine ideal for

which he has been searching. . . . And within the tough-guy framework of the genre, Marlowe's homoerotic intimacy can pass unnoticed" ("Twentieth-Century Crime Fiction," 74–75). I do not think Marlowe's homoerotic intimacy can pass unnoticed; it cannot, and as Legman and others attest, it did not.

58. Abbott, *The Street Was Mine*, 87.
59. McCann, *Gumshoe America*, 144, 150.
60. Ibid., 149, 194.
61. Relatedly, Denning has noted the link "between proletarian literature and the popular hard-boiled thrillers of gangsters and detectives, a link that can . . . be seen in the work of Dashiell Hammett, Horace McCoy, and Chester Himes" (*The Cultural Front*, 221).
62. McCann, *Gumshoe America*, 1.
63. Conrad, "The Private Dick," 60.
64. As Julian Symons notes, "When [Chandler] read Max Beerbohm he felt that he too belonged to an age of grace and taste from which he had been exiled. 'So I wrote for *Black Mask*. What a wry joke'" ("An Aesthete Discovers," 27).
65. Conrad, "The Private Dick," 60.
66. Hammett, *The Maltese Falcon*, 96.
67. Ibid., 144–45.

3. WILLIAM S. BURROUGHS'S MODERNIST GENRE DECADENCE

1. Carlyle, *Sartor Resartus*, 217.
2. Wells, *The Time Machine*, 54, 56.
3. Ibid., 51, 70, 66, 69.
4. Ibid., 110.
5. Ibid., 114–15.
6. Ibid., 115–16, 148.
7. Burroughs, *Letters*, 178, 181.
8. Burroughs, *Cities of the Red Night*, 243.
9. Ibid., 154.
10. Ibid., 158, 155, 158.
11. Quoted in Glick, *Materializing Queer Desire*, 129.
12. Ibid.
13. Apter, "Spaces of the Demimonde," 143.
14. For an account of decadence and its relationship to modernism, see Calinescu, *Five Faces of Modernity*, 151–211.
15. Apter, "Spaces of the Demimonde," 144.
16. Pittock, *Spectrum of Decadence*, 208.

NOTES TO PAGES 97–103

17. Burroughs, *The Place of Dead Roads*, 183.

18. Burroughs. *Junky*, 150.

19. Ibid., 135.

20. Ibid., 131.

21. Burroughs, *A Word Virus*, 16.

22. Ibid., 20, 21.

23. Ibid.

24. Burroughs, *Junky*, 4.

25. Ibid., 73.

26. Glick, *Materializing Queer Desire*, 129, 130.

27. Burroughs, *Letters*, 119–20, quoted in Glick, *Materializing Queer Desire*, 128.

28. Glick, *Materializing Queer Desire*, 128–29.

29. In *Queer Burroughs*, Russell similarly reads this passage as a piece of "camp self-consciousness": "Lawrence of Arabia and 'all manner of right Joes' may well have been masculine-identified gay men, but openly acknowledging their queer potential is in itself a subversive act, as Burroughs himself self-consciously indicates—'boy can I turn a phrase.' Is he merely commenting on his literary skills, or noting the 'turning' (resignification) of the all-American 'Joe Public' into a queer 'right Joe'?" In his correspondence, writes Russell, Burroughs would erect "a seemingly strict definition of the gender differences that constitute the two supposedly oppositional labels of 'fag' and 'queer,' while confusing both positions by repeatedly shifting between their two extremes" (10, 11–12).

30. Burroughs, *Queer*, 39–40, boldface in original.

31. As Murphy observes in *Wising Up the Marks*, this passage draws parodically on "the psychiatric 'confession' of deviance" and is "less a coming-out narrative than a simultaneous parody of a coming-out narrative and of a confession of homosexual psychopathology" (60).

32. Quoted in Sante, "The Invisible Man."

33. Russell observes that Burroughs's fantasies of gay revolutionary violence are developed in reaction to Mattachine Society founder Donald Webster Cory's counsel of "turning the other cheek" (quoted in Russell, *Queer Burroughs*, 41). Burroughs, conversely: "This citizen says a queer learns humility, learns to turn the other cheek, and returns love for hate . . . I never swallowed the other cheek routine, and I hate the stupid bastards who won't mind their own business. They can die in agony for all I care" (*Letters*, 105–6, quoted in Russell, 42).

34. Burroughs, *Junky*, 2.

35. Burroughs, *Place of Dead Roads*, 23.

36. Ibid., 25.

37. Burroughs, *Cities*, 34.

38. Burroughs, *Place of Dead Roads*, 168.

39. Ibid., 72.

40. Ibid., 48, 72.

41. Burroughs's Clem Snide—the "private asshole"—points toward an idealized synthesis of genre-fiction continence (the hard shell of the private detective) with decadent interiority (signified by the asshole) and therefore suggests a somewhat different solution than that achieved in Kim Carsons. The asshole recurs throughout Burroughs's fiction, from the comic "talking asshole" routine in *Naked Lunch* (discussed in the following section) to the erotic lyricism of the "The Miracle of the Rose" chapter in *The Wild Boys*. At its most obscene, the Burroughsian asshole converts Nietzschean anxiety about what's "under the skin" into revolting slapstick, as when *Queer* describes Bobo's "sticky end": "He was riding in the Duc de Ventre's Hispano-Suiza when his falling piles blew out of the car and wrapped around the rear wheel. He was completely gutted, leaving an empty shell sitting there on the giraffe-skin upholstery. Even the eyes and the brain went, with a horrible shlupping sound" (40). But the "private asshole" cannot fall victim to this fate, because he tempers the "horrible shlupping sound" of his insides with the codes of an (always already parodied) genre-fiction machismo, with the cool stares of those tough guys and "shootists" of Burroughs's adventure-fiction world.

42. In *Junky*, a drug buyer named Louis "looked like an 1890 portrait" (44). In *Naked Lunch*, there are "1890 cops" and a "vast empty hotel lobby in 1890 style" (17, 34). Examples can be multiplied.

43. Shaviro, "Burroughs' Theater," 203.

44. Quoted in Annette Michelson, ed., *Andy Warhol*, 1.

45. For a discussion of Burroughs that makes brief reference to Warhol in the context of discussing "fascination," see Harris, *William Burroughs and the Secret of Fascination*, 6–7.

46. Burroughs, *Place of Dead Roads*, 260–61.

47. Ibid., ellipses in original.

48. I adapt "Darwinesque" from Morse Peckham's "Darwinistic," which refers to imaginative, metaphoric, or figurative appropriations of Darwin's thought, thereby distinguishing the (non- or pseudoscientific) "Darwinistic/Darwinesque" from the more properly scientific "Darwinian." See Peckham, quoted in C. Williams, *Transfigured World*, 142.

49. Sparks examines the "medical gothic at the *fin de siècle*" and observes that "[t]he literature of the era personifies the suspect power of the scientist or

surgeon in figures like Dr. Jekyll or Dr. Moreau, among whose moral crimes include experimentation for its own sake rather than towards the alleviation of pain and suffering" (*The Doctor*, 112). Hurley sums up the impact of evolutionary thought on the "*fin-de-siècle* Gothic" thus: "[T]he Darwinian narrative of the evolution of species was a narrative within which any combination of morphic traits, any transfiguration of bodily form, was possible; species integrity was undone and remade according to the immediate, situational logic of adaptation to the environment" (*The Gothic Body*, 6). On the impact of Darwinian thought on Victorian realism (but not on H. G. Wells or science fiction), see Beer, *Darwin's Plots;* and Levine, *Darwin and the Novelists*. Levine treats Victorian novelists' ambivalent assimilation and negotiation of a world unmoored from absolutes in the wake of evolutionary thinking. Beer traces the effects of Darwin's metaphors as they "take on a life of their own" (8) as the determinative mythoi of the second half the nineteenth century.

50. Burroughs, *Naked Lunch*, 119–20, 119.
51. Burroughs and Gysin, *Third Mind*, 2.
52. Burroughs, *Ah Pook Is Here*, 66, 67.
53. Burroughs and Odier, *The Job*, 199.
54. Pound and Fenollosa, *The Chinese Written Character*, 52.
55. Burroughs, *Ah Pook Is Here*, 65. Burroughs cites not Fenollosa but the brilliant quack Alfred Korzybski for teaching him about the perniciousness of verbs of identity. For a good popular summary of Korzybski's ideas and their influence on science fiction, see Konstantinou, "The Eccentric Polish Count."
56. Burroughs and Odier, *The Job*, 34, 59.
57. See Jean-Michel Rabaté: "The link between the creation of a language and the foundation of a city or state is one of Pound's major motifs in the *Cantos*" (*Language, Sexuality*, 8). Pound's linguistically oriented political philosophy is rooted in his understanding of Confucianism, since, as Alec Marsh writes, "The opening of the *Ta Hio* [which Pound translated] tells us to look into our hearts and ascertain the correct definition of words, then through self-discipline we can put our house in order" ("Politics," 97). And Feng Lan discusses the relationship between Pound's "etymographic" approach to the Chinese ideogram (in which "the authenticity and truthfulness of the ideogrammic sign system" is excavated by "decompos[ing] a character into a number of smallest meaningful units, and then reorganiz[ing] their sememes to reproduce the supposedly primordial idea") and a politicized epistemology: Pound's Confucianism "gave his theory of precise language a profound epistemological and ontological foundation, a theory that championed a redeemed language not only as the key to social problems, but also

as the bridge for reconnecting the human world with the world of nature as well as with the world of transcendental eternity" ("Confucius," 328, 330). Ira Nadel has discussed Pound's "visualization of history" in the Confucian Cantos: "The 'picture writing' of the Chinese ideogram gave Pound the model that enhanced the visibility not only of metaphor but of history" ("Visualizing History," 165). Jackson observes that Pound "sees the artifex, whether poet or politician, as cleaving to certain key values," first of which is "concreteness." "Concreteness is almost Pound's epistemological cornerstone and its importance extends from his briefest, most subjective poem to his broadest political conception" ("The Poetic Politics," 997–98).

58. Burroughs and Odier, *The Job*, 11.

59. See Guillory, "Genesis of the Media Concept." Guillory mentions science fiction in the context of the seventeenth-century language theorist John Wilkins, whose anti-alphabetic "real character" eerily prefigures, to my mind, Burroughs's hieroglyphic fixations: "But Wilkins's real character famously bypasses alphabetic script; his ideographic writing was intended to free writing from the purpose only of representing spoken words and so enable the real character to establish an unambiguous and permanently fixed relation between symbols and ideas, on the one side, and things, on the other. Locke saw that this was an error, but it is worth specifying what kind of error. Today we would say that Wilkins hoped to correct the communicative deficiency of language by means of a technological fix. This recourse, which has the same sort of charm as much science fiction, also has something of that genre's capacity to leap beyond conceptual safe ground for something new and strange" (336).

60. Quoted in Simon James, *Maps of Utopia*, 65.

61. Ibid.

62. Ibid.

63. Wilde, *The Picture of Dorian Gray*, 47.

64. Wells, *The Island of Dr. Moreau*, 63.

65. Ibid., 34.

66. Ibid., 178.

67. Ibid., 91, 98.

68. Ibid., 133.

69. Ibid., 74–75.

70. Burroughs, *The Soft Machine*, 173–74.

71. Burroughs and Gysin, *Third Mind*, 131.

72. Burroughs and Odier, *The Job*, 13.

73. Burroughs and Gysin, *Third Mind*, 17.

74. Burroughs, *The Ticket That Exploded*, 49–50.

75. Quoted in Miles, *William Burroughs*, 96.

76. Burroughs and Odier, *The Job*, 137.

77. Ibid., 96.

78. For a concise history of the imaginative ramifications of the "missing link," see Beer, *Forging the Missing Link*.

79. See Dowling, *Language and Decadence*, 133, for a discussion of the resonance between Bourget's influential definition of literary decadence and the new linguistic theories of the period.

80. Burroughs, *Rub Out the Words*, 22.

81. Miles, *William Burroughs*, 93.

82. Quoted in Pericles Lewis, "To Make a Dadaist Poem."

83. Tzara, "Dada Manifesto."

84. Burroughs, *Rub Out the Words*, 132.

85. Lydenberg, *Word Cultures*, 55. Lydenberg, luckily, does not follow her own advice.

86. Burroughs and Gysin, *Third Mind*, 2.

87. In *The Western Lands*, Burroughs credits Norman Mailer's *Ancient Evenings* (1983) "for inspiration" regarding the treatment of Egyptian mythology. In this connection, it is curious to note Mailer's linkage of hieroglyphic writing to biology in *The Armies of the Night* (1968), a connection that Burroughs would reverse: "[P]erhaps the history of the past was another tissue, spiritual, no doubt, without physical embodiment, unless its embodiment was in the cuneiform hieroglyphics of the chromosome (so much like primitive writing!) . . ." (109).

88. Quoted in Bernheimer, *Decadent Subjects*, 10.

89. Lemair, introduction to Burroughs and Gysin, *Third Mind*, 20.

90. Burroughs and Odier, *The Job*, 178.

91. Burroughs, *Junky*, 99.

92. Rainey, "Taking Dictation," 125.

93. Sword, *Ghostwriting Modernism*, 84–85.

94. Lotringer, ed., *Burroughs Live*, 497.

95. Sword, *Ghostwriting Modernism*, 17–18.

96. Ibid., 101.

97. Burroughs and Gysin, *Third Mind*, 70.

98. Sword, *Ghostwriting Modernism*, 18. As Burroughs says at the beginning of *Towers Open Fire*, the cut-up film he and Antony Balch made in 1963, "Gentlemen, this was to be expected. After all he's been a medium all his life" (William S. Burroughs and Antony Balch, *Towers Open Fire*, accessed September 14, 2014, https://www.youtube.com/watch?v=dlQKPYfP0CM).

99. Agamben, *Stanzas*, 53.
100. Grimstad, "Notes on Burroughs."
101. Burroughs, *The Western Lands*, 1.
102. Ibid., 1–2.
103. Ibid., 2.
104. Ibid., 3, 4. In fact, the actual Goethe lines do not form a couplet, but an ABAB quatrain. Burroughs misquotes the German as: "Wenn Du dies nicht hast dieses Sterben und Werden, / Bist du nur ein trübe Gast auf der dunklen Erden." The poem is "Selige Sehnsucht," and Burroughs was evidently quoting from memory; the lines actually run: "Und so lang du das nicht hast, / Dieses: Stirb und werde! / Bist du nur ein trüber Gast / Auf der dunklen Erde." As far as I can discover, the translation is Burroughs's own.
105. Lotringer, *Burroughs Live*, 497.
106. Burroughs, *Western Lands*, 165.
107. Clune, *Writing Against Time*, 20.
108. Goldstone, *Fictions of Autonomy*, 26.
109. Olsen, "Prelude," 288.
110. Ibid., 280.
111. Ibid.
112. Lydenberg, *Word Cultures*, 71.
113. Sherry, *Modernism and the Reinvention of Decadence*, 57.
114. Burroughs, *Western Lands*, 258.

4. DJUNA BARNES'S CROSS-GENDERED CONCEITS

1. Barnes, *Interviews*, 381.
2. See http://www.oprah.com/style/the-history-of-coco-chanel.
3. Chaney, *Coco Chanel*, 109.
4. Barnes, *Interviews*, 382.
5. Thoreau, *A Year*, 112.
6. See Simon, *Chanel*, 14.
7. Quoted in ibid., 13. "Chanel modelled a body image that could be achieved only through rigorous dieting and undergarments that flattened and bound the breasts and any other body parts that might interrupt an outfit's line" (13).
8. Ibid., 20.
9. Ibid., 75.
10. See ibid., 11.
11. Ibid., 61.
12. Barnes, *Interviews*, 379.
13. Burstein, *Cold Modernism*, 146, 130.

14. Barnes, "Against Nature," 88, quoted in Gillespie, "'The Triumph,'" 7.
15. Blyn, "*Nightwood's* Freak Dandies," 513.
16. For the definitive overview of nineteenth-century female aestheticism, see Schaffer, *The Forgotten Female Aesthetes.* For the gender politics of modernist decadence, see Mahoney, *Literature and Politics,* 153–93. The fictional characters most pertinent to the female decadents in Barnes might be those of Beresford Egan (1905–84), in whose work appears the "radically strange and striking character Anna Beryl Foster. Anna is a female dandy whose sexual adventurousness, same-sex relationships, and detachment are represented by Egan in wholly approving terms" (Mahoney 177).
17. Messerli, foreword to Barnes, *Interviews,* 377.
18. See Cottom, *International Bohemia,* 1–2.
19. Ibid., 2.
20. Ibid.
21. Ibid., 21.
22. Davidson, "Pregnant Men," 215.
23. Barnes, *Nightwood,* 30.
24. Meredith, *The Ordeal of Richard Feveral,* 355.
25. Ibid., 356, 357.
26. Ibid., 359, 364.
27. Rachilde's *The Marquise de Sade* offers something like the anti-*Nightwood,* insofar as the excessive interiority of its decadent heroine is turned outward—in sadism—rather than inward, in the lovelorn masochism typical of Barnes.
28. Butler, *Gender Trouble,* 187.
29. Garber, *Vested Interests,* 385.
30. Barnes, *Nightwood,* 85.
31. See Garber, *Vested Interests,* 377–87. Garber supplements Freud's case study with reference to a later psychotherapist of the Wolf-Man's, Dr. Ruth Brunswick. As in Meredith, transgendered fantasy involves a mirror, in this case the Wolf-Man's wife's pocket mirror, with which he compulsively looks at his nose: "The Wolf-Man, in short, had . . . become a 'woman,' become his wife" (378). Garber reports on several cross-dressing dreams shared by the Wolf-Man with Brunswick.
32. Ibid., 388.
33. Butler, *Gender Trouble,* 187.
34. Barnes, *Nightwood,* 84–85.
35. Nietzsche, *Gay Science,* 122, quoted in Bernheimer, 22; Garber, *Vested Interests,* 389.
36. Barnes, *Nightwood,* 85.

37. Gilbert, "Costumes of the Mind," 403, 415.
38. Gubar, "Blessings in Disguise," n.p.
39. My discomfort with certain kinds of celebratory readings of Barnes is conso-
    nant with Shin's complaint that "the [critical] tendency to gloss over Barnes's
    nihilism and to draw out feel-good elements—the mere presence of sexual
    deviance, the overtly (and fleetingly) anti-patriarchal—gets in the way of
    reading Barnes's oeuvre holistically, that is, as a whole in terms of form and
    context" ("Apocalypse for Barnes," 182).
40. Gilbert, "Costumes of the Mind," 403.
41. Blyn, in order to reject it, observes this "commonplace in the criticism"
    ("*Nightwood*'s Freak Dandies," 522n2).
42. See Hardie, "Repulsive Modernism," 119.
43. Carlston, *Thinking Fascism*, 50. In its emphasis on Barnes's debt to decadence,
    recent critical consensus is in agreement with Kannenstine's pathbreaking
    1977 *The Art of Djuna Barnes*, which saw that "[t]he theme of decadence is of
    course everywhere in [*Nightwood*]" (100).
44. Weir, *Decadent Culture*, 180–81, 183–84.
45. Ibid, 186.
46. Barnes, *Book of Repulsive Women*, 27, 28.
47. Sherry, *Modernism and the Reinvention of Decadence*, 280.
48. Gagnier, "Global Circulation," 70.
49. Weir, *Decadent Culture*, 185.
50. Barnes, *Ryder*, 100.
51. T. S. Eliot, introduction to Barnes, *Nightwood*, xxii.
52. Kannenstine, too, "hear[s] echoes of the metaphysical poets" (*Art of Djuna
    Barnes*, 104).
53. Kaup identifies Barnes as a practitioner of the "neobaroque," a category asso-
    ciated with the Spanish poet Góngora, himself sometimes considered "deca-
    dent" ("The Neobaroque," 90).
54. Riffaterre, "Decadent Paradoxes," 66.
55. Ibid., 78.
56. Blyn, "*Nightwood*'s Freak Dandies," 504.
57. Riffaterre, "Decadent Paradoxes," 70.
58. See Gardner, *The Metaphysical Poets*, xx.
59. Johnson, *The Major Works*, 678.
60. Gardner, *The Metaphysical Poets*, xxiii, xxvi.
61. Donne, indeed, is quoted (by Dr. O'Connor) in *Nightwood*, specifically
    his sermon of March 28, 1619, "Preached to the Lords upon Easter Day":
    "Donne says, 'We are all conceived in close prison, in our mothers' wombs

we are close prisoners all. When we are born, we are but born to the liberty of the house—all our life is but a going out to the place of execution and death. Now was there ever any man seen to sleep in the Car, between Newgate and Tyburn? Between the prison and the place of execution, does any man sleep?' Yet he says, 'Men sleep all the way.' How much more, therefore, is there upon him a close sleep when he is mounted on darkness" (104). O'Connor's "mounted on darkness" is a characteristically opaque phrase, apparently completing an argument but resistant to paraphrase or elucidation. As Daniella Caselli observes, "Nightwood favours conceptual antitheses that, like in John Donne . . . use syllogism as a mechanism; the novel is a method of persuasion without a thesis to demonstrate" (Improper Modernism, 158).

62. Barnes, Nightwood, 61–62.

63. Ibid., 165.

64. Singer, A Metaphysics of Fiction, 49, 58.

65. Barnes, Nightwood, 95.

66. Ibid., 34.

67. In "A Story Beside(s) Itself," Victoria L. Smith observes, relatedly, that Barnes's "relentless metaphors and similes . . . are so thickly wrapped around each other that we lose sight of the object but begin to see shadows of something long forgotten or lost" (203). Smith emphasizes not the autonomy developed by the vehicle in Barnes's unfurling metaphors but, rather, the sense that the tenor is unnamable, that it gestures toward an absence that, in her larger reading, she connects to Freudian melancholia in general and to the historically specific set of losses experienced by lesbians, gay men, and Jews.

68. Riffaterre, "Decadent Paradoxes," 68.

69. Analogously, Katz reads Pater's metaphors in "The Child in the House" as destabilizing the relationship between tenor and vehicle: "The metaphors themselves seem to initiate a process of decay that passes out of the realm of the metaphorical as well as out of control. . . . they begin to take on an autonomy that appears increasingly threatening, indeed that promises an ominous self-dissolution" (Impressionist Subjects, 37).

70. Quoted in Bernheimer, Decadent Subjects, 10.

71. Weir, Decadent Culture, 185. Eliot's quotation is from his introduction to Nightwood, xviii.

72. Kannenstine, The Art of Djuna Barnes, xvi.

73. Barnes, Nightwood, 45. Delany mentions the possibility that Barnes's Isaiahan "Watchman, What of the Night?" derives from a poem of Pater's (About Writing, 179).

74. Pater, *Renaissance*, 70.
75. C. Williams, *Transfigured World*, 3.
76. Ibid., 45, 59, 5, 10.
77. Garber, *Vested Interests*, 387.
78. For a compelling analysis of the relationship between the transgender and the transhistorical in *Nightwood*, see Shin, "Djuna Barnes, History's Elsewhere." For Shin, "Dateless languages complement the queer mythmaking of Barnes's characters to reimagine the West's paternal heritage and map out historically erased queer experience" (26).
79. Barnes, *Nightwood*, 97.
80. Ibid, 173.
81. Kannenstine, *The Art of Djuna Barnes*, xvi–xvii.
82. Caselli, *Improper Modernism*, 170.
83. Barnes, *Nightwood*, 44.
84. And so on for another several hundred words. Nordau, *Degeneration*, 7–8.
85. Ibid., 11.
86. Ibid., 5.
87. Seitler, "'Down on All Fours," 534, 553. For other treatments of Barnes and degeneration, see Heise, "Degenerate Sex and the City"; and Azzarello, *Queer Environmentality*.
88. Barnes, *Nightwood*, 44, 41, 56.
89. De Man, "The Epistemology of Metaphor," 19. De Man is offering an interpretive summary of Locke.
90. Clare Taylor, *Women, Writing, and Fetishism*, 160, 165.
91. Quoted in ibid., 152.
92. Scott, *Refiguring Modernism*, 73.
93. Nordau, *Degeneration*, 315.
94. Barnes, *Nightwood*, 179.
95. Tyrus Miller, *Late Modernism*, 159.
96. Burke, *Language as Symbolic Action*, 244, 246.
97. Singer, *A Metaphysics of Fiction*, 72.
98. For a reading of horror and the "fantastic tale" as major outgrowths of aesthetic decadence, see Pittock, *Spectrum of Decadence*, 108.
99. Blyn, "*Nightwood*'s Freak Dandies," 507.
100. Letter to Chester Page, quoted in Clare Taylor, *Women, Writing*, 188.
101. Seitler, "Down On All Fours," 526, 530.
102. Barnes, *Nightwood*, 126–27.
103. Paul West, afterword to *Ryder*, 248.

104. Chu, *Do Metaphors Dream?*, 112, 3, 9. Chu locates the metaphysical conceit at the origin of science fiction, and names specifically Donne's "Valediction: Forbidding Mourning" (11).
105. Ibid., 65.
106. Barnes, *At the Root of the Stars*, 62.
107. Clare Taylor reads *Madame Collects Herself* as "a premature critique on psychoanalytic theories of the masquerade and gendered embodiment: what is it that precisely makes the woman?" (182).
108. Barnes, *At the Root of the Stars*, 62.
109. Ibid.
110. Nordau, *Degeneration*, 9.

5. THE PSYCHOPATHIC DANDY

1. Quoted in Mailer, *The Executioner's Song*, 404–5.
2. I am speaking primarily of *representations* of the sociopath; I am not interested in the clinical profiles of "actual" sociopaths, though as it happens they are overwhelmingly male.
3. Lindner, *Rebel without a Cause*, 6.
4. *Bonnie and Clyde*, DVD.
5. As Mendelssohn recounts, the association of dandiacal aestheticism with advertising and commodification was strong enough in the nineteenth century that skeptical Americans could refer to Wilde, during his lecture tour, as an "a$$-thete" (*Henry James, Oscar Wilde*, 58).
6. Highsmith, *Ripley Under Water*, 206.
7. Goffman, *Asylums*, 320.
8. Seltzer, *Serial Killers*, 108.
9. Adorno, *The Authoritarian Personality*, 763.
10. Lindner, *Rebel*, 6.
11. Trask, *Camp Sites*, 135.
12. Edelman, *No Future*, 39–40.
13. Mailer, *Advertisements for Myself*, 206, 207, 209.
14. Ibid., 211, 207, 211.
15. Mishima, *Confessions of a Mask*, 41.
16. Ibid., 27.
17. Ibid., 101.
18. Ibid., 104–5.
19. Ibid., 183.
20. Ibid., 90–91.
21. Ibid., 108, 228, 126.

22. Edelman, *No Future*, 4.
23. Ibid., 9.
24. Ibid., 153.
25. In her *New York Times* review of *The Executioner's Song*, Joan Didion writes, "The very subject of 'The Executioner's Song' is that vast emptiness at the center of the Western experience, a nihilism antithetical not only to literature but to most other forms of human endeavor, a dread so close to zero that human voices fadeout, trail off, like skywriting" ("I Want to Go Ahead and Do It").
26. Lyotard, *Jacques Monory*, 196.
27. Ibid., 142–43, 102.
28. Apocalypse, as Mario Praz suggests, has always been a secret wish of decadent literature, which "show[s] not so much the terror, as the attraction, of disaster" (*The Romantic Agony*, 381).
29. Trask, *Camp Sites*, 135.
30. Greven, "Queer Ripley," 122.
31. Trask, *Camp Sites*, 135, 145, 144.
32. Highsmith, *The Talented Mr. Ripley*, 38, 40.
33. Ibid., 58, 59.
34. Ibid., 201.
35. Ibid., 234.
36. Highsmith, *Ripley Under Ground*, 325.
37. Highsmith, *Talented Mr. Ripley*, 85.
38. Cassuto, *Hard-Boiled Sentimentality*, 136.
39. Highsmith, *The Boy Who Followed*, 132.
40. Ibid., 144.
41. Ibid., 187.
42. Ibid., 204.
43. Ibid., 322.
44. Ibid., 323.
45. Highsmith, *Ripley Under Water*, 41.
46. Ibid., 105.
47. Highsmith, *Ripley Under Ground*, 505.
48. Highsmith, *Ripley Under Water*, 201.
49. Ibid., 87.
50. Ibid., 112.
51. Highsmith, *Talented Mr. Ripley*, 25.
52. Wilkinson, *American Tough*, 13.
53. Mailer, *Mind of an Outlaw*, 48.
54. Ibid., 45.

55. For a good overview of the debates around "The White Negro," see Douglas Taylor, "Three Lean Cats." See also Szalay's *Hip Figures*, which rehabilitates "The White Negro" as the master key to the racial politics of American progressivism.

56. The Beats exemplify this tendency—Ivy League–educated writers (Ginsberg, Kerouac, Burroughs) partake of hipness only through contact with figures like Neal Cassady and Hubert Huncke (the latter actually middle-class but projecting marginality), who function, as it were, as hip's native informants.

57. Mailer, *Mind of an Outlaw*, 41.

58. *The Wild One*, DVD.

59. Quoted in Mailer, *Mind of an Outlaw*, 41.

60. But it was Brando's genius to play Johnny with minimal theatricality, as an actual psychopath in a melancholy key. It is perhaps not surprising that an adherent of method acting would approach the role in this way, since "the method" calls for an ambiguous immersion in and performance of a character type analogous to the hipster's performative immersion in the sensory and psychic life of the psychopath. From Brando as Kowalski in *Streetcar* through Al Pacino's Michael Corleone and Tony Montana, Robert De Niro's Travis Bickle, and so on, method acting is practically synonymous, in the popular imagination, with playing psychopaths.

61. Kesey, *One Flew Over*, 12–13.

62. Goodin suggests an even longer lineage for McMurphy: not only is he like "a Western hero coming into a strange saloon" but like "a saga hero into a strange meadhall" (*The Poetics of Protest*, 147).

63. Kesey, *One Flew Over*, 123.

64. Ibid., 90.

65. Ibid., 39.

66. Ibid., 42.

67. Ibid., 190.

68. Ibid., 228, 231.

69. Ibid., 229.

70. Ellis, *American Psycho*, 375. Elizabeth Young observes that Bateman's "surface" monologue might be read in the register of parody: "This sophomoric philosophizing appears to be delivered seriously, although it is nonsensical placed against the enormity of the crimes Patrick claims to have committed" (Young and Cavenay, *Shopping in Space*, 112). The indeterminately parodic nature of Bateman's "philosophizing" rhymes with Snooty's ambiguously parodic "behaviorism."

71. McCarthy, "Love and Death in the Pacific."

72. Ellis, *American Psycho*, 5, 4–5, 8.

73. Jameson, *Postmodernism*, 12. Critics have devised a number of suggestive labels for the late-century antinovel to which Ellis's work belongs, alongside the output of novelists such as Jay McInerney, Dennis Cooper, Tama Janowitz, and Kathy Acker. Young and Cavenay suggest "blank generation fiction," "which establishes, through Richard Hell's anthem of the same name, the necessary link with punk and conveys something of the flat, stunned quality of much of the writing" (*Shopping in Space*, intro.). Annesley, similarly, suggests "blank fictions" in his study of that title. Hume's category of "aggressive fictions" is more capacious and therefore somewhat less precise, including as it does not only work by writers of Ellis's generation and disposition but also by such diverse figures as Philip Roth, Ishmael Reed, and Philip K. Dick. However, Hume's description of one mode of "aggressive fiction" fits Ellis nicely: it is "anti-hermeneutic" and "encourages a kind of reader masochism" (*Aggressive Fictions*, xiii).

74. Annesley has examined the consonance between late twentieth-century "blank fiction" and the Victorian fin de siècle, both of which "appear to articulate a similar response to shifts in the economic organisation of their respective societies" (115). His key text is not *American Psycho* but Ellis's second novel, *The Rules of Attraction*, with its presiding dandy, Richard: "Echoes of Dorian Gray's and Des Esseintes's epicurean tastes reverberate in Ellis's description of Richard's consumption of British post-punk. . . . In these terms he seems intent on turning himself into a kind of late twentieth-century dandy" (116).

75. Ellis, *American Psycho*, 179, ellipses in original.

76. Felski, *The Gender of Modernity*, 100.

77. Ellis, *American Psycho*, 179.

78. Characteristically, the French tradition articulates the link between decadent aestheticism and murderous psychopathy much more explicitly than the English. One thinks inter alia of the visionary sadism of Lautréamont's *Maldoror* (1869), in which the eponymous protagonist eviscerates an "unfortunate child" through her vagina (129)—a variety of mutilation that will be repeated by Bateman—and of Huysmans's *Là-bas* (1891), a classic of decadence featuring extended, horrific set pieces describing the ritualized child murders committed by Gilles de Rais. *Dorian Gray* acknowledges its debt to its more extreme French forebears with the corrupting book, widely presumed to be Huysmans's *À Rebours*, given to Dorian by Lord Wotton.

79. See Weinreich, " 'Into the Void.' " For more on Baudrillard and Ellis, see Baelo-Allué, "Bret Easton Ellis's Controversial Fiction," 110.

80. Sherry, *Ezra Pound and Radical Modernism*, 5. Sherry provides a cultural and political history of this aesthetic dichotomy, which is shown to inform Lewis's and Pound's attraction to authoritarian political systems.

81. Baudrillard, *Simulacra and Simulation*, 162.

82. Ellis, *American Psycho*, 374.

83. Indeed, the desert is something of a stock trope for psychopathy and murderousness, for instance in Norman Mailer's *The Executioner's Song* (1980) and in the fiction of Paul Bowles.

84. Burstein, *Cold Modernism*, 66.

85. F. Ferguson, *Pornography*, 151.

86. Ellis, *American Psycho*, 304.

87. Lewis, *Snooty Baronet*, 48.

88. Burstein, *Cold Modernism*, 76.

89. Ngai, *Our Aesthetic Categories*, 92.

90. Ibid., 59, 4.

91. Ibid., 92.

92. Ellis, *American Psycho*, 343.

93. F. Ferguson, *Pornography*, 150.

94. Serpell, "Repetition," 62. For a reading of *American Psycho* as a "representation of normative masculinity taken to its extremes" (63) in reaction to shifting gender norms in postmodernity, see Storey, "'And As Things Fell Apart.'"

95. Edwards, *Wyndham Lewis*, 4. Between modernism proper and Ellis's postmodernism lies the *nouveau roman*, about which, as Jameson puts it, there is "the widespread impression that [it] had something to do with *things* (and therefore with descriptions)" (*Postmodernism*, 135). And the *nouveau roman*, too, exhibited a distinct interest in the psychopath, as demonstrated for instance by the (possible) child-murdering narrator of Robbe-Grillet's *Le Voyeur* (1955).

96. Mailer, *Mind of an Outlaw*, 439.

97. Ellis, *American Psycho*, 139.

98. Ibid., 51.

99. Serpell, "Repetition," 63.

100. Ibid., 47–48, for a concise overview of the book's initial reception.

101. Seltzer, *Serial Killers*, 64. Seltzer mentions *American Psycho* specifically, which, he says, "advertises, and trades on, the analogies, or causal relations, between these two forms of compulsive repetition, consumerism and serial killing" (64–65).

102. Vermeule, *Why Do We Care?*, 31.

103. Ibid., 144.

104. Kotsko, *Why We Love Psychopaths*, 6.

105. Ngai, *Our Aesthetic Categories*, 62.

106. Ellis, *American Psycho*, 77.

107. Lyotard, *Jacques Monory*, 111.

108. Ibid., 196.

109. Quoted in Weinreich, "'Into the Void,'" 73; ibid., 66.

110. Lyotard, *Jacques Monory*, 111, 137.

111. Ibid., 113–14.

112. Ibid., 140.

113. Ibid., 127, 130, 122.

114. Ibid., 154.

115. Ibid., 127.

116. F. Ferguson, *Pornography*, 151.

117. As Katz puts it, "Abstraction powerfully reencloses the subject, reestablishes that dream of autonomy which impressionism begins by denying" (*Impressionist Subjects*, 14).

118. Schoene-Harwood, *Writing Men*, 68. And Jachimiak observes that Kubrick's film version, in rendering Alex and his droogs iconic, also reduces *A Clockwork Orange* to mere advertising: "Its bootboy kick reduced to that of lame parody, *A Clockwork Orange* no longer scares, now it just sells" ("'Putting the Boot In,'" 159). Furthermore, "Kubrick's on-screen realisation of the Korova milk bar . . . is a nightmare extension of modernity's witnessing of a chrome-and-neon-enhancing Americanisation" (150). The seamless application of its rebellious iconicity to advertising has much in common with Brando and the Triumph motorcycle in *The Wild One*.

119. Burgess, *A Clockwork Orange*, 4. Elsewhere, Alex refers to his pajamas, "plain green, the heighth of bedwear fashion" (111); "two malchicks dressed at the heighth of fashion, as it was at this time (still thin trousers but no like cravat any more, more of a real tie)" (118); to himself "dressed in the heighth of nasdat fashion" (128); and to him and his accomplices "dressed in the heighth of fashion, which in those days was these very wide trousers and a very loose black shiny leather like jerkin over an open-necked shirt with a like scarf tucked in" (207). This list is not exhaustive. For other readings sensitive to Alex's dandyism, see Sumner, "Humanist Drama"; Schoene-Harwood, *Writing Men*; and Jachimiak, "'Putting the Boot In.'" Sumner reads Alex's commitment to fashion as a sign that "he unknowingly courts his own servitude" (57). For Schoene-Harwood, "The droogs' identity is a strenuous, adopted pose"; their "incongruous outfit is not of their own making but fastidiously tailored after the fashion of the day which, in turn, reflects the hegemonic gender dictates of the totalitarian patriarchy in which they live" (67). Both Sumner and Schoene-Harwood, then, read the putative hyperindividualism of the droogs' costume as a sign of their deeper servitude to norms that

oppress and control them. Jachimiak reports that the real-life social effect of Kubrick's film was the permission it granted macho skinhead culture to leaven its machismo with glam: the film "allowed members of the otherwise hypermasculine and homophobic skinhead subculture to dip the toes of their Doc Martens into the sequined water of the far more feminised glam rock style" (157).

120. Burgess, *A Clockwork Orange*, 14.
121. Ibid., 92, 157.
122. Ibid., 47.
123. Ibid., 205.
124. O'Connell, "The Libertine," 224.
125. Ibid., 227.
126. Burgess, "Introduction," x.
127. Ibid., viii.
128. Burgess, *A Clockwork Orange*, 210.
129. Edelman, *No Future*, 19.
130. Burgess, *A Clockwork Orange*, 210, 215, 217.
131. Ibid., 217–18.
132. O'Connell, "The Libertine," 126.
133. Tom (Matt Damon) in *The Talented Mr. Ripley*, DVD.

CODA

1. Baumgardner, "Williamsburg," 95.
2. "Discussion," in Greif, Ross, and Tortorici, *What Was the Hipster?*, 31–75, 66.
3. Greif, "Epitaph for the White Hipster," 145.
4. Greif writes of hipsterism in terms of subcultural styling more generally, a connection that can also be brought to bear on dandyism: "The essence of subculture is distinction. It can give a positive profile to unavoidable experiences of difference; you may join subculture when you are philosophically or ideologically out of step with the mainstream, or in some way handicapped in the dominant mainstream social competition" ("Epitaph," 160).
5. Lerner, *10:04*, 3.
6. Ibid., 4.
7. Ibid., 27.
8. Ibid., 158.
9. Ibid., 19.
10. Greif, "Positions," 12.
11. Ibid., 9.
12. Bourdieu, *The Field of Cultural Production*, 281n11.

13. Wolff, "Gender and the Haunting of Cities," 24.
14. Felski, *The Limits of Critique*, 94. For an insightful examination of the midcentury (not the twenty-first century) hipster's relationship to criticality, see Konstantinou's *Cool Characters*. As Konstantinou says, the hipster "symbolically resisted the dominant culture using attitudinal strategies that intellectuals and critics increasingly prized" (52).
15. Lerner, *10:04*, 47.
16. Ibid., 133–34.
17. Ibid., 233.
18. Ibid., 238.
19. Menand, *Discovering Modernism*, 17.
20. Lerner, *10:04*, 240.
21. Greif, "Positions," 8.
22. Ibid., 10. According to Greif, one version of twenty-first-century hipsterism simply swaps out blackness for the white lower middle class: "As the 'White Negro' had once fetishized blackness, the 'white hipster' fetishized the violence, instinctiveness, and rebelliousness of low-middle-class suburban or country whites" (10). This dynamic describes the hard-partying *Vice Magazine* hipster pretty well; it doesn't tell us too much, though, about the intellectualized hipster I am focusing on.
23. Greif, "Positions," 10.
24. Ibid., 10, 8. On the '50s hipster's specialized claims to knowledge, Greif cites Anatole Broyard, who "focused on the password language of hip slang" (8). Broyard's "A Portrait of the Hipster" (*Partisan Review*, June 1948) is canonical.
25. Ibid., 12, emphasis in original.
26. Konstantinou, *Cool Characters*, 215.
27. Schwenger, *The Masculine Mode*, 110.

BIBLIOGRAPHY

UNPUBLISHED SOURCES

Garden of Eden manuscript and typescript, in the Hemingway Papers, The John F. Kennedy Library. Massachusetts.

PUBLISHED SOURCES

Abbott, Megan E. *The Street Was Mine: White Masculinity in Hardboiled Fiction and Film Noir.* New York: Palgrave Macmillan, 2002.

Adams, James Eli. *Dandies and Desert Saints.* Ithaca: Cornell University Press, 1995.

Adorno, Theodor, et al. *The Authoritarian Personality.* New York: Harper and Brothers, 1950.

Agamben, Giorgio. *Stanzas: Word and Phantasm in Western Culture.* Translated by Ronald L. Martinez. Minneapolis: University of Minnesota Press, 1993.

Altman, Meryl. "Posthumous Queer: Hemingway Among the Others." *Hemingway Review* 30.1 (2010): 129–41.

Anderson, Amanda. *The Powers of Distance: Cosmopolitanism and the Cultivation of Detachment.* Princeton: Princeton University Press, 2001.

Annesley, James. *Blank Fictions: Consumerism, Culture and the Contemporary American Novel.* London: Pluto Press, 1998.

Apter, Emily. "Spaces of the Demimonde/Subcultures of Decadence: 1890–1990." In Constable, Denisoff, and Potolsky, 142–56.

Armstrong, Tim. *Modernism. Technology, and the Body.* Cambridge: Cambridge University Press, 1998.

Arvidson, Heather. "Personality, Impersonality, and the Personified Detachment of Wyndham Lewis." *Modernism/modernity* 25.4 (November 2018): 793–816.

Azzarello, Robert. *Queer Environmentality.* Burlington: Ashgate, 2012.

Baccolini, Rafella, and Tom Moylan, eds. *Dark Horizons: Science Fiction and the Dystopian Imagination.* New York: Routledge, 2003.

Baelo-Allué, Sonia. *Bret Easton Ellis's Controversial Fiction: Writing Between High and Low Culture.* London: Continuum, 2011.

Bak, John S. *Homo americanus: Ernest Hemingway, Tennessee Williams, and Queer Masculinities.* Madison: Farleigh Dickinson University Press, 2009.

Bakhtin, M. M. *The Dialogic Imagination.* Translated by Caryl Emerson and Michael Holquist. Austin: University of Texas Press, 1981.

Barbey d'Aurevilly, Jules. *On Dandyism and Beau Brummell.* Translated by Douglas Ainslie. London and Boston: J. M. Dent, 1896.

Barnes, Djuna. "Against Nature: In Which Everything That Is Young, Inadequate and Tiresome Is Included in the Term Natural." *Vanity Fair* (August 1920).

———. *At the Root of the Stars: The Short Plays.* Los Angeles: Sun and Moon Press, 1995.

———. *The Book of Repulsive Women: Eight Rhythms and Five Drawings.* Los Angeles: Sun and Moon Press, 1994.

———. *Interviews.* Edited by Alyce Barry. Washington, DC: Sun and Moon Press, 1985.

———. *Nightwood.* New York: New Directions, 2006.

———. *Ryder.* With illustrations by the author and an afterword by Paul West. Champaign, IL, and London: Dalkey Archive, 2010.

Barthes, Roland. *The Language of Fashion.* Translated by Andy Stafford. Edited by Andy Stafford and Michael Carter. London: Bloomsbury Academic, 2006.

Baudelaire, Charles. *La Fanfarlo.* 1847. Translated by Edward K. Kaplan. New York: Melville House, 2012.

———. *The Prose Poems and La Fanfarlo.* Translated by Rosemary Lloyd. Oxford: Oxford University Press, 1994.

Baudrillard, Jean. *Simulacra and Simulation.* Translated by Sheila Faria Glaser. Ann Arbor: University of Michigan Press, 1994.

Baumgardner, Jennifer. "Williamsburg, Year Zero." In Greif, Ross, and Tortorici, 92–96.

Beekman, E. M. "Raymond Chandler and an American Genre." *Massachusetts Review* 14.1 (1973): 149–73.

Beer, Gillian. *Darwin's Plots: Evolutionary Narrative in Darwin, George Eliot and Nineteenth-Century Fiction.* London: Routledge & Kegan Paul, 1983.

———. *Forging the Missing Link.* Cambridge: Cambridge University Press, 1992.

Berlant, Lauren. *The Female Complaint.* Durham: Duke University Press, 2008.

Bernheimer, Charles. *Decadent Subjects.* Baltimore: Johns Hopkins University Press, 2002.

Bidney, Martin. *Patterns of Epiphany.* Carbondale: Southern Illinois University Press, 1997.

Bloom, Harold, ed. *Hemingway.* New York: Chelsea, 1987.

Blyn, Robin. "*Nightwood*'s Freak Dandies: Decadence in the 1930s." *Modernism/modernity* 15.3 (2008): 503–26.

Bockris, Victor, comp. *With William Burroughs: A Report from the Bunker.* New York: St. Martin's Griffin, 1996.

Boone, Joseph Allen. *Libidinal Currents.* Chicago: University of Chicago Press, 1996.

Boswell, James. *The Life of Samuel Johnson L.L.D.* New York: Modern Library, n.d.

Bourdieu, Pierre. *The Field of Cultural Production: Essays in Art and Literature.* New York: Columbia University Press, 1993.

Braudy, Leo. *The Frenzy of Renown: Fame and Its History.* Oxford: Oxford University Press, 1986.

Brown, Bill. *The Sense of Things: The Object Matter of American Literature.* Chicago: University of Chicago Press, 2003.

Buchbinder, David. *Masculinities and Identities.* Melbourne: Melbourne University Press, 1994.

Burgess, Anthony. *A Clockwork Orange.* New York: Ballantine Books, 1993.

——. "Introduction: A Clockwork Orange Resucked." In Burgess, *A Clockwork Orange,* v–xi.

Burke, Kenneth. *Language as Symbolic Action.* Berkeley: University of California Press, 1966.

Burroughs, William S. *Ah Pook Is Here and Other Texts.* London: John Calder, 1979.

——. *Cities of the Red Night.* New York: Picador, 1981.

——. *Junky.* Melbourne: Penguin, 1993.

——. *The Letters of William S. Burroughs, 1945–1959.* New York: Penguin, 1994.

——. *Naked Lunch.* New York: Grove Press, 1990.

——. *The Place of Dead Roads.* London: Fourth Estate, 1983.

——. *Queer.* New York: Penguin, 1987.

——. *Rub Out the Words: The Letters of William S. Burroughs, 1959–1974.* Edited by Bill Morgan. New York: Ecco, 2012.

——. *The Soft Machine.* New York: Grove Press, 1992.

——. *The Western Lands.* New York: Penguin, 1987.

——. *The Wild Boys.* New York: Grove Press, 1994.

——. *A Word Virus: The William S. Burroughs Reader.* Edited by James Grauerholz and Ira Silverberg. New York: Grove Press, 1998.

Burroughs, William S., and Brion Gysin. *The Third Mind.* New York: Viking Press, 1978.

Burroughs, William S., and Daniel Odier. *The Job.* New York: Grove Press, 1974.

Burstein, Jessica. *Cold Modernism: Literature, Fashion, Art.* University Park: Pennsylvania State University Press, 2012.

Burwell, Rose Marie. *Hemingway: The Postwar Years and the Posthumous Novels.* Cambridge: Cambridge UP, 1996.

Butler, Judith. *Gender Trouble*. London: Routledge, 2006.

Calinescu, Matei. *Five Faces of Modernity*. Durham: Duke University Press, 1987.

Canning, Richard. Introduction to Firbank, *Vainglory*.

Carlston, Erin G. "'Acting the Man'—Wyndham Lewis and the Future of Masculinity." *Modernism/modernity* 25.4 (November 2018): 771–91.

———. *Thinking Fascism: Sapphic Modernism and Fascist Modernity*. Palo Alto: Stanford University Press, 1998.

Carlyle, Thomas. *Sartor Resartus*. 1837. Reprint, Oxford: Oxford University Press, 2008.

Caselli, Daniella. *Improper Modernism: Djuna Barnes's Bewildering Corpus*. Burlington: Ashgate, 2009.

Cassuto, Leonard. *Hard-Boiled Sentimentality: The Secret History of American Crime Stories*. New York: Columbia University Press, 2008.

Chai, Leon. *Aestheticism: The Religion of Art in Post-Romantic Literature*. New York: Columbia University Press, 1990.

Chandler, Raymond. *Later Novels and Other Writings*. New York: Library of America, 1995.

———. *The Raymond Chandler Omnibus: The Big Sleep, Farewell, My Lovely, The High Window, The Lady in the Lake*. New York: Random House, 1964.

———. *The Raymond Chandler Papers: Selected Letters and Nonfiction, 1909–1959*. Edited by Tom Hiney and Frank MacShane. New York: Grove Press, 2002.

Chaney, Lisa. *Coco Chanel: An Intimate Life*. New York: Penguin, 2011.

Cheng, Anne Anlin. *Second Skin: Josephine Baker and the Modern Surface*. Oxford: Oxford University Press, 2011.

Christ, Carol T. *Victorian and Modern Poetics*. Chicago: University of Chicago Press, 1986.

Christianson, Scott R. "Tough Talk and Wisecracks." *Journal of Popular Culture* 23 (Fall 1989): 151–62.

Chu, Seo-Young. *Do Metaphors Dream of Literal Sleep? A Science-Fictional Theory of Representation*. Cambridge, MA: Harvard University Press, 2010.

Cleland, John. *Fanny Hill*. 1749. Reprint, Project Gutenberg e-text, 2008. http://www.gutenberg.org/files/25305/25305-h/25305-h.htm.

Clune, Michael. *Writing Against Time*. Stanford: Stanford University Press, 2013.

Cohen, Ed. *Talk on the Wilde Side*. Oxford: Oxford University Press, 1992.

Comley, Nancy R., and Robert Scholes. *Hemingway's Genders*. New Haven: Yale University Press, 1994.

Connolly, Cyril. *The Rock Pool*. 1936. Reprint, Norfolk, CT: New Directions, n.d.

Conrad, Peter. "The Private Dick as Dandy." *Times Literary Supplement*, January 20, 1978.

Constable, Liz, Dennis Denisoff, and Matthew Potolsky, eds. *Perennial Decay*. Philadelphia: University of Pennsylvania Press, 1999.

Corber, Robert. *Homosexuality in Cold War America: Resistance and the Crisis of Masculinity*. Durham: Duke University Press, 1997.

Cottom, Daniel. *International Bohemia: Scenes of Nineteenth-Century Life*. Philadelphia: University of Pennsylvania Press, 2013.

Davidson, Michael. "Pregnant Men: Modernism, Disability and Biofuturity in Djuna Barnes." *Novel: A Forum on Fiction* 43.2 (2010): 207–26.

Dearborn, Mary V. *Ernest Hemingway: A Biography*. New York: Knopf, 2017.

Delany, Samuel. *About Writing*. Middletown: Wesleyan University Press, 2006.

Dellamora, Richard. *Masculine Desire: The Sexual Politics of Victorian Aestheticism*. Chapel Hill: University of North Carolina Press, 1990.

——, ed. *Postmodern Apocalypse*. Philadelphia: University of Pennsylvania Press, 1995.

De Man, Paul. "The Epistemology of Metaphor." In Sacks, 11–28.

Denning, Michael. *The Cultural Front*. London: Verso, 1996.

Dickens, Charles. *Bleak House*. 1853. Reprint, New York: Bantam Dell, 1983.

——. *Great Expectations*. 1861. Reprint, Boston: Estes and Lauriat, 1881.

Didion, Joan. "I Want to Go Ahead and Do It." *New York Times*, October 7, 1979.

Doan, Laura, and Jane Garrit, eds. *Sapphic Modernities*. New York: Palgrave Macmillian, 2006.

Doctorow, E. L. "Braver Than We Thought." *New York Times*, May 18, 1986.

Douglas, Ann. Introduction to Silverberg, *Word Virus*.

Dowling, Linda. *Hellenism and Homosexuality in Victorian Oxford*. Ithaca: Cornell University Press, 1994.

——. *Language and Decadence in the Victorian Fin de Siècle*. Princeton: Princeton University Press, 1986.

Dreiser, Theodore. *Sister Carrie*. New York: Harper and Brothers, 1900.

D'Souza, Aruna, and Tom McDonough. *The Invisible* Flâneuse?: *Gender, Public Space, and Visual Culture in Nineteenth-Century Paris*. Manchester: Manchester University Press, 2006.

Easthope, Anthony. *What a Man's Gotta Do: The Masculine Myth in Popular Culture*. London: Routledge, 1990.

Eby, Carl. "'He Felt the Change So That It Hurt Him All Through': Sodomy and Transvestic Hallucination in Hemingway." *Hemingway Review* 23.1 (2005): 77–95.

——. *Hemingway's Fetishism: Psychoanalysis and the Mirror of Manhood*. Albany: SUNY Press, 1999.

Edel, Leon. "The Art of Evasion." In Weeks, *Hemingway*.

Edelman, Lee. *No Future: Queer Theory and the Death Drive.* Durham: Duke University Press, 2004.

Eden, Rick A. "Detective Fiction as Satire." *Genre* 16 (Fall 1983): 279–95.

Edwards, Paul. *Wyndham Lewis: Painter and Writer.* New Haven: Yale University Press, 2000.

Eliot, T. S. *Selected Essays.* New York: Harcourt and Brace, 1964.

Elliot, Bridget. "Art Deco Hybridity, Interior Design, and Sexuality Between the Wars." In Doan and Garrit, 109–32.

Ellis, Bret Easton. *American Psycho.* New York: Vintage, 1991.

Ellmann, Richard. *Oscar Wilde.* New York: Vintage, 1988.

Espey, John J. *Ezra Pound's* Mauberley: *A Study in Composition.* Berkeley: University of California Press, 1955.

Feldman, Jessica R. *Gender on the Divide: The Dandy in Modernist Literature.* Ithaca: Cornell University Press, 1993.

———. *Victorian Modernism: Pragmatism and the Varieties of Aesthetic Experience.* Cambridge: Cambridge University Press, 2002.

Felski, Rita. *The Gender of Modernity.* Cambridge: Harvard University Press, 1995.

———. *The Limits of Critique.* Chicago: University of Chicago Press, 2015.

Ferguson, Christine. "Decadence as Scientific Fulfillment." *PMLA* 117.3 (May 2002): 465–78.

Ferguson, Frances. *Pornography, the Theory: What Utilitarianism Did to Action.* Chicago: University of Chicago Press, 2004.

Fiedler, Leslie. *Love and Death in the American Novel.* New York: Anchor, 1992.

Fillin-Yeh, Susan, ed. *Dandies: Fashion and Finesse in Art and Culture.* New York: New York University Press, 2001.

Firbank, Ronald. *Vainglory.* New York: Penguin, 2012.

Firchow, Peter. *Friedrich Schlegel's Lucinde and The Fragments.* Minneapolis: University of Minnesota Press, 1971.

Fitzgerald, F. Scott. *This Side of Paradise and The Last Tycoon.* 1920 and 1941. Reprint, New York: Scribner's, 1969.

Foldy, Michael S. *The Trials of Oscar Wilde: Deviance, Morality, and Late-Victorian Society.* New Haven: Yale University Press, 1997.

Freedman, Jonathan. *Professions of Taste: Henry James, British Aestheticism and Commodity Culture.* Stanford: Stanford University Press, 1990.

Gaggin, John. *Hemingway and Nineteenth-Century Aestheticism.* Ann Arbor: UMI Research Press.

Gagnier, Regenia. "The Global Circulation of the Literatures of Decadence." *Literature Compass* 10.1 (2013): 70–81.

———. *Idylls of the Marketplace: Oscar Wilde and the Victorian Public*. Stanford: Stanford University Press, 1986.

———. *Individualism, Decadence and Globalization: On the Relationship of Part to Whole, 1859–1920*. London: Palgrave MacMillan, 2010.

Garber, Marjorie. *Vested Interests: Cross-Dressing and Cultural Anxiety*. London: Routledge, 1997.

Gardner, Helen. *The Metaphysical Poets*. Oxford: Oxford University Press, 1961.

Garelick, Rhonda. *Rising Star: Dandyism, Gender and Performance in the Fin de Siècle*. Princeton: Princeton University Press, 1998.

Gautier, Théophile. *Mademoiselle de Maupin*. 1834. Translation, Paris, London, and New York: Société des Beaux-Arts, 1905.

Gigante, Denise. *Taste: A Literary History*. New Haven: Yale University Press, 2005.

Gilbert, Sandra M. "Costumes of the Mind: Transvestism as Metaphor in Modern Literature." *Critical Inquiry* 7.2 (1980): 391–417.

Gillespie, Margaret. "'The Triumph of the Epicene Style': *Nightwood* and Camp." *Miranda* 12 (2016): 1–14.

Glass, Loren. *Authors Inc.: Literary Celebrity in the United States, 1880–1980*. New York: New York University Press, 2004.

Glick, Elisa. *Materializing Queer Desire: Oscar Wilde to Andy Warhol*. Albany: SUNY Press, 2009.

Glickman, Susan. "The World as Will and Idea: A Comparative Study of *An American Dream* and *Mr. Sammler's Planet*." *Modern Fiction Studies* 28.4 (1982): 569–82.

Goffman, Erving. *Asylums*. New York: Anchor Books, 1961.

———. *Interaction Ritual: Essays on Face-to-Face Behavior*. New York: Pantheon, 1982.

Goldman, Jonathan. *Modernism Is the Literature of Celebrity*. Austin: University of Texas Press, 2011.

Goldstone, Andrew. *Fictions of Autonomy*. Oxford: Oxford University Press, 2013.

Goodin, George. *The Poetics of Protest: Literary Form and Political Implication in the Victim-of-Society Novel*. Carbondale: Southern Illinois University Press, 1985.

Green, Martin. *Children of the Sun: A Narrative of Decadence in England after 1918*. London: Constable, 1977.

Greif, Mark. "Epitaph for the White Hipster." In Greif, Ross, and Tortorici, 142–67.

———. "Positions." In Greif, Ross, and Tortorici, 4–13.

Greif, Mark, Kathleen Ross, and Dayna Tortorici, eds. *What Was the Hipster?* New York: n+1 Foundation, 2010.

Greven, David. "Queer Ripley: Minghella, Highsmith, and the Antisocial." In Schwanebeck and McFarland, 121–38.

Grimstad, Paul. "Notes on Burroughs." *Raritan* 36.2 (2016): 52.

Gross, Miriam, ed. *The World of Raymond Chandler.* London: Weidenfeld and Nicolson, 1977.

Gubar, Susan. "Blessings in Disguise: Cross-Dressing as Re-Dressing for Female Modernists." *Massachusetts Review* 22.3 (Autumn 1981): 477–508.

Guetti, James. "Aggressive Reading: Detective Fiction and Realistic Narrative." In Van Dover, 139–44.

Guillory, John. "Genesis of the Media Concept." *Critical Inquiry* 36.2 (2010): 321–62.

Halmi, Nicholas. "Symbolism, Imagism, and Hermeneutic Anxiety: A Response to Andrew Hay." *Connotations* 23.1 (2013/14): 129–39.

Hammett, Dashiell. *Complete Novels.* New York: Library of America, 1999.

———. *The Maltese Falcon.* 1929. Reprint, New York: Vintage, 1989.

Haralson, Eric. *Henry James and Queer Modernity.* Cambridge: Cambridge University Press, 2003.

Hardie, Melissa Jane. "Repulsive Modernism: Djuna Barnes's 'The Book of Repulsive Women.'" *Journal of Modern Literature* 29.1 (2005): 118–32.

Harris, Oliver. *William Burroughs and the Secret of Fascination.* Carbondale: Southern Illinois University Press, 2003.

Harris, Oliver, and Ian MacFayden, eds. *Naked Lunch at 50.* Carbondale: Southern Illinois University Press, 2009.

Hassan, Ihab. "The Subtracting Machine." In Skerl and Lydenberg, 53–68.

Hay, Andrew. "On the Shore of Interpretation: The Theory and Reading of the Image in Imagism." *Connotations* 21.2–3 (2011/12): 304–26.

Hazlitt, William. *Essayist and Critic: Selections from His Writings.* London: Frederick Warne, 1889.

Heise, Thomas. "Degenerate Sex and the City: Djuna Barnes's Urban Underworld." *Twentieth-Century Literature* 55.3 (2009): 287–321.

Hemingway, Ernest. *Across the River and into the Trees.* New York: Scribner's, 1950.

———. *Death in the Afternoon.* New York: Scribner's, 1932.

———. *For Whom the Bell Tolls.* New York: Scribner's, 1940.

———. *The Garden of Eden.* New York: Scribner's, 1986.

———. *Green Hills of Africa.* New York: Scribner's, 1935.

———. "An Interview with George Plimpton." In Bloom, 136.

———. *Islands in the Stream.* New York: Scribner's, 1970.

———. *A Moveable Feast.* New York: Scribner's, 1960.

———. *The Nick Adams Stories.* New York: Scribner's, 2003.

———. *Selected Letters of Ernest Hemingway, 1917–1961.* Edited by Carlos Baker. New York: Scribner, 1981.

Herring, Philip. *Djuna: The Life and Work of Djuna Barnes.* New York: Penguin, 1995.

Higgins, Lesley. *The Modernist Cult of Ugliness: Aesthetic and Gender Politics.* New York: Palgrave Macmillan, 2002.

Highsmith, Patricia. *The Boy Who Followed Ripley.* New York: W.W. Norton, 2008.

————. *Ripley Under Water.* New York: W.W. Norton, 1991.

————. *The Talented Mr. Ripley.* New York: Norton, 1993.

————. *The Talented Mr. Ripley, Ripley Under Ground, Ripley's Game.* New York: Everyman's Library, 1999.

Hiney, Tom. *Raymond Chandler: A Biography.* New York: Atlantic Monthly Press, 1997.

Homburger, Eric, ed. *Ezra Pound: The Critical Heritage.* London and Boston: Routledge and Kegan Paul, 1972.

Horsley, Lee. *Twentieth-Century Crime Fiction.* Oxford: Oxford University Press, 2005.

Hulme, T. E. *Speculations.* London: Kegan Paul, 1924.

Hume, Kathryn. *Aggressive Fictions: Reading the Contemporary American Novel.* Ithaca: Cornell University Press, 1998.

Hurley, Kelly. *The Gothic Body.* Cambridge: Cambridge University Press, 1996.

Huysmans, J. K. *À Rebours.* Translated as *Against the Grain* by John Howard. New York: Albert and Charles Boni, 1922.

Hyde, H. Montgomery. *The Trials of Oscar Wilde.* London: William Hodge and Company, 1948.

Irwin, John T. *Unless the Threat of Death Is Behind Them: Hardboiled Fiction and Film Noir.* Baltimore: Johns Hopkins University Press, 2006.

Jachimiak, Peter Hughes. "'Putting the Boot In: *A Clockwork Orange*, Post-'69 Youth Culture and the Onset of Late Modernity." In Roughley, 147–64.

Jackson, Thomas H. "The Poetic Politics of Ezra Pound." *Journal of Modern Literature* 3.4 (1974): 987–1011.

Jaffe, Aaron. *Modernism and the Culture of Celebrity.* Cambridge: Cambridge University Press, 2005.

Jaffe, Aaron, and Jonathan Goldman, eds. *Modernist Star Maps.* Burlington: Ashgate, 2010.

James, Henry. *The Golden Bowl.* Oxford: Oxford University Press, 2009.

————. *Novels, 1886–1890.* Library of America, 43. New York: Literary Classics of the United States, 1989.

James, Simon J. *Maps of Utopia: H. G. Wells, Modernity, and the End of Culture.* Cambridge: Cambridge University Press, 2012.

Jameson, Fredric. *Archaeologies of the Future: The Desire Called Utopian and Other Science Fictions*. London: Verso, 2005.

———. *Fables of Aggression: Wyndham Lewis, the Modernist as Fascist*. Berkeley: University of California Press, 1979.

———. *Postmodernism: Or, The Cultural Logical of Late Capitalism*. Durham: Duke University Press, 1991.

———. "Wyndham Lewis as Futurist." *Hudson Review* 26.2 (Summer 1973): 295–329.

Johnson, Samuel. *The Major Works*. Edited by Donald Greene. Oxford: Oxford University Press, 2000.

Joselit, David. "Notes on Surface: Toward a Genealogy of Flatness." *Art History* 23.1 (March 2000): 19–34.

Justice, Hilary Kovar. "The Consolation of Critique: Food, Culture, and Civilization in Ernest Hemingway." *Hemingway Review* 32.1 (2012): 16–38.

Kane, Michael. *Modern Men: Mapping Masculinity in English and German Literature, 1880–1930*. London: Cassell, 1999.

Kannenstine, Louis. *The Art of Djuna Barnes*. New York: New York University Press, 1977.

Katz, Tamar. *Impressionist Subjects: Gender, Interiority, and Modernist Fiction in England*. Urbana: University of Illinois Press, 2000.

Kaup, Monika. "The Neobaroque in Djuna Barnes." *Modernism/modernity* 12.1 (2005): 85–110.

Kemp, Wolfgang. *The Desire of My Eyes: The Life and Work of John Ruskin*. Translated by Jan Van Heurck. New York: Farrar, Straus, and Giroux, 1992.

Kennedy, Gerald. *Imagining Paris*. New Haven: Yale University Press, 1993.

Kenner, Hugh. *A Homemade World*. Baltimore: Johns Hopkins University Press, 1989.

———. *The Pound Era*. Berkeley: University of California Press, 1971.

———. *Wyndham Lewis*. Norfolk, CT: New Directions, 1954.

Kermode, Frank. *The Romantic Image*. London: Routledge and Kegan Paul, 1957.

———. *The Sense of an Ending: Studies in the Theory of Fiction*. Oxford: Oxford University Press, 1967.

Kesey, Ken. *One Flew Over the Cuckoo's Nest*. New York: Penguin, 2002.

Knowles, Marika. "The Microcosm as Interior in Théophile Gautier's 'Marilhat.'" In Lasc, 3–18.

Konstantinou, Lee. *Cool Characters: Irony and American Fiction*. Cambridge, MA: Harvard University Press, 2016.

———. "The Eccentric Polish Count Who Influenced Sci-Fi's Greatest Writers." *io9*, accessed September 14, 2014. http://io9.com/the-eccentric-polish-count-who -influenced-classic-sfs-g-1631001935.

Kotsko, Adam. *Why We Love Sociopaths: A Guide to Late Capitalist Television*. Ropley: Zero Books, 2012.

Lan, Feng. "Confucius." In Nadel, *Ezra Pound in Context*, 324–34.

Lasc, Anca I., ed. *Visualizing the Nineteenth-Century Home: Modern Art and the Decorative Impulse*. New York: Routledge, 2016.

Lautréamont. *Maldoror and Poems*. Translated by Paul Knight. New York: Penguin Classics, 1988.

Lavar, James. *Dandies*. London: Weidenfeld and Nicolson, 1968.

Lemair, Gérard-Georges. Introduction to Burroughs and Gysin.

Lerner, Ben. *10:04*. New York: Faber and Faber, 2014.

Levenson, Michael. *A Genealogy of Modernism*. Cambridge: Cambridge University Press, 1984.

Levine, George. *Darwin and the Novelists: Patterns of Science in Victorian Fiction*. Cambridge, MA: Harvard University Press, 1988.

Lewis, Pericles. "To Make a Dadaist Poem." *Yale Modernism Lab*, accessed September 14, 2014. http://modernism.research.yale.edu/wiki/index.php/To_Make_a_Dadaist_Poem.

Lewis, Stephen E. "Love and Politics in Wyndham Lewis's *Snooty Baronet*." *MLQ* 61.4 (2000): 617–49.

Lewis, Wyndham. *The Art of Being Ruled*. Edited by Reed Way Dasenbrock. Santa Rosa: Black Sparrow Press, 1989.

——, ed. *BLAST*. London: The Bodley Head, 1914.

——. *Blasting and Bombardiering*. 1937. Reprint, Berkeley: University of California Press, 1967.

——. *The Demon of Progress in the Arts*. London: Methuen, 1954.

——. *Malign Fiesta*. 1955. Reprint, London: Calder Books, 1966.

——. *Snooty Baronet*. 1932. Reprint, Santa Barbara: Black Sparrow Press, 1984.

——. *Tarr*. London: Calder, 1968.

——. *Tarr: The 1918 Version*. Reprint, Santa Rosa: Black Sparrow Press, 1990.

Lindner, Robert. *Rebel without a Cause*. New York: Other Press, 2003.

Lodge, David. "Objections to William Burroughs." In Skerl and Lydenberg.

Lotringer, Sylvère, ed. *Burroughs Live: The Collected Interviews of William S. Burroughs, 1960–1997*. Cambridge, MA: Semiotext(e), distributed by MIT Press.

Lott, Eric. *Love and Theft: Blackface Minstrelsy and the American Working Class*. Oxford: Oxford University Press, 1993.

Love, Heather K. "Forced Exile: Walter Pater's Queer Modernism." In Mao and Walkowitz, 19–43.

Lydenberg, Robin. *Word Cultures: Radical Theory and Practice in William S. Burroughs' Fiction*. Urbana: University of Illinois Press, 1987.

Lyotard, Jean-François. *Jacques Monory.* London: Black Dog Publishing, 1998.

Lytton, Edward Bulwer. *Pelham, or, The Adventures of a Gentleman.* Boston: Little, Brown, 1893.

Mahoney, Kristin. *Literature and the Politics of Post-Victorian Decadence.* Cambridge: Cambridge University Press, 2015.

Mailer, Norman. *Advertisements for Myself.* New York: Putnam, 1959.

———. *The Executioner's Song.* 1980. Reprint, New York: Grand Central Publishing, 2012.

———. *Mind of an Outlaw: Selected Essays.* New York: Random House, 2013.

Mann, Philip. *The Dandy at Dusk: Taste and Melancholy in the Twentieth Century.* London: Head of Zeus, 2017.

Mao, Douglas. *Solid Objects: Modernism and the Test of Production.* Princeton: Princeton University Press, 1998.

Mao, Douglas, and Rebecca Walkowitz, eds. *Bad Modernisms.* Durham: Duke University Press, 2006.

Marsh, Alec. "Politics." In Nadel, *Ezra Pound in Context,* 96–105.

Matz, Jesse. *Literary Impressionism and Modernist Aesthetics.* Cambridge: Cambridge University Press, 2001.

McCann, Sean. *Gumshoe America: Hard-Boiled Crime Fiction and the Rise and Fall of New Deal Liberalism.* Durham: Duke University Press, 2000.

McCarthy, Mary. "Love and Death in the Pacific." *New York Times,* April 22, 1984.

McCullum, E. L., and Mikko Tuhkanen, eds. *The Cambridge History of Gay and Lesbian Literature.* Cambridge: Cambridge University Press, 2016.

Meisel, Perry. *The Cowboy and the Dandy.* Oxford: Oxford University Press, 1998.

Menand, Louis. *Discovering Modernism: T. S. Eliot and His Context.* Oxford: Oxford University Press, 1987.

Mendelson, Edward. "Who Was Ernest Hemingway?," *New York Review of Books,* August 2014.

Mendelssohn, Michèle. *Henry James, Oscar Wilde, and Aesthetic Culture.* Edinburgh: Edinburgh University Press, 2007.

Meredith, George. *The Egoist.* 1879. Reprint, Peterborough: Broadview Press, 2010.

———. *The Ordeal of Richard Feveral.* New York: Scribner's Sons, 1917.

Meyers, Jeffrey. "T. S. Eliot's Green Face Powder: A Mystery Solved." *Yeats Eliot Review* 28, no. 3–4 (Fall–Winter 2011): 33.

Michaels, Walter Benn. *Our America: Nativism, Modernism, and Pluralism.* Durham: Duke University Press, 1995.

Michelson, Annette, ed. *Andy Warhol.* Cambridge, MA: MIT Press, 2001.

Michelson, Peter. "Beardsley, Burroughs, Decadence, and the Poetics of Obscenity." *Tri-Quarterly Review* 12 (1968): 139–55.

Miles, Barry. *William Burroughs: A Portrait.* New York: Virgin, 1992.

Miller, Monica. *Slaves to Fashion: Black Dandyism and the Styling of Black Diasporic Identity.* Durham: Duke University Press, 2009.

Miller, Tyrus. *Late Modernism.* Berkeley: University of California Press, 1999.

Mishima, Yukio. *Confessions of a Mask.* Translated by Meredith Weatherby. New York: New Directions, 1958.

Moddelmog, Debra A. *Reading Desire: In Pursuit of Ernest Hemingway.* Ithaca: Cornell University Press, 1999.

Moers, Ellen. *The Dandy: From Brummell to Beerbohm.* New York: Viking Press, 1960.

Moody, A. David. *Ezra Pound: Poet.* Volume 1. Oxford: Oxford University Press, 2009.

Murphy, Timothy S. "Random Insect Doom: The Pulp Science Fiction of *Naked Lunch.*" In Harris and MacFayden, 223–33.

———. *Wising Up the Marks.* Berkeley: University of California Press, 1997.

Nadel, Ira, ed. *The Cambridge Companion to Ezra Pound.* Cambridge: Cambridge University Press, 1999.

———. ed. *Ezra Pound in Context.* Cambridge: Cambridge University Press, 1996.

———. "Visualizing History: Pound and the Chinese Cantos." In Rainey, 151–66.

Newman, John Henry. *Apologia Pro Vita Sua and Six Sermons.* Ed. Frank M. Turner. New Haven: Yale University Press, 2008.

Nietzsche, Friedrich. *The Gay Science.* Translated by Walter Kaufmann. New York: Vintage, 1974

Ngai, Sianne. *Our Aesthetic Categories: Zany, Cute, Interesting.* Cambridge, MA: Harvard University Press, 2012.

Nicholls, Peter. *Modernisms: A Literary Guide.* Berkeley and Los Angeles: University of California Press, 1995.

Nichols, Ashton. *The Poetics of Epiphany: Nineteenth-Century Origins of the Modern Literary Moment.* Tuscaloosa: University of Alabama Press, 1987.

Nordau, Max. *Degeneration.* Lincoln: University of Nebraska Press, 1993.

Norman, Will. "The Big Empty: Chandler's Transatlantic Modernism." *Modernism/modernity* 20.4 (2013): 747–70.

North, Michael. *Reading 1922.* Oxford: Oxford University Press, 1998.

Oates, Joyce Carol. "The Simple Art of Murder." *New York Review of Books,* December 1995, accessed January 8, 2013.

O'Connell, Lisa. "The Libertine, the Rake, and the Dandy: Personae, Styles, and Affects." In McCullum and Tuhkanen, 218–38.

O'Keeffe, Paul. *Some Sort of Genius.* Berkeley: Counterpoint, 2000.

Okura, Lynn. "How Coco Became Chanel." *Oprah.com,* accessed May 30, 2019. http://www.oprah.com/style/the-history-of-coco-chanel.

Olsen, Lance. "Prelude: Nameless Things and Thingless Names." In Sander, 274–92.

Paglia, Camille. *Sexual Personae.* New York: Vintage, 1991.

Pater, Walter. *Appreciations.* London: Macmillan, 1889.

———. *Studies in the History of the Renaissance.* 1873. Reprint, Oxford: Oxford University Press, 2010.

Peckham, Morse. "Darwinism and Darwinisticism." *Victorian Studies* 3 (September 1959): 19–40.

Pittock, Murray G. H. *Spectrum of Decadence: The Literature of the 1890s.* London: Routledge, 1993.

Plain, Gill. *Twentieth-Century Crime Fiction: Gender, Sexuality, and the Body.* Edinburgh: Edinburgh University Press, 2001.

Porter, Dennis. *The Pursuit of Crime.* New Haven: Yale University Press, 1981.

Pound, Ezra. *New and Selected Poems and Translations.* Edited by Richard Sieburth. New York: New Directions, 2010.

Pound, Ezra, and Ernest Fenollosa. *The Chinese Written Character as a Medium for Poetry.* New York: Fordham University Press, 2008.

Praz, Mario. *The Romantic Agony.* 2nd ed. Oxford: Oxford University Press, 1950.

Quéma, Anne. *The Agon of Modernism.* Lewisburg: Bucknell University Press, 1999.

Rabaté, Jean-Michel. *Language, Sexuality, and Ideology in Ezra Pound's Cantos.* London: Macmillan, 1986.

Rainey, Lawrence, ed. *A Poem Containing History.* Ann Arbor: University of Michigan Press, 1997.

———. "Taking Dictation." *Modernism/modernity* 5.2 (1998): 123–53.

Ratcliffe, Carter. "Dandyism and Abstraction in a Universe Defined by Newton." In Fillin-Yeh, 101–26.

Rieff, Philip. *The Triumph of the Therapeutic: Uses of Faith after Freud.* Wilmington: ISI Books, 2006.

Riffaterre, Michael. "Decadent Paradoxes." In Constable, Denisoff, and Potolsky, 65–82.

Roach, Joseph. *It.* Ann Arbor: University of Michigan Press, 2007.

Rohman, Carrie. *Stalking the Subject: Modernism and the Animal.* New York: Columbia University Press, 2009.

Rosenfeld, Paul. "The Case of Ezra Pound." *The American Mercury,* January 1944. Reprinted in Homburger, 355–57.

Roughley, Alan R., ed. *Anthony Burgess and Modernity*. Manchester: Manchester University Press, 2008.

Russell, Jamie. *Queer Burroughs*. New York: Palgrave, 2001.

Ryan, Judith. *The Vanishing Subject: Early Psychology and Literary Modernism*. Chicago: University of Chicago Press, 1991.

Sacks, Sheldon, ed. *On Metaphor*. Chicago: University of Chicago Press, 1978.

Sander, David. *Fantastic Literature: A Critical Reader*. Westport: Praeger, 2004.

Sante, Luc. "The Invisible Man." *New York Review of Books*, May 1984.

Saunders, Max. *Self Impression: Life-Writing, Autobiografiction, and the Forms of Modern Literature*. Oxford: Oxford University Press, 2010.

Schaffer, Talia. *The Forgotten Female Aesthetes: Literary Culture in Late-Victorian England*. Charlottesville: University Press of Virginia, 2009.

Schmid, Marion. "Decadence and the Fin de Siècle." In Watt, 51–58.

Schoene-Harwood, Berthold. *Writing Men: Literary Masculinities from Frankenstein to the New Man*. Edinburgh: Edinburgh University Press, 2000.

Schwanebeck, Wieland, and Douglas McFarland, eds. *Patricia Highsmith on Screen*. Basingstoke: Palgrave MacMillan, 2018.

Schwartz, Sanford. *The Matrix of Modernism*. Princeton: Princeton University Press, 1985.

Schwenger, Peter. "The Masculine Mode." In Showalter, 101–12.

———. *Phallic Critiques: Masculinity and Twentieth-Century Literature*. London: Routledge and Kegan Paul, 1984.

Scott, Bonnie Kime. *Refiguring Modernism*. 2 vols. Bloomington: Indiana University Press, 1996.

Sedgwick, Eve Kosofsky. *Epistemology of the Closet*. Berkeley: University of California Press, 1990.

———. *Tendencies*. Durham: Duke University Press, 1993.

Seitler, Dana. *Atavistic Tendencies: The Culture of Science in American Modernity*. Minneapolis: University of Minnesota Press, 2008.

———. "'Down on All Fours: Atavistic Perversions and the Science of Desire from Frank Norris to Djuna Barnes." *American Literature* 73.3 (2001): 525–62.

Self, Will. Introduction to William S. Burroughs, *Junky*. Melbourne: Penguin, 2003.

Seltzer, Mark. *Serial Killers: Death and Life in America's Wound Culture*. New York: Routledge, 1998.

Serpell, Namwali. "Repetition and the Ethics of Suspended Reading in *American Psycho*." *Critique: Studies in Contemporary Fiction* 51.1 (2010): 47–73.

Shaviro, Steven. "Burroughs' Theater of Illusion: *Cities of the Red Night*." In Skerl and Lydenberg, 197–208.

Sherry, Vincent. *Ezra Pound and Radical Modernism*. Oxford: Oxford University Press, 1993.

———. *Modernism and the Reinvention of Decadence*. Cambridge: Cambridge University Press, 2014.

Shin, Ery. "The Apocalypse for Barnes." *Texas Studies in Language and Literature* 57.2 (2015): 182–209.

———. "Djuna Barnes, History's Elsewhere, and the Transgender." *Journal of Modern Literature* 37.2 (2014): 20–38.

Showalter, Elaine, ed. *Speaking of Gender*. New York and London: Routledge, 1989.

Simon, Linda. *Chanel*. London: Reaktion Books, 2011.

Simpson, Mark. *Male Impersonators: Men Performing Masculinity*. London: Cassell, 1994.

Sinfield, Alan. *The Wilde Century: Effeminacy, Oscar Wilde, and the Queer Moment*. London: Cassell, 1994.

Singer, Alan. *A Metaphysics of Fiction*. Tallahassee: University Press of Florida, 1983.

Skerl, Jennie. *William S. Burroughs*. Boston: Twayne, 1985.

Skerl, Jennie, and Robin Lydenberg, eds. *William S. Burroughs at the Front*. Carbondale: Southern Illinois University Press, 1991.

Smith, Barbara Herrnstein. *Poetic Closure: A Study of How Poems End*. Chicago: University of Chicago Press, 2007.

Smith, Erin A. *Hard-Boiled: Working-Class Readers and Pulp Magazines*. Philadelphia: Temple University Press, 2000.

Smith, Victoria L. "A Story Beside(s) Itself: The Language of Loss in Djuna Barnes's *Nightwood*." *PMLA* 114.2 (1999): 194–206.

Spackman, Barbara. *Decadent Genealogies: The Rhetoric of Sickness from Baudelaire to d'Annunzio*. Ithaca: Cornell University Press, 1989.

Sparks, Tabitha. *The Doctor in the Victorian Novel*. Burlingston: Ashgate, 2009.

Spilka, Mark. *Hemingway's Quarrel with Androgyny*. Lincoln: University of Nebraska Press, 1990.

Stearns, Peter N. *American Cool: Constructing a Twentieth-Century Emotional Style*. New York: NYU Press, 1994.

Stoneback, H. R. "Memorable Eggs 'in Danger of Getting Cold' and Mackeral 'Perilous with Edge-Level Juice': Eating in Hemingway's Garden." *Hemingway Review* 8.2 (1989): 21–29.

Storey, Mark. "'And As Things Fell Apart': The Crisis of Postmodern Masculinity in Bret Easton Ellis's *American Psycho* and Dennis Cooper's *Frisk*." *Critique: Studies in Contemporary Fiction* 41.1 (2005): 57–72.

Stowell, Peter H. *Literary Impressionism: James and Chekhov.* Athens: University of Georgia Press, 1980.

Strychacz, Thomas. *Hemingway's Theaters of Masculinity.* Baton Rouge: Louisiana State University Press, 2003.

Stubbs, Neil. "'Watch Out How That Egg Runs': Hemingway and the Rhetoric of American Road Food." *Hemingway Review* 33.1 (2013): 79–85.

Sumner, Charles. "Humanist Drama in *A Clockwork Orange.*" *Yearbook of English Studies* 42 (2012): 49–63.

Surette, Leon. *The Birth of Modernism: Ezra Pound, T. S. Eliot, W. B. Yeats, and the Occult.* Toronto: McGill-Queen's University Press, 1993.

Sussman, Herbert. *Victorian Masculinities.* Cambridge: Cambridge University Press, 1995.

Suvin, Darko. "Theses on Dystopia 2001." In Baccolini and Moylan, 199–214.

Swinburne, Algernon Charles. *A Year's Letters.* Portland, ME: Charles Mosher, 1901.

Sword, Helen. *Ghostwriting Modernism.* Ithaca: Cornell University Press, 2002.

Symons, Julian. "An Aesthete Discovers the Pulps." In Gross, 19–29.

Szalay, Michael. *Hip Figures: A Literary History of the Democratic Party.* Stanford: Stanford University Press, 2012.

———. *New Deal Modernism.* Durham: Duke University Press, 2000.

Tanner, Stephen L. "The Function of Simile in Raymond Chandler's Novels." In Van Dover, 167–76.

Tanner, Tony. *City of Words.* New York: HarperCollins, 1971.

Taylor, Charles. *A Secular Age.* Cambridge, MA: Harvard University Press, 2007.

Taylor, Clare L. *Women, Writing, and Fetishism 1890–1950: Female Cross-Gendering.* Oxford: Oxford University Press, 2003.

Taylor, Douglas. "Three Lean Cats in a Hall of Mirrors: James Baldwin, Eldridge Cleaver, and Norman Mailer on Race and Masculinity." *Texas Studies in Language and Literature* 52.1 (2010): 70–101.

Thoreau, Henry David. *A Year in Thoreau's Journals: 1851.* New York: Penguin, 1993.

Trask, Michael. *Camp Sites: Sex, Politics, and Academic Style in Postwar America.* Palo Alto: Stanford University Press, 2013.

Trotter, David. *Paranoid Modernism: Literary Experiment, Psychosis, and the Professionalization of English Society.* Oxford: Oxford University Press, 2001.

Tzara, Tristan. "Dada Manifesto on Feeble Love and Bitter Love." http://www.391 .org/manifestos/1920-dada-manifesto-feeble-love-bitter-love-tristan-tzara .html#.VCnbJVa4mlI.

Van Dover, J. K., ed. *Critical Response to Raymond Chandler.* Westport: Greenwood Press, 1995.

Vermeule, Blakey. *Why Do We Care about Literary Characters?* Baltimore: Johns Hopkins University Press, 2010.

Vonnegut, Kurt. *A Man Without a Country.* New York: Random House, 2007.

Watt, Adam, ed. *Marcel Proust in Context.* Cambridge: Cambridge University Press, 2014.

Weeks, Robert P., ed. *Hemingway: A Collection of Critical Essays.* Englewood Cliffs: Prentice-Hall, 1962.

Weinreich, Martin. "'Into the Void': The Hyperrealism of Simulation in Bret Easton Ellis's 'American Psycho.'" *Amerikastudien/American Studies* 49.1 (2004): 65–78.

Weir, David. *Decadence and the Making of Modernism.* Amherst: University of Massachusetts Press, 1996.

———. *Decadent Culture in the United States.* Albany: SUNY Press, 2009.

Wells, H. G. *The Island of Dr. Moreau.* New York: Garden City, 1896.

———. *The Time Machine.* New York: Henry Holt, 1895.

———. *The War of the Worlds.* 1897. Reprint, New York: Barnes and Noble Classics, 2004.

White, Allon. *The Uses of Obscurity.* London: Routledge, 1981.

Widiss, Benjamin. *Obscure Invitations: The Persistence of the Author in Twentieth-Century American Literature.* Stanford: Stanford University Press, 2011.

Wilde, Oscar. *The Complete Works of Oscar Wilde.* London: Collins, 1966.

———. *The Picture of Dorian Gray.* 1891. Reprint, Hertfordshire: Wordsworth Editions Limited, 2001.

———. *Poems and Essays.* London: Collins, 1956.

Wilkinson, Rupert. *American Tough: The Tough-Guy Tradition and American Character.* New York: HarperCollins, 1986.

Williams, Carolyn. *Transfigured World: Walter Pater's Aesthetic Historicism.* Ithaca: Cornell University Press, 1989.

Williams, Rosalind. *Dream Worlds: Mass Consumption in Late Nineteenth-Century France.* Berkeley and Los Angeles: University of California Press, 1982.

Wilstach, Frank Jenners. *A Dictionary of Similes.* Boston: Little Brown, 1917.

Winant, Gabriel. "Not Every Kid Bond Matures." *n+1.* https://nplusonemag.com/online-only/book-review/not-every-kid-bond-matures/.

Witemeyer, Hugh. "Early Poetry 1908–1920." In Nadel, 43–58.

Wolff, Janet. "Gender and the Haunting of Cities (or, the Retirement of the *Flaneur*)." In D'Souza and McDonough, 18–31.

Young, Elizabeth, and Graham Cavenay. *Shopping in Space: Essays on America's Blank Generation Fiction.* London: Serpent's Tail, 1993.

Young, Philip. *Ernest Hemingway: A Reconsideration.* Pennsylvania State University Press, 1965.

FILMS

American Psycho. DVD. Directed by Mary Harron. 2000. Santa Monica: Lions Gate, 2005.

Bonnie and Clyde. DVD. Directed by Arthur Penn. 1967. Burbank: Warner Brothers, 1999.

Kiss Kiss Bang Bang. Directed by Shane Black. 2005.

The Long Goodbye. Directed by Robert Altman. 1973.

The Maltese Falcon. DVD. Directed by John Huston. 1941. Burbank: Warner Brothers, 2010.

The Talented Mr. Ripley. DVD. Directed by Anthony Minghella. 1999. Burbank: Warner Brothers, 2007.

Towers Open Fire. Online. Directed by Anthony Balch and William S. Burroughs. 1963. Accessed September 14, 2014. https://www.youtube.com/watch?v=dlQK PYfP0CM.

The Wild One. DVD. Directed by Lázsló Benedek. 1953. Culver City: Columbia, 1998.

INDEX

RECENT BOOKS IN THE SERIES
CULTURAL FRAMES, FRAMING CULTURE

Lightning Source UK Ltd.
Milton Keynes UK
UKHW041835250220
359324UK00001B/21